T5-ACP-624

The Vertical File
and Its Alternatives

The Vertical File and Its Alternatives
A Handbook

Clara L. Sitter

1992
LIBRARIES UNLIMITED, INC.
Englewood, Colorado

Copyright © 1992 Libraries Unlimited, Inc.
All Rights Reserved
Printed in the United States of America

No part of this publication may be reproduced, stored in a retrieval system, or transmitted, in any form or by any means, electronic, mechanical, photocopying, recording, or otherwise, without the prior written permission of the publisher.

LIBRARIES UNLIMITED, INC.
P.O. Box 6633
Englewood, CO 80155-6633

Library of Congress Cataloging-in-Publication Data

Sitter, Clara Loewen.
   The vertical file and its alternatives : a handbook / Clara L. Sitter.
   xv, 256 p. 17x25 cm.
   Includes bibliographical references and index.
   ISBN 0-87287-910-0
   1. Vertical files (Libraries)--Handbooks, manuals, etc.
2. Library materials--Handbooks, manuals, etc.   I. Title.
Z691.S58   1992
025.3'42--dc20   91-42253
                                                                        CIP

*To Les
for all that he does for me;*

*to our children,
Susan and Scott,
who are my inspiration;*

*and to my parents
for their loving encouragement.*

Contents

Preface xiii
Acknowledgments xv

1 – INTRODUCTION TO SUPPLEMENTARY RESOURCES 1
   What Are Vertical Files and Why Have Them? 1
   What Are the Characteristics of Vertical-File Materials or
      Supplementary Resources? 2
   What Kinds of Things Go in a Vertical File? 4
   When Do You Have a Special Collection? 4
   Who Should Collect and Use Supplementary Resources? 5
   What Do You Need to Build a Collection? 7
   How Do You Get Started? 8

Part I
Acquisition, Processing, and Management of Materials

2 – LOCATING RESOURCES 10
   Indexes 10
   Books – General 12
   Books – Specialized 16
   Bibliographies and Publications Lists 20
   Periodicals and Newspapers 21
   Directories 21
   Summary Recommendations 22
   Notes 22

3 – SELECTION 24
   The Cost of Free Materials 24
   Guidelines for the Acquisition of Supplementary Materials . 25
   Summary Recommendations 26

4 – ORDERING 27
   How to Place an Order 27
   How to Prepare a Request 29
   How to Facilitate Mailing 30
   How to Simplify Payment 30
   How to Keep Track of Orders 30
   Your Ordering Alternatives 31
   Summary Recommendations 31
   Notes 31

5 — INITIAL PROCESSING AND LABELING ... 32
Initial Processing ... 32
Labeling ... 33
Notes to Files ... 36
Summary Recommendations ... 36
Notes ... 36

6 — ORGANIZATION ... 37
Types of Organization ... 37
    Alphabetical by Subject — The Dictionary Arrangement ... 38
    Classified by Subject — Dewey or Library of Congress (LC) Arrangement ... 38
    Sequential by Number — Accession Number Arrangement ... 39
Subject Heading Alternatives ... 40
    Subject-Headings Lists Written for Vertical Files ... 40
    Standard Subject Headings for the Book Collection ... 41
    Subject Headings from Indexes and Guides ... 42
    Establishing Your Own Subject-Headings List ... 43
Index Alternatives ... 44
    Self-indexing ... 45
Summary Recommendations ... 48
Notes ... 48

7 — PRESERVATION AND PROTECTION ... 49
Flat, Single Items ... 49
    Protective Housing ... 50
    Mounting ... 50
    Laminating ... 52
    Encapsulation ... 52
Multiple Pages ... 52
    Reinforcements ... 53
    Protective Housing ... 54
Film Media ... 54
Summary Recommendations ... 54
Notes ... 54

8 — HOUSING ... 56
External Housing Units ... 56
Internal Filing Devices ... 57
Summary Recommendations ... 60
Notes ... 60

9 — PROMOTION ... 62
Summary Recommendations ... 63

10 — CIRCULATION ... 64
Manual Circulation ... 64
Automated Circulation ... 66
Circulation Procedures ... 67
Summary Recommendations ... 67

Contents / ix

11 – WEEDING 68
   Purpose of Weeding 68
   Negative Factors to Consider When Weeding 68
   When to Weed 69
   Summary Recommendations 70
   Notes 71

Part II
Supplementary Materials and Special Collections

**12 – SUPPLEMENTARY MATERIALS FOR INFORMATION
      FILES** 74
   Annual Reports 74
   Art Reproductions 75
   Association Information 77
   Bibliographies 78
   Biographical Sketches and Obituaries 80
   Calendars 82
   Cartoons 83
   Charts and Drawings 84
   Clippings 85
   College Catalogs 87
   Coloring Books 88
   Comic Books 89
   Court Cases 90
   Directories 91
   Documents (Facsimile) 92
   Election Issues 94
   Exhibition Catalogs 95
   Forms 96
   Government Documents 96
   Guides 98
   Holiday Items 99
   Instructions 100
   Interviews 101
   Lesson Plans and Curriculum Guides 102
   Librettos 103
   Magazines (Free) 104
   Magazines (Sample) 105
   Mail-Order Catalogs 106
   Manuals 107
   Newsletters 108
   Notebook Inserts 109
   Oral History 110
   Pamphlets 111
   Patterns, Stencils, and Templets 113
   Photographs 114
   Pictures 115
   Portraits 116

x / Contents

    Postcards..117
    Posters..118
    Programs, Playbills, and Reviews............................119
    Reference Materials (Discarded).............................120
    Reports...121
    Reprints..122
    Schedules...123
    Scripts...124
    Sheet Music and Song Sheets.................................125
    Speeches..126
    Study Guides and Worksheets.................................127
    Tests...128
    Time Lines..130
    Transcripts...131
    Travel Brochures..132
    Wheels and Other Manipulatives..............................133
    Notes...134

13 – OTHER FREE AND INEXPENSIVE SUPPLEMENTARY
    MATERIALS..138
    Cassette Tapes..138
    Computer Programs...140
    Films, Filmstrips, and Videotapes...........................141
    Flags...142
    Flash Cards...143
    Games...144
    Microforms..145
    Puzzles...147
    Slides..148
    Transparencies..149
    Notes...150

14 – SUPPLEMENTARY MATERIALS FOR PERSONAL
    FILES OF LIBRARIANS AND TEACHERS.........................152
    Book Jackets..152
    Bookmarks...153
    Book-Talks..155
    Bulletin-Board Materials....................................156
    Buttons and Bumper Stickers.................................157
    Clip Art..158
    Flannel-Board Materials.....................................159
    Handouts..160
    Lettering Guides..161
    Masks...162
    Miniature Books...162
    Publishers' Catalogs..163
    Puppets...164
    Notes...166

15 – SPECIAL COLLECTIONS OF SUPPLEMENTARY MATERIALS 167
Map Collections 169
Career Collections 171
Local History Collections 175
Notes 179

Appendix – Vendors 181

Glossary 213

Bibliography 229

Index 237

Preface

The first edition of this work, titled *The Vertical File and Its Satellites*, was written by Shirley Miller and published by Libraries Unlimited in 1971. The response it received indicated the need for a comprehensive contemporary handbook on the subject of vertical files. The second edition was published in 1979. It was an enlarged and expanded work that included the many developments taking place in the eight years between editions. It introduced new resources, new products, and new techniques. Many of the additions were responses to the feedback received from librarians working with vertical files. Even more changes have occurred since the 1979 edition. There are now many alternatives: format, sources, ways in which we can acquire resources, how we organize and store them, and alternatives in supplementary materials themselves.

This work is intended as an updated text on vertical files and supplementary materials and was originally planned as a third edition of Miller's title. Some of her original text is retained, so the author would like to acknowledge those contributions in providing the foundation for this work. In this book the general approach and the coverage of topics has been changed, making the emphasis on alternatives—alternatives in types of materials and sources as well as in policies and procedures in ordering, processing, and management.

Supplementary materials and information about them is available from many sources. This work provides a starting point for establishing collections of supplementary materials and directs readers to examples of basic resources. For libraries with established collections, this book can be a working tool for outlining some of the options in the acquisition, processing, and management of materials and provides direction to additional sources.

No one has all of the answers. In fact there can be no right answer because situations are too different. We have learned a lot about supplementary materials over the years from experience and from reading and writing about vertical files and special collections; but nearly every day something new comes to our attention that relates in some way to supplementary resources.

We hope that you are excited about the opportunities and the alternatives that are part of working with supplementary materials. We hope that you are energized by the many options for acquiring, organizing, and managing supplementary materials. And finally, we hope that you are inspired by the opportunity to create a constantly changing collection that is uniquely valuable to your users.

The area of supplementary materials is continually changing. A work of this type needs constant revision, so it is my hope that readers will make suggestions for the next edition. Comments may be sent to me at the University of Alaska Anchorage, Consortium Library, 3211 Providence Drive, Anchorage, Alaska 99508.

Acknowledgments

The first thanks go to my husband, Les Sitter, who read the manuscript more times than he can remember, and second to my friend and colleague at the University of Alaska Anchorage, Cathie Innes-Taylor, who also read parts of the manuscript through several versions. Thanks to other Anchorage librarians who read sections and gave me their suggestions: Diane Brenner, Nancy Hesch, Patricia Pauley, Alden Rollins, Marjorie Segal, and Bill Siemens. A special thanks to Blanche Woolls from the University of Pittsburgh School of Library and Information Science for her suggestions and encouragement.

Many thanks to David Loertscher, acquisitions editor at Libraries Unlimited, for his help and for getting me started on the project. Additional thanks to the staff at Libraries Unlimited, who have been very helpful.

Finally, I want to acknowledge the support I have received from the two library directors I served under while working on this project: Jack O'Bar, director before his retirement in June 1990, and Barbara Sokolov, director since July 1990. The support of these administrators along with a University of Alaska Anchorage faculty grant allowed me to complete the manuscript on a timely schedule.

1
Introduction to Supplementary Resources

Vertical files and supplementary collections vary a great deal from library to library. Some libraries give full processing and integrated shelving to everything in their collection while others may have the same kinds of materials in cabinet after cabinet of vertical files. There are few rules for vertical files, so there is a lot of room to "do it your way." Individual libraries determine what kinds of materials go into their supplementary collections and how the materials will be organized and managed.

The description above leads us to assume that it is the way we handle supplementary materials that determines whether a particular item is destined for the vertical file or "vertical-file treatment." If you treat a resource like vertical-file material, it will become vertical-file material. This book describes vertical files and supplementary materials and suggests some of the alternatives for their acquisition, organization, and management.

WHAT ARE VERTICAL FILES AND WHY HAVE THEM?

For many years librarians thought of vertical files as collections of pamphlets, clippings, pictures, and maps. Early terms related to pamphlet and leaflet information include *broadside, chapbook, festschrift, handbill, newsbook*, and *small press publication*. Newer terms given to elements of this broad range of miscellaneous printing include *underground publications, alternative publications, curiosa*, and *gray literature*. The ALA (American Library Association) *Glossary of Library and Information Science* defines vertical file as follows:

> **vertical file** 1. A collection of materials such as pamphlets, clippings, and pictures, which, because of their shape and often their ephemeral nature, are filed in drawers for easy reference. 2. A case of drawers in which materials may be filed vertically.

The collections of these materials in the past have been called *ephemera* and *fugitive*. Neither quite describes the subject of this book. *Ephemera* (materials of transitory interest) is not quite right because some items we discuss will be of lasting interest. *Fugitive* (hard to find) is another misnomer because most materials are very easy to locate. A more modern term, *information files* (files of data), is broader in scope but implies that the material is print or graphic and suggests that the material will be in files. Our discussions include materials that are not limited to vertical file cabinets or limited by format. *Supplementary materials* (complementary to the main collection) is a term broad enough to include all kinds of materials and carries no implication of limits. *Supplementary materials* is the best term to describe the subject of this book.

Descriptive terms that indicate the subject or type of material in special collections of supplementary materials include *clippings file, picture file, pamphlet file*, or *report file*. You may call one group of materials your *travel* or *country file* if it is limited by geography. You may call another *biographical* if it is about people; another might be *career* or *vocational*; another could be called *maps* or simply *pamphlet file*. You will call your materials the name that best describes them for your library. You may even call your general collection the *vertical file*.

WHAT ARE THE CHARACTERISTICS OF VERTICAL-FILE MATERIALS OR SUPPLEMENTARY RESOURCES?

The characteristics we associate with vertical-file materials relate to the size, format, subject, purpose, approach, source, availability, cost, and shelf life. Most supplementary materials will have one or more of the following characteristics:

- fit in the vertical-file cabinet
- offer unique information
- focus on a small segment of knowledge
- provide current information
- have a short shelf life
- are written in simple, concise language
- are presented in an appealing format
- are available from sources other than your usual vendor
- are free or inexpensive

Format. Certain formats are easily managed as vertical-file materials. Leaflets, clippings, reprints, and pictures are examples of formats that are probably best handled in files. General policies about the disposition of certain formats can be established to simplify the decision-making when materials are received.

Characteristics of Vertical-File Materials or Supplementary Resources / 3

Size. Most materials for vertical files will be concise. A simplification of the issue of size is to think of items for the vertical file as those things that might get lost on the shelf if they were cataloged. Most pamphlets will be 50 pages or less, but you may want to include longer items in the file such as reports, catalogs, or directories, which may be 100 pages or more. Your file cabinets will fill quickly if you include many book-length items. Items such as maps, pictures, or posters should fit in the file flat or folded in a hanging folder, file, or envelope. Alternative housing should be considered for larger items.

Subject. Materials on specific or unusual topics are often easier to find in the vertical file than on the shelf if they are organized alphabetically by subject. The patron can often bypass the index and go directly to the files.

Shelf life. Many of the items in the vertical file are important for only a brief time. If the relevance for your collection is a year or less, then the vertical file may be a good way to handle the information. Examples include current class schedules for your local university or college, election materials, and reviews of a traveling production coming to your community.

Source. Much of the vertical-file information will be acquired from sources other than standard publishers or book and periodicals jobbers. Examples include associations, commercial companies, special-interest groups, and governments or government agencies. A policy may be established to house all materials from special groups as vertical-file materials.

Purpose. Ask yourself why the author or publisher produced the material. Information received from associations, special-interest groups, businesses, and government agencies often reflects the perspective or bias of the group. Much of the material provides an excellent resource, but you may choose to keep it in a temporary status rather than adding it to your permanent collection.

Availability. Much of the free and inexpensive material available in the vertical file is also available to the public for the asking. Adding the source and cost to items in your files will be an aid to users who want to acquire materials for themselves.

Cost. Many of the items in the vertical file are available free or at very little cost. Unless otherwise noted, *inexpensive* will refer to items that are $10 or less. Discussions about audiovisual items such as computer programs, audiotapes, films, slides, and videotapes for supplementary collections will be limited to include only materials that are free or inexpensive. Current prices are given in this work so that the reader will have a general idea of the cost, but most items are subject to regular price increases. (Nothing is really free. Although many supplementary materials are free or inexpensive, you will invest time, supplies, and space. It is important to keep in mind these hidden costs when you select materials.)

Treatment. The quick-and-easy treatment and the temporary status of materials are probably the most distinguishing characteristics of items for the vertical file. Almost any kind of material in your library can be given the vertical-file treatment.

Vertical-file and supplementary materials will have several of these characteristics but not necessarily all of them. The characteristics discussed relate to vertical-file materials in general, but other characteristics may be present in special kinds of supplementary materials.

WHAT KINDS OF THINGS GO IN A VERTICAL FILE?

Vertical files contain many of the supplementary materials found in libraries. In the broadest sense these supplementary resources include everything that is not in the regular collection. Materials such as maps, government documents, and reports that are supplementary in one library may be the main collection of another library. Historically, supplementary materials were either print or graphic, but there are now a growing number of miscellaneous items that are neither. People learn in many different ways, so librarians should be open minded in their consideration of the kinds of items they consider for addition to the collection.

Print. Pamphlets and clippings are the most frequently collected print materials, but vertical files may also include such things as annual reports, association flyers, bibliographies, biographical sketches, bookmarks, bulletins, career guides, college catalogs, comic books, court decisions, curriculum guides, election materials, exercises, exhibit catalogs, flyers, forms, government documents, guides, handouts, how-to guides, instructions, interviews, lesson plans, librettos, local history, magazine samples, mail-order catalogs, manuals, newsletters, notebook insert guides, photocopies, playbills, programs, publisher catalogs, recipes, reports, reprints, reviews, schedules, scripts, sheet music, speeches, study guides, telephone books, tests, trade catalogs, transcripts, translations, and travel brochures.

Graphics. Maps and pictures top the list of graphic materials, but other graphic materials for consideration include art reproductions, book jackets, calendars, cards, cartoons, drawings, charts, clip art, greeting cards, patterns, photographs, placemats, portraits, postcards, posters, reproductions, and time lines.

Miscellaneous. Some miscellaneous supplementary materials (audio, visual, or realia) you may find in your library include audiotapes, records and discs, book-talks, bulletin-board materials, busts, buttons, computer programs, conversion wheels, cut-outs, decorations, films, flags, flash cards, games, holiday items, interviews, lettering guides, masks, microfiche, miniature books, models, money, music, oral history, pins, puzzles, puppets, sculpture, projection slides, transparencies, and videotapes. Some of these will be a part of the regular collection in many libraries, but all of them can be considered for a vertical file or supplementary collection in other libraries.

WHEN DO YOU HAVE A SPECIAL COLLECTION?

Decisions to create special collections are very individual. Most libraries have a few special collections. Various parts of the supplementary materials of a library can be pulled together (apart from the rest of the collection) to form a special collection. What qualifies for a special collection? Decisions are often based on format or subject, with consideration for the size of the special collection.

Format. Special collections based on format will include materials of the same format but on a variety of subjects. For example, a picture file would probably have pictures on all subjects. Traditionally, special collections of supplementary materials have included clippings, maps, pamphlets, and pictures along with perhaps government documents and audiovisual materials. All of these are "special" because of their format. Some special formats may be a part of the regular collection in some libraries and supplementary in others.

The combination of format and quantity will often determine whether you establish a special collection of materials. Large collections of materials such as maps, catalogs, newsletters, scripts, sheet music, or reports may be easier for users to find or for staff to manage if they are separated from the rest of the supplementary materials.

Subject. Special collections may also be special because of the topic. Special collections based on subject will likely include a variety of formats. For example, a music collection might contain biographical information about musicians, portraits, interviews, lesson plans, librettos, posters, sheet music, scripts, time lines, and study guides.

There is, of course, a very wide range of subjects that could be collected. Teachers will have special collections of materials based on the subjects they teach, associations or clubs may have special collections based on the interests of the members, academic libraries may have special collections based on curriculum emphasis, and public libraries will have special collections based on the needs of their users. Topics for general subject collections include art, biography, business, college, career, drama, education, holiday, health, language, literature, music, science, social studies, travel/countries.

Quantity. A special collection will be less likely to be overlooked if it is of substantial size. There is no specific formula for a special collection based on numbers, but if you have a collection of several hundred items or the equivalent of several file cabinet drawers, you may want to consider a special collection. There is some risk of confusing your users by creating too many special collections, but advantages of special collections are that they can be placed near related materials and can be promoted separately.

WHO SHOULD COLLECT AND USE SUPPLEMENTARY RESOURCES?

Almost all librarians and teachers benefit from collecting and using supplementary materials of one kind or another. Small school and public libraries collect supplementary materials to fill gaps when they cannot buy more expensive materials. Large libraries collect supplementary materials because they want to offer both breadth and depth in the subject areas they cover. Librarians and teachers develop personal and classroom collections to enhance their work with individuals and groups.

This book was written for the small public or school library with little or no budget for supplementary materials. Throughout are suggestions for larger public and academic libraries, which, it is assumed, have a budget for supplementary materials.

Small public libraries. Small public libraries or those with practically no budget for supplementary materials can develop a vertical-file collection. There is a great deal of free material available for the asking. Librarians who have no funds except for postage and who have time or help can build sizable collections on a shoestring. This book is for you.

Examples of some items for consideration include selected annual reports, art reproductions, bibliographies, biographical sketches, calendars, charts, clippings, court cases, documents, election materials, government documents, guides, handouts, instructions, interviews, mail-order catalogs, manuals, maps, newsletters, pamphlets, pictures, postcards, reports, reprints, speeches, time lines, and travel brochures.

School libraries. School libraries probably vary as much as public libraries in the range of support in staff and funding. Regardless of the size of the school or the size of the budget, there never seems to be enough time or money. With a budget of a few hundred dollars and volunteer help, many schools have put together fine vertical-file collections.

Examples of items for consideration by school libraries include art reproductions, bibliographies, calendars, cartoons, charts, clippings, college catalogs, court cases, documents, flash cards, games, guides, handouts, instructions, interviews, lettering guides, maps, pamphlets, photographs, pictures, portraits, postcards, posters, puzzles, reports, reprints, schedules, scripts, slides, speeches, study guides, tests, time lines, and travel or country brochures.

Larger public libraries. Larger public libraries will probably make use of a number of free resources along with some purchased items in developing collections for travel, local history, newsletters, and pamphlets. Friends of libraries groups and volunteers can be a great help in the acquisition, organization, and management of vertical files and special collections in their public libraries. Funding for vertical-file collections in public libraries varies. A vertical-file budget of, say, $500 to $1,000 could be used to purchase some individual items, and more expensive collections could be funded through the materials-collection budget.

College and university libraries. College and university libraries may focus more on purchased items and less on free materials. Examples of purchased collections would be annual reports, art reproductions, college catalogs, charts, pamphlet collections, PhoneFiche, and time lines. Some alternatives for purchase are indicated in the footnotes. Special collections in college and university libraries may include materials such as federal and state government documents, maps, and test files. University libraries that cover a broad range of subjects are more likely to need complete sets of materials than are school and public libraries that may have more narrowly defined collections. Academic libraries may budget $1,000 or more for materials. Materials purchased as expensive sets, such as college catalogs, annual reports, or PhoneFiche, are considered a part of the serial or book collection.

Special libraries. Special libraries vary so widely in purpose, scope, and funding that it is difficult to make any comments that will be helpful to special libraries as a group. It is expected that librarians working with vertical files in special libraries will benefit from the general suggestions in part 1 of this work. There are few references to specific materials for special libraries.

Teacher or classroom collections. Teacher or classroom collections are included because a number of specific kinds of supplementary materials discussed will be collected by the classroom teacher for personal or classroom files. It is assumed that in most cases budgeted funds for the development of collections will go to the school library for common collections that can be used by all teachers in the school and that most teachers will be interested in free and inexpensive materials or materials they can develop themselves. Teachers who spend their own time and resources to develop personal collections of materials to enhance their teaching will find suggestions in this book. Personal files can be managed differently than collections used by a number of people.

Possible materials include items such as book-talks, bulletin-board materials, buttons, cartoons, charts, clip art, clippings, computer programs, felt pictures, flash cards, games, guides, handouts, holiday materials, lesson plans, magazine samples, maps, masks, music (recorded or sheet music), photographs, pictures, portraits, postcards, posters, puppets, puzzles, reprints, slides, study guides, tests, time lines, and transparencies. Other possibilities include relevant bibliographies, art reproductions, biographical sketches, career profiles, court cases, flags, foreign money, and wheels and other manipulatives.

Librarian's files. The librarian's files are included as a separate category because there are a number of materials the librarian may prefer to keep for personal use. Examples include bibliographies, book jackets, bookmarks, book-talks, bulletin-board materials, buttons, clip art, felt pictures, forms, greeting cards, guides, handouts, magazine samples, pathfinders, and puppets.

All collections will benefit from adding information that is not available from other sources or that offers a different approach. Each collection will reflect the individual needs of that particular library or classroom as well as the amount of time and money available to develop the collection.

WHAT DO YOU NEED TO BUILD A COLLECTION?

Building a collection of supplementary materials is an area of high payoff for the dollars invested, but there is more than money involved. Commitment is essential. If you are in a small library, a school library, or a classroom setting, you must be committed to the importance of supplementary materials. If you are in a large library system, it is also critical to have the support of the library administration for continuing development. In addition to commitment you need the following:

- *Budgeted funds* for some purchases and a few supplies ($500 to $1,000 per year is a moderate allocation for a small collection). Additional money is required if you need to buy file cabinets or a large number of supplies. Many libraries get supplies from their general supplies, run the postage through the office expense, buy resources from petty cash, or order only "free" materials. Try to keep things simple and be aware of the costs.

- *Space* to house the materials and to provide for library use. You need tables and chairs near your materials, and it is useful to patrons to have a photocopy machine located near the vertical file.

- *Time* to supervise the acquisition, processing, and management of the materials. Ideally, coordination will be by one staff person, but volunteers or rotating help can be used for some tasks.

HOW DO YOU GET STARTED?

If you are really "tuned in" to supplementary materials, you will find them everywhere. They will be in the doctor's office, at the grocery store, the drugstore, the copy center, even as placemats in restaurants where you eat. They will come to you from organizations, periodicals, newspapers, and many other unexpected sources. Many of these finds will be excellent additions to your collection. There are several techniques and tools for actively building your supplementary collections. Save found items that you think will be useful to your users for later reference. Begin with the following:

1. Clip the local newspaper.

2. Order pamphlets out of magazines you read.

3. Canvas your city for materials. Sources in many cities include banks, car dealers, the chamber of commerce, city hall, the local health department, credit unions, dentists and doctors, health associations (e.g., American Cancer Society), hospitals, organizations (e.g., American Red Cross), political party headquarters, travel agencies, visitor centers, fairs, and special shows.

4. Begin an active, systematic approach to developing your collection by following the suggestions in this book.

Part 1, "The Acquisition, Processing, and Management of Materials," discusses 10 steps in the life of supplementary materials. The topics addressed include acquisition—locating sources, selection, and ordering; processing—initial processing, organization, preservation and protection, and housing; and management—promotion, circulation, and weeding.

Part 2, "Supplementary Materials and Special Collections," discusses the different types of supplementary materials and special collections. Most of the materials discussed are for information files, but also included is a section on other free and inexpensive materials and one for items for the personal files of librarians and teachers. Specific information about acquisition, processing, and management, indicating special problems and alternatives, is given for each type of material. Part 2 also discusses special collections (maps, career and local history materials, etc.) based on format and subject.

Additional information in the book includes an appendix of vendors, with addresses and resources for vertical-file projects; a glossary of terms related to working with supplementary materials; a bibliography with some annotations; and an index with subject, author, and title entries.

This book is a starting point if you are a volunteer or a library staff member just beginning a vertical file. For the experienced librarian working with an established collection, this book reviews basic principles, offers ideas for options in developing and managing collections, and makes suggestions for pursuing additional materials.

Your materials will be as valuable as you make them. Vertical-file and supplementary materials collections can be an excellent resource in even the smallest, most underfunded libraries. These materials have the potential to be the most unique and exciting feature distinguishing your collection from that of other libraries.

Part I
Acquisition, Processing, and Management of Materials

Part 1 addresses the acquisition, processing, and management of supplementary materials in a broad sense. General sources and guides for locating materials are discussed, as are principles and options for selection and ordering. More specific sources are included in part 2 where the specific type of material is covered.

The steps in the process of handling supplementary materials have been identified: locating resources, selection, ordering, initial processing, organization, preservation and protection, housing, promotion, circulation, and weeding. For most materials this is a cycle beginning with locating resources and ending with weeding before beginning the process again (see figure 2.1).

There are many options for handling materials, from the first step of locating resources to the final one of weeding. Libraries that do not have guidelines for supplementary materials may find it helpful to establish some basic principles, policies, and procedures. Areas for decision-making are indicated in the following discussion of the steps in the processing of materials.

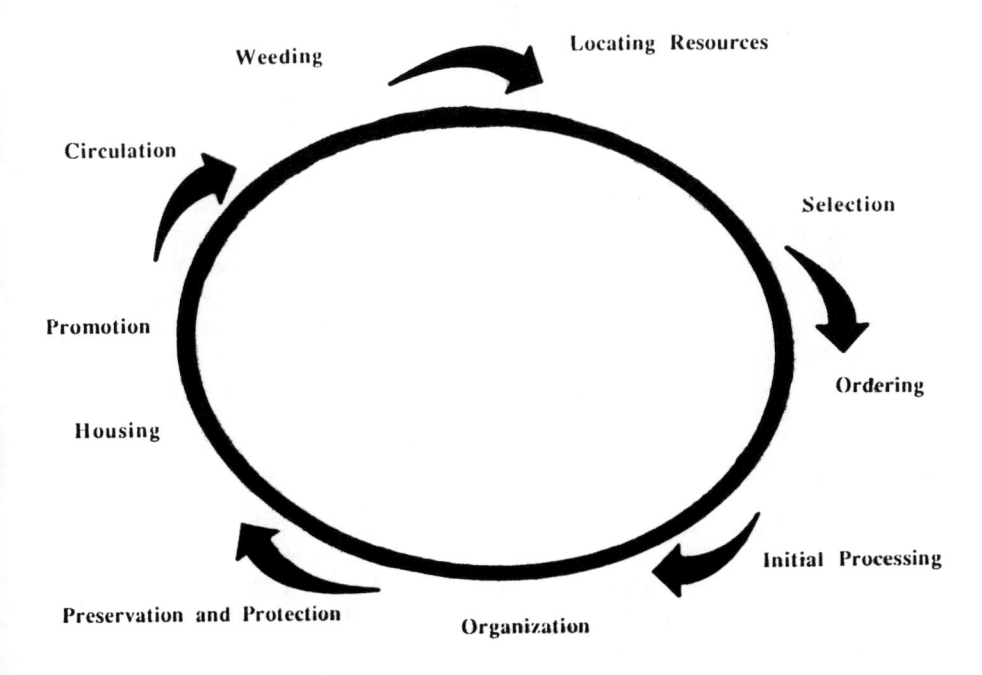

Fig. 2.1. Steps in the processing of materials.

2
Locating Resources

You can locate resources by using some basic tools such as indexes, books, bibliographies and publication lists, periodicals and newspapers, and directories. Some of these resources can be shared among libraries, but the best ones you may want to buy for use as working tools for your own collection and to make them available to your patrons. Current prices are included for most of the resources discussed so that the reader will have an idea of the cost involved. The possibility of price increases should be considered when ordering. The reader is cautioned that the prices of these resources, just as any prices for items listed in the tools, may be incorrect. Some examples in each category are discussed and others simply listed for your information.

INDEXES

Three indexes stand out as sources of vertical-file materials: *Vertical File Index* (see figure 2.2), *Information America*, and *Monthly Catalog of U.S. Government Publications*. There are other indexes such as *PAIS* (see figure 2.3) and *Hospital Literature Index*, that also give sources of supplementary materials.[1]

Vertical File Index. New York: H. W. Wilson Company, monthly except in August. ($45 per year) This is the resource most often listed when the subject of vertical files is discussed. It is a subject index to current pamphlets and other free and inexpensive items including charts, posters, and maps. Entries are arranged by subject headings and then subarranged alphabetically by title. Each entry has complete bibliographic information and ordering instructions and usually includes a brief descriptive annotation. There is a separate title index. A supplementary section, "References to Current Topics," contains selected periodical citations. Quarterly and semiannual issues cumulate the subject headings for the current volume.

Information America. (3 issues each year for $80) This publication is an option for libraries that can afford the price. The entries are arranged by source; many pamphlets and other publications are listed by title with price. There is an index to free and inexpensive materials, but it seems almost easier to look through the entries.[2]

Food
  See also
  Nutrition

Food allergy
  Food allergies. 36p 1989 Am. Council on Sci. & Health, 1995 Broadway, 18th Floor, New York, NY 10023-5860 $3 plus 75¢ stamped #10 s.a.e.; send payment with order
    This pamphlet identifies various types of food allergies and sensitivities and includes information on common allergenic foods, symptoms, diagnosis, and treatment. A glossary is also provided.

Food contamination
  For our kids' sake; how to protect your child against pesticides in food, by Anne Witte Garland. 87p il 1989 Sierra Club, Store Orders, 730 Polk St., San Francisco, CA 94109 $6.95 plus $3 postage & handling; send payment with order; CA residents add sales tax
    This book, based on a National Resources Defense Council study, explains the threat pesticides in foods pose to children. It describes ways to protect yourself against pesticides when buying and preparing produce and lists 25 common fruits and vegetables with the 5 pesticides most often detected in each. It also outlines ways to get organic food into local supermarkets, to help farmers reduce reliance on pesticides and to improve food safety.
  Pesticides and food safety. 28p figs 1989 Am. Council on Sci. & Health, 1995 Broadway, 18th Floor, New York, NY 10023-5860 $3 plus 75¢ stamped #10 s.a.e.; send payment with order
    The chemicals discussed in this booklet are limited to those that are monitored by the FDA. It takes the position that there is no scientific evidence that residues in food from approved use have ever been the cause of illness or death in either adults or children. Contents include pesticide regulation, determining safety and residue limits, government monitoring, and nutrition.

G

Games
  Beyond winning; sports and games all kids want to play, by Lawrence Rowen. 94p il 1990 Fearon Teacher Aids, Box 280, Carthage, IL 62321 $6.95 send payment or purchase order
  Great games to play with groups; a leader's guide, by Frank W. Harris. 96p il 1990 Fearon Teacher Aids, Box 280, Carthage, IL 62321 $6.95 send payment or purchase order

Gases
  See also
  Radon

German reunification question
  See also German reunification question in Part 3
  Gorbachev's interview with Pravda. (News & views from the USSR) 6p 1990 Soviet Embassy, Inf. Dept., 1706 18th St. NW, Washington, DC 20009 free
    These are the answers given by Soviet President Mikhail Gorbachev to questions from the newspaper Pravda on German unification. The interview was published on February 21.

Gifted children
  A program to meet the emotional and social needs of gifted and talented adolescents, by Edmund L. Barnette. (Professional P90-7) repr 4p 1990 Chronicle Guidance Publs. Inc., Moravia, NY 13118 $2 plus $1 postage & handling on orders to $10; 10% postage on orders over $10; send payment with order; minimum order 2 items
    This article is a report on the Ozark Summer Communications Institute for Gifted and Talented Adolescents workshop sponsored by the Mountain Home School District. Reprinted from May 1989 Journal of Counseling and Development.

Fig. 2.2. *Vertical File Index*, March 1991, sample page. Copyright © 1991 by The H. W. Wilson Company. Material reproduced with permission of the publisher.

GREECE
See also this heading used as a subheading under appropriate main headings.

Environmental policy
Legislation

Karakostas, Ioannis. Neue Entwicklungen des Umweltschutzes im griechischen Zivilrecht. *Z Umweltpol und Umweltrecht 13:295-310 S '90*
Overview of provisions relating to environmental protection in the Greek civil code.
Summary in English.

Finance
Statistics

† Greece. Nat. Statis. Service. Public finance statistics, 1984-1985. '89 144p tables charts (ISSN 0256-3568) pa 500 drachmas ($8) —*Lycourgon 14-16, Athens, Greece*
Includes data for earlier years.
Text in both Greek and English.

Government and politics

Tachos, Anastase. Le contrôle interne de l'administration publique en Grèce. chart *R Internat Droit Comparé p 967-82 Jl/S '90*
Constitutional and legal basis of the petition process.

GREENHOUSE EFFECT, ATMOSPHERIC

Barron, William and Peter Hills. Climatic concerns: possible energy implications for selected lower income Asian nations. tables *Energy Policy 18:819-27 N '90*
Examines fossil carbon emissions by fuel type and consuming sector in China, India, Indonesia, and Thailand in terms of their national energy plans.

Mitchell, George J. World on fire: saving an endangered earth. '91 viii+247p bibl index (LC 90-8578) (ISBN 0-684-19231-4) $22.50 —*Scribner.*; $29.95—*Collier Macmillan Can*
Major global environmental concerns and possible US remedial actions on national and international levels; some emphasis on the greenhouse effect.

Robertson, David. The global environment: are international treaties a distraction? bibl tables chart *World Economy (London) 13:111-27 Mr '90*
View that global environment problems should be best addressed within national policies and regulations; with particular reference to global warming.

Starr, Chauncey and Milton F. Searl. Global energy and electricity futures: demand and supply alternatives. bibl tables charts *Energy Systems and Policy 14:53-83 Ja/Mr '90*
Estimates of developments to the year 2060, with emphasis on the greenhouse effect and options for nonfossil power sources.

Treaties

† Resources for the Future. Energy and Natural Resources Div. Lessons from other international agreements for a global CO2 accord. Morrisette, Peter M. and others. O '90 65p bibl tables chart map (Discussion pa. ENR91-02) pa $5 payment with order —*Resources for the Future*
Discusses five international agreements, 1959-87, addressing environmental controls.

Fig. 2.3. Sample page from *PAIS International in Print*. Reprinted with permission.

Monthly Catalog of United States Government Publications. This catalog lists all publications of the U.S. government. It is helpful to have, but you can do quite nicely with some of the free indexes: *Consumer Information Catalog, New Books, Government Books for You.* You can receive the free indexes regularly by requesting them from Consumer Information Center, P.O. Box 100, Pueblo, Colorado 81002.

BOOKS—GENERAL

A good place to start is with some books of sources.[3] Two series are available, the twelve titles of the Educators Progress Service and Carol Smallwood's books. Several of the Educators Progress Service books cover general topics, but most of them treat specific subject areas or specific types of materials. Carol Smallwood's books on sources of free and inexpensive materials address both general and specific topics. Some of the best general books are listed here.

Educators Index of Free Materials. Randolph, Wisconsin: Educators Progress Service, Inc., annual. ($45.75) This annual is the oldest of the series of guides in the Educators Progress Series on General Sources. It lists pamphlets and brochures for the most part but does include a section on visual and audiovisual aids including charts, pictures, posters, magazines, newsletters, and maps. The 100th edition, published in 1991, includes 2,821 items with more than 30 percent new listings. New items are asterisked (*) for easy update by regular readers. Arrangement is by curricular area and the volume is indexed by title, subject, and source. It is punched and housed in a three-ring notebook. This is a basic resource for secondary teachers and librarians and a good source of print material.

Elementary Teachers Guide to Free Curriculum Materials. Randolph, Wisconsin: Educators Progress Service, Inc., annual. ($23.75) This volume is revised annually in the summer with standing orders shipped in July and August. The 1991 edition lists 1,986 items from 578 sources with more than 50 percent new titles. Arrangement is by curricular categories. There are indexes for titles, subjects, and sources. Entries are annotated and include charts, pictures, and maps as well as pamphlets. The company publishes a number of other specific resources in subject areas along with guides to free materials in various formats including films, filmstrips, slides, audio, video, and computer materials. It is an outstanding resource for elementary teachers and librarians.

Educators Grade Guide to Free Teaching Aids. Randolph, Wisconsin: Educators Progress Service, Inc., annual. ($43.95) This guide is revised each summer for use during the school year. The 37th edition, 1991, includes more than 2,100 items with 57 percent new titles from 635 sources, of which 211 are new. New items are asterisked (*), so updating is easy for people who order the resource each year. This is a selective list including only about 50 percent of materials examined. Arrangement is by curricular categories with indexes for title, subject, and source. There is a separate section for teacher reference and professional growth materials. This edition appears to be very much like the *Elementary Teachers Guide to Free Curriculum Materials* except for the introductory section, the addition of five sample teaching units (primary through middle school) and a 30-page supplement. The resource comes punched with a three-ring binder.

Exceptional Free Library Resource Materials. Littleton, Colorado: Libraries Unlimited, 1984. This guide by Carol Smallwood lists more than 850 free materials available from government agencies, businesses, and nonprofit organizations. The book is organized into 27 broad subject categories. It is a selective list and all materials have been evaluated. The appendix has several useful lists including "Cooperative Extension Service State Offices," "NASA Regional Film Libraries," "State Labor Information Offices," "State Travel Information Bureaus," and "U.S. Forest Service Regional Offices."

Free Resource Builder for Librarians and Teachers. Jefferson, North Carolina: McFarland, 1986. ($19.95) This resource, compiled by Carol Smallwood, provides more than 3,000 addresses of government, business, and nonprofit organizations that offer materials of interest to educators (see figure 2.4). Specific materials are not listed. The addresses are arranged by broad subject areas including business and finance, consumer affairs, environment, government and legal affairs, health, library and archive usage, and travel and geography. Multiresource agencies, special aids, and resource management are also included. There is a subject index. This resource is useful if you want to send

14 / 2—Locating Resources

159 Federal Reserve Bank of Boston
Bank and Public Services Department
Boston MA 02106

160 Federal Reserve Bank of New York
Public Information Department
33 Liberty St.
New York NY 10045

161 Federal Reserve Bank of Philadelphia
Public Information Department
P.O. Box 66
Philadelphia PA 19105

162 Federal Reserve Bank of Cleveland
Public Information Center
P.O. Box 6387
Cleveland OH 44101

Fig. 2.4. Sample page from *Free Resource Builder*. From *Free Resource Builder for Librarians and Teachers* © 1986 by Carol Smallwood by permission of McFarland & Company, Inc., Publishers, Jefferson, North Carolina.

a blanket request for materials; otherwise you will have to write for a catalog and then request specific materials. The list of addresses is not likely to change as quickly as a list of specific titles.

A Guide to Selected Federal Agency Programs and Publications for Librarians and Teachers. Littleton, Colorado: Libraries Unlimited, 1986. ($25.50) Carol Smallwood's guide is organized by agency and indexed by subject. Agency name, address, and phone number are given along with the date it was established, the objectives of the agency, curriculum application, subjects (suggested vertical-file headings based on *Sears*), locations of regional offices, publications, audiovisuals, library locations, and special services (see figure 2.5). Additional information includes acronyms and abbreviations, federal information centers, land-grant university film libraries, sea-grant programs, and subject bibliographies published by the Government Printing Office.

WOMEN'S RIGHTS NATIONAL HISTORICAL PARK
National Park Service
P.O. Box 70
Seneca Falls, NY 13148
(315) 568-2991

Date Established: 1980

Objectives of the Agency: Preserve and interpret the significant sites associated with the first women's rights convention, held in Seneca Falls in 1848.

Curriculum: History, women's studies

Subjects: America—history
 Feminism
 Women—civil rights
 Women—U.S.
 Women's liberation movement

Publications: Fact sheets. Flyers. On the park and personalities connected with the women's rights movement.

Selected List of Books and Pamphlets

"Answers to Frequently Asked Questions about the Park." n.d. 3p. free.
 Answers to such questions as what the park is, and who organized the first women's rights convention.

"The Bloomer Costume and Dress Reform." n.d. 6p. free.
 Describes the introduction of knee-length skirts worn over baggy pantaloons as a convenient form of dress. Includes public reaction, use, and arguments.

"Declaration of Sentiments." n.d. 2p. free.
 Modeled on the Declaration of Independence, the Declaration of Sentiments of 1848, asserted the rights of women. Includes the names of the men and women who signed the declaration.

Fig. 2.5. Sample page from *Guide to Selected Federal Agency Programs and Publications for Librarians and Teachers* by Carol Smallwood (Littleton, Colo.: Libraries Unlimited, 1986).

BOOKS – SPECIALIZED

In addition to their general guides, Educators Progress Service and Carol Smallwood each have a number of specialized guides. Specialized guides to supplementary resources are also available from a variety of other sources including commercial publishers, educational institutions, organizations, and government agencies.[4] Titles that follow are representative of the guides available.

Specialized guides from The Educators Progress Service, Inc., include print and nonprint materials in various subject areas. Each includes multimedia and is arranged in the same general format with lists for films (16mm), filmstrips and slides, tapes (audio and video), scripts and transcriptions, and printed materials. Each section is grouped by broad subject area with a descriptive annotation. New entries are asterisked (*). Each work is indexed by title, subject, and source. Each of the titles from the Educators Progress Service is revised annually, usually in the summer, for use during the next school year. The revision policy helps to keep the lists current. These resources are used by classroom teachers. District media centers may subscribe to the entire set, although there is some overlap in coverage. Entries are pulled from the publishers' titles of print materials and the following audiovisual titles that are available in individual titles.

Guide to Free Computer Materials. Randolph, Wisconsin: Educators Progress Service, annual. ($36.95) This title was introduced in 1983. The volume lists films, disks, videotapes, brochures, pamphlets, articles, and other materials related to computers. The 1991 edition includes a new feature listing more than 2,000 titles of "shareware" for Apple, IBM, Macintosh, and Commodore computers. The title is released in April. A special feature is a 104-page glossary of computer terminology.

Free Audio and Video Materials. Randolph, Wisconsin: Educators Progress Service, annual. ($23.95) This 1991 resource includes 2,470 selected titles of audio and video materials available for free loan. Nearly 75 percent of the entries in the 1991 edition are for videotapes.

Free Films. Randolph, Wisconsin: Educators Progress Service, annual. ($27.95) The 51st edition of this title claims to be the only complete guide to all films available free of cost (no rental fee) throughout the United States. The 2,215 titles included represent the broad range of subjects of interest to schools, libraries, and industries. All entries are for 16mm films and are available for loan only.

Free Filmstrips and Slides. Randolph, Wisconsin: Educators Progress Service, annual. ($20.50) Included are filmstrips, slides, and transparencies, of which nearly 75 percent are slides. Most materials are for loan, but a few titles may be retained.

Titles in specific subject areas include the following.

Free Home Economics and Consumer Education Materials. Randolph, Wisconsin: Educators Progress Service, annual. ($23.00) The 8th edition (1991) lists 1,310 titles, of which nearly half are new. Forty-two percent of materials listed are print. About one-quarter of the entries are videotapes, with very few new films or filmstrips. The work is revised annually in August.

Free Science Materials. Randolph, Wisconsin: Educators Progress Service, annual. ($26.25) The title for the 1991-1992 school year includes in its 32nd edition a total of 1,520 free items. Nearly 35 percent of the entries are films, with print materials making up 30 percent and the rest including listings for audiotapes, videotapes, slides, and filmstrips.

Free Guidance Materials. Randolph, Wisconsin: Educators Progress Service, annual. ($25.95) This resource lists more than 2,180 guidance items, of which nearly 25 percent are new to the 1991 edition. It is a multimedia listing, and about 35 percent of the items are available as free-loan films; a quarter of the items are free print materials. The remainder are videotapes, audiotapes, slides, audiodiscs, filmstrips, and transparencies. Materials are grouped under categories of career planning, social-personal, responsibility, and use of leisure time.

Free Health, P.E. & Recreational Materials. Randolph, Wisconsin: Educators Progress Service, annual. ($26.75) The 24th edition (1991) lists more than 2,000 items, of which about 33 percent are printed materials including charts, posters, magazines, and pamphlets. In this edition 41 percent of the entries are new and, like all others in the series, are marked with an asterisk (*) for easy identification by regular users of the series. Information on sports and recreation fitness, nutrition, diseases, mental health, sex education, first aid, and family health is included.

Free Social Studies Materials. Randolph, Wisconsin: Educators Progress Service, annual. ($27.95) Social studies topics included are citizenship, communications, transportation, exhibits, geography, history, magazines, maps, social problems, world affairs, teacher reference, and professional growth materials. Of the 2,570 titles in the 1991 31st edition, about 25 percent are print materials and about 25 percent of the total items are new to this edition.

The following three specialized books were compiled by Carol Smallwood.

Current Issues Resource Builder: Free and Inexpensive Materials for Librarians and Teachers. Jefferson, North Carolina: McFarland, 1989. ($19.95) This source lists 280 topics including acid rain, AIDS, the homeless, literacy, and teenage parenting. The nearly 300-page directory lists sources with information about the focus and interests of the organization (see figure 2.6). State and regional offices are included with addresses and telephone numbers. Some specific titles are given. The topical guide is really an index to the directory and makes up three-quarters of the pages in the work. All materials lists are, by Smallwood's definition (under $16), free or inexpensive.

An Educational Guide to the National Park System. Metuchen, New Jersey: Scarecrow Press, 1989. ($39.50) This is a key to the wealth of information available through the National Park Service of the U.S. Department of the Interior (see figure 2.7). The National Park System includes 327 sites in various classifications including national parks, battlefields, memorials, and other types of sites. Entries are arranged by type and grouped under forty-seven broad subject headings. The guide is indexed by classification and title. Each entry includes the name, address, telephone number, acreage, year authorized or established, directions for locating, purpose, description of site, facilities, free print materials with annotations, audiovisual list, sales list, suggested curriculum applications, and suggested *Sears* subject headings. This publication is useful for teachers and librarians.

The Jefferson Foundation. 1529 18th St., N.W., Washington DC 20036, (202) 234-3688. Helps students and teachers meet Jefferson's challenge to review the Constitution. The foundation is a nonpartisan, nonadvocacy, nonprofit organization. Services: publications. Format of materials: curriculum guides. Cost. Grades 11-12, college, adult. American government. Ordering aids: "The Jefferson Meeting on the Constitution: The Constitution in the Classroom." 14 pp. Description of materials, order form. Selected examples: "Guide for Teachers Packet." Includes guide for teachers and a set of eight issue discussion guides. $12.00. "To Make and Alter Their Constitutions of Government, Article V and Amendment by Convention." One in the eight issue discussion guides that range from 16 to 37 pages. 75¢.

Johnson Institute. 7151 Metro Blvd., Minneapolis MN 55435, (800) 231-5165. Chemical dependence intervention, prevention and education. Services: publications, audiovisuals, videos, seminars, consultation. Format of materials: audiovisuals, booklets, books, coloring books, conference/program/workshop models/guides, curriculum guides, guides, packets/kits, videos. Cost. K-12, college, adult. Alcoholism, drug abuse, drunk driving, mental health, religion. Ordering aids: "Publications, Films and Audiocassettes." 46 pp. Title, author, description, format, pages, ISBN number, price. Selected examples:

Joint Center for Political Studies. Associates Program, Suite 400, 1301 Pennsylvania Ave., N.W., Washington DC 20004, (202) 626-3500. Seeks to unite black and white business and labor leaders, scholars, legislators, journalists and provide an open nonpartisan forum to discuss black Americans and society as a whole. Services: meetings, conferences, symposia, publications, research, literature searches, news packages. Format of materials: booklets, books, bulletins, case studies, monographs, newsletters, reports. Cost. Grades 10-12, college, adult. Black Americans. Ordering aids: "Introducing 3 New Books." 2 pp. Title, author, date, description, catalog number, pages, ISBN number, price. "Introducing Two New Books." 2 pp. Title, author, date, description, catalog number, pages, ISBN number, price. "Selected JCPS Publications." 2 pp. Title, date, catalog number, price, author/editor, order blank. Selected examples: "Mobilizing the Black Community: The Effects of Personal Contact Campaigning on Black Voters." 35 pp. Evaluation of the effects of personal contact, outlines ways of increasing black voter turnout. $4.95. "The Nineteen Eighties: Prologue and Prospect." 22 pp. Reviews the progress made by blacks, problems, opportunities. $2.95.

Fig. 2.6. Sample page from *Current Issues Resource Builder*. From *Current Issues Resource Builder: Free and Inexpensive Materials for Librarians and Teachers* © 1989 by Carol Smallwood by permission of McFarland & Company, Inc., Publishers, Jefferson, North Carolina.

INVENTORS / 129

- WRIGHT BROTHERS
National Memorial. c/o Cape Hatteras National Seashore, Route 1, Box 675, Manteo, NC 27954. (919) 441-7430. 431.40 acres. National Memorial, 1927; transferred from War Department, 1933; redesignated, 1953. Eastern North Carolina, on the outer banks of North Carolina about midway between Kitty Hawk and Nags Head on Byp. U.S. 158, about 10 miles from Cape Hatteras National Seashore.

Commemorate the first sustained flight in a heavier-than-air vehicle in 1903 by Wilbur and Orville Wright. Exhibits, full-scale reproductions of 1902 glider and 1903 flying machine, 60-foot Wright Monument shaft standing on the site of many glider experiments, reconstruction of the Wrights' 1903 camp. Visitor center. Food and lodging in Manteo.

Free Print Material:
"Camping Information." 2 pages. Description of Cape Hatteras National Seashore, names of campgrounds, ranger-conducted activities, fees, reservations, and other user information.
"In the Park." 12 pages. Newspaper format. Visitor information about Wright Brothers National Memorial, Fort Raleigh National Historic Site, Cape Hatteras National Seashore. Photos, schedules of activities, articles, maps, sales items.
"Wright Brothers." 12-fold. Narrative chronology from September 13, 1900 to the first flight December 17, 1903. Photos, maps, biographical information about the Wright brothers, what to see at the memorial.

Sales/Audiovisual List:
Items from the Eastern National Park and Monument Association included in "In the Park" described above. Includes: books, miscellaneous, children's books, slides, puzzles, posters, note cards, model kits.

Suggested Curriculum Application:
AMERICAN HISTORY
NORTH CAROLINA STATE AND LOCAL STUDIES
SOCIAL STUDIES

Suggested Sears Subject Heading:
FLIGHT
INVENTORS
NORTH CAROLINA--DESCRIPTION AND TRAVEL--GUIDES
NORTH CAROLINA--PUBLIC LANDS
U.S.--DESCRIPTION AND TRAVEL--GUIDES
WRIGHT, ORVILLE, 1871-1948
WRIGHT, WILBUR, 1867-1912

Fig. 2.7. Sample page from *An Educational Guide to the National Park System*. Reprinted by permission from *An Educational Guide to the National Park System* by Carol Smallwood (Metuchen, N.J.: Scarecrow Press, Inc. 1989). Copyright © 1989 by Carol Smallwood.

Health Resource Builder: Free and Inexpensive Materials for Librarians and Teachers. Jefferson, North Carolina: McFarland, 1988. ($15.95) Here is a topical approach to health resources from federal and state agencies, nonprofit associations, and a few commercial sources. Each entry includes the name, address, and telephone number of the source with a description of materials available. Examples of specific titles are given, but most are described generally with no prices listed. Useful appendix material includes state and regional offices of public agencies; a national health observances calendar; and a list of hotlines, telecommunications devices for the deaf (TDD), and other special telephone numbers. There is a detailed index. This volume is helpful to anyone building information files in health.

BIBLIOGRAPHIES AND PUBLICATIONS LISTS

In addition to books, there are a number of other ways to find supplementary materials. Many organizations, companies, government agencies, and special interest groups offer bibliographies and publications lists that are helpful in locating materials. It is important to be selective since materials available from these sources may be somewhat biased or may contain a plug for the product or the company. There are many fine materials available from these sources. The following examples illustrate the diversity that is possible.[5]

Dow Jones & Company, Inc., publishers of the *Wall Street Journal*, offers a list of educational materials that may be requested by writing to the Western Representative Educational Service Bureau, Dow Jones & Company, Inc., P.O. Box 2000, Riverside, California 92516.

The American Classical League issues a catalog of teaching materials for teachers of Latin, Greek, and the classical humanities. The 35-page list includes books and pamphlets in Latin, greeting cards, classroom accessories, coins, computer software, a directory of classical associations, fun and learning materials, historical novels, Latin games, posters, maps, charts, slides, and tape recordings. Most materials are available from the American Classical League.

American Fiber Manufacturers Association, Inc., formerly Man-Made Fiber Producers Association, Inc., includes history in its 1988 *Man-Made Fibers Guide* along with names of generic fibers, tradenames, and names and addresses of artificial fibers producers.

The United States Superintendent of Documents is the source of major guides to specific subjects and fields of interest that are published as a series called Subject Bibliographies. There have been hundreds published over the years on many diverse topics. *Subject Bibliography Index* will help in locating specific lists.

Metropolitan Life and Affiliated Companies is an example of a company that issues an extensive list of educational materials for libraries, schools, and other groups or individuals. The latest catalog is a 16-page listing of materials in the areas of personal and family health, safety and first aid, health risks, nutrition and fitness, and worksite health promotion. Materials available include pamphlets, reprints of articles, bookmarks, posters, cards, videotapes, cookbooks, and other promotional materials. There is a nominal charge for most items. Many can be ordered in quantities for distribution to patrons.

The Library of Congress catalog lists a number of free items among its books, pamphlets, serials, sound recordings, videos, and other miscellaneous items. Individual items are available from the Library of Congress, the issuing office, or from the Superintendent of Documents.

The American Humane Association has an eight-page catalog of materials of animal care and protection including books, booklets, classroom teaching kits for elementary students at three levels, reproducible articles with clip art, bookmarks, posters, flyers, stickers, pins, videotapes, a newsletter, a quarterly magazine, T-shirts, and other items. All items have a small charge.

The publications catalog of the League of Women Voters of the United States includes an eight-page listing of materials available. General areas of interest are how to be politically effective, election services, debates, government, international relations, natural resources, social policy, and public relations. Most items are under $3 with an approximate 30 percent discount for members. Booklets, flyers, and posters make up the majority of the listings.

PERIODICALS AND NEWSPAPERS

Many popular periodicals have regular columns listing free and inexpensive materials that would be appropriate for vertical files. The following are suggestions to check for general-interest topics: *Better Homes and Gardens, Changing Times, Family Handyman, Good Housekeeping, McCall's,* and *Seventeen*. You can also check other periodicals such as *English Journal, Library Journal, NASA Report to Educators, School Library Journal,* and *Wilson Library Bulletin*.

Newspapers frequently offer information on pamphlets or brochures that you can request. Generally the references are in articles on specific topics. Be alert to these sources as you read or clip the newspaper.

DIRECTORIES

Probably the best source for information about organizations is the annual *Encyclopedia of Associations* (Detroit, Michigan: Gale Research Inc., 3 volumes, 26th ed., 1992, $305). The 26th edition for 1992 includes more than 22,000 active associations, organizations, clubs, and other nonprofit membership groups. This is an expensive resource but would be worth a trip to the closest large library to get addresses for associations related to the information you need. Frequently libraries discard superseded sets, so perhaps you can get one that is just a year old.

United States Government Manual from the U.S. Government Printing Office is an excellent source of information on the structure of our system. Your own local telephone directory is one of the quickest and easiest ways to get ideas and information from local chapters of organizations and agency offices. Many will have the information or can give you the address to write for information.

World Chamber of Commerce Directory (P.O. Box 1029, Loveland, Colorado 80539) is available each June for $24. It contains addresses for U.S. and foreign chambers of commerce, state boards of tourism, foreign tourist information bureaus, and U.S. and foreign embassies.

22 / 2—Locating Resources

There are many options for locating sources of materials for vertical files and supplementary materials collections. The reader is encouraged to select one or two that best fit the library's needs. The section on vendors lists resources that have been discussed as well as additional sources including addresses, telephone numbers, and a guide to some of the specific titles and types of materials available from each source.

SUMMARY RECOMMENDATIONS

- Examine basic tools for locating resources by visiting another library or requesting titles on interlibrary loan.

- Buy a few tools or sources that best fit your needs.

NOTES

[1] *PAIS International in Print* began in January 1991, incorporating *PAIS Bulletin* and *PAIS Foreign Language Index*. The Public Affairs Information Service compiles this selective index to the latest materials including books, pamphlets, government publications, reports of public and private agencies and periodical articles relating to business, economic and social conditions, public administration, and international relations. Price or free status is indicated for materials. Many inexpensive items are listed. Subscription is $495 per year for 12 monthly issues. This resource is also on CD-ROM and online. *Hospital Literature Index* is a quarterly index on hospital and other health-care administration and is published by the American Hospital Association Resource Center ($200 per year for nonmembers). A feature in each issue, "Recent Acquisitions of the AHA Resource Center," lists pamphlets, reports, theses, new journals, audiovisual materials, and books that have been added to the American Hospital Association Library. If you have access to this tool, the feature can lead you to supplementary material in the health care area.

[2] This publication began in 1977 as *Sources: A Guide to Print and Nonprint Materials Available from Organizations, Industry, Government Agencies, and Specialized Publishers*, distributed by Gaylord in association with Neal-Schuman Publishers. The title was changed in 1983 with the beginning of volume 6. To date there have been two editions of selected resources from this periodical published under the title *Information America: Sources of Print and Nonprint Materials Available from Organizations, Industry, Government Agencies and Specialized Publishers*. The first edition was in 1985 and the second edition in 1990.

[3] For another general source see Fran Malin and Richard Stanzi, compilers, *Information America: Sources of Print and Nonprint Materials Available from Organizations, Industry, Government Agencies and Specialized Publishers*, 2d ed. (New York: Neal-Schuman Publishers, 1990) ($150). "This work updates and expands the 1985 edition and brings together some 3,000 substantial entries, selected and revised from ten volumes of the periodical Information America." See also Matthew Lesko, *Information U.S.A.*, rev. ed. (New York: Viking, 1986)

($22.95). This 1,253-page paperback contains a wealth of information to help you locate items from the various agencies in the federal government. The book is written to the general public so you will want to make it available on your reference shelf as well as glean ideas from it for your vertical-file materials.

[4]Another example of a title in a specific subject area is Bruce Nash and Allan Zullo, *Freebies for Sports Fans* (New York: Simon & Schuster, 1990) ($4.95). This is a directory of more than 160 free and inexpensive (less than $1) items for young fans. Vertical-file additions can be found in entries for pamphlets, newsletters, magazines, and newspapers related to the rules, equipment, history, and safety of various sports. Novelty items including trading cards, decals, stickers, buttons, and pins will interest young readers. This inexpensive paperback is bound to be a best-seller.

[5]Other examples include the American Bar Association, American Association of Petroleum Geologists, and American Association for State and Local History. Additional information including addresses and telephone numbers is included in the section on vendors.

3
Selection

Many of the principles you apply to choosing other materials for your collection will also apply to the selection of items to add to your vertical files or supplementary materials collections. The fact that many of these materials are free or inexpensive should not distort your perception of the importance of good selection policies. Because there is so much material available (and much of it from commercial and special-interest groups) it is even more important to be careful in the selection of material you add to your collection.

Care in selection cannot be emphasized too much but remember that the opportunity to expand the scope of subjects covered in your collection with free or inexpensive items is one of the main reasons for establishing your supplementary collection. This collection can provide a broad coverage of subjects with little investment. At the same time, you want to add depth to the areas of interest that are already developed in your collection. Alternative formats and presentation styles are other factors to seek out when selecting materials.

Selection is one of the most important steps in building your information files, but you are bound to make a few mistakes. When something you have ordered turns out to be inappropriate, throw it out before you process it. You are ordering most supplementary materials without the benefit of reviews, so many decisions will have to be made after the material is received. Evaluating supplementary materials will become easier as you do it more often. An active weeding system will give you an opportunity to reevaluate materials on a regular basis.

THE COST OF FREE MATERIALS

Every item you place in your library costs you in time, supplies, and space, in addition to the price of the item. Although many supplementary materials are "free" or inexpensive to acquire, it is important to remember the hidden costs when you are selecting materials. Estimate that each item will cost you at least one hour of time. Figure the cost based on the hourly rate or average rate of the people who work with the materials. Looking at resources with that perspective will help you be more selective. If it is necessary for you to process a purchase order, then that cost should be figured as well. The average cost to process a purchase order in larger institutions may be on the order of $75.

GUIDELINES FOR THE ACQUISITION OF SUPPLEMENTARY MATERIALS

It will be helpful to establish basic guidelines for developing your collection of supplementary materials along with some general policies and procedures for processing and managing the items. These guidelines will ensure consistency for teachers and librarians and facilitate the training of new employees or volunteers who may wish to help in the library. When you consider adding specific kinds of supplementary materials to your collection, you may find the list of questions in figure 3.1 helpful. You will notice that many questions reflect the criteria for all materials in the library as well as for supplementary materials.

Need or Place in the Collection

1. Will these materials be used? Yes No
   If not, do you have a good reason to acquire them? Yes No
2. Will the materials be used often? Yes No
   If not, can you justify getting them? Yes No
3. Is this the only source of this kind of information in your library? Yes No
   If not, will it add to the collection? Yes No
4. Does your collection need this viewpoint? Yes No
   If not, does it add information? Yes No

Presentation

5. Is this format desirable? Yes No
   If not, do you really want it? Yes No
6. Is this material easy to use? Yes No
   If not, do you have a good reason to add it? Yes No

Authority

7. Is the material accurate? Yes No
   If not, should you even consider it? Yes No
8. Is the material from a reliable source? Yes No
   If not, do you have a good reason to add it? Yes No
9. Is the material objective?* Yes No
   If not, can you justify putting it in the collection? Yes No
10. Is the name and address of the source on the item? Yes No
    If not, have you written it on the item? Yes No

Timeliness

11. Was the item published within the past three years? Yes No
    If not, is it valuable for historical reasons? Yes No
12. Is the date printed on the material? Yes No
    If not, have you written the date of receipt on the material? Yes No

*You must discipline yourself to limit the propaganda-type material that will fill your files if you are not very selective in choosing your additions.

Fig. 3.1. Questions to ask yourself when considering materials.

If you cannot answer each question with a yes, you need to look carefully at the material in hand to be sure that you really want to add it to your collection. Questions 7, 8, and 9 are critical. If you get a no on any of the questions, you should probably reject the material.

If you have the space and time, your supplementary materials collection can add both breadth and depth to your book collection, but the managing of supplementary materials can be an overwhelming task if you allow the collection to grow without a plan. Avoid the temptation to get something just because it is free. Avoid the temptation to keep something just because it is there.

SUMMARY RECOMMENDATIONS

- Establish guidelines for the acquisition and retention of supplementary materials.

- Include your collection development priorities in your guidelines.

- Start with a few kinds of materials and expand slowly.

4
Ordering

Under ordering, several issues are discussed including means of placing the order, the message, mailing, payment, record-keeping, and alternatives. Ordering principles, policies, and procedures will be similar for all types of supplementary materials. Unique ordering problems for specific types of supplementary materials are addressed in the section dealing with that particular type of material.

HOW TO PLACE AN ORDER

There are several means of placing orders: postcards, computer-generated letters, photocopied form letters, individually written letters and cards, or telephone calls.

Postcards. These are appropriate for most routine requests for free materials.

Form postcards. These are even better time-savers and can be tailored to special needs. For instance, if you are requesting college catalogs or information from local chambers of commerce, art galleries, or some other group of sources, you can tailor your requests to the group. See figure 4.1 for an example.

Supplementary Materials Coordinator
University of Alaska Anchorage Library
3211 Providence Drive
Anchorage, Alaska 99508

Please send one copy each of the following free materials for use in our library. If there is a charge, please advise us before sending the material.

We appreciate your help in assisting us to build a collection of supplementary materials to enrich our library collection.

Requested by Clara L. Sitter, Supplementary Materials Coordinator.

Fig. 4.1. Sample form postcard.

28 / 4—Ordering

Form letters. These offer little advantage over form postcards and require more postage unless you are ordering a number of titles from that source. Figure 4.2 provides a sample form letter for occasions when they are appropriate.

UNIVERSITY OF ALASKA, ANCHORAGE

3211 Providence Drive
Anchorage, Alaska 99508
SAN 300-2497

LIBRARY SYSTEM

Dear Sponsor:

Please send one copy each of the following free materials for use in our library. If there is a charge, please advise us before sending the materials.

We appreciate your help in assisting us to build a collection of supplementary materials to enrich our library.

Sincerely,

Clara L. Sitter
Supplementary Materials Coordinator

A DIVISION OF THE UNIVERSITY OF ALASKA STATEWIDE SYSTEM OF HIGHER EDUCATION

Fig. 4.2. Sample form letter.

Personalized individual letters. These are generally not worth the extra time involved unless they can be computer generated. They are recommended in the following situations, however:

- when special explanations are necessary or personalized attention is being requested,
- if the source is an unusual one that is unaccustomed to handling requests for materials, or
- if the supply of the item is limited, in which case a personal letter may have a slight advantage.

Telephone orders. These are an option since many sources have toll-free 800 telephone numbers. It will take much more time to locate the right person for the order, place the order, and provide mailing information than it will to address a card or an envelope. This is recommended only when you need something in a rush.

HOW TO PREPARE A REQUEST

1. Use your institution's logo or letterhead.
2. Keep it brief. Most requests will be handled by clerks who do not want to read a long letter.
3. Designate a particular person, position, or collection to receive materials. If you do not want to use personal names, use File Librarian or Career Collection, which facilitates the sorting of mail.
4. Include a mailing label for faster returns. (You can get peelable mailing labels for postcards, but be sure to include a notation that it is to be used for the return mailing.)
5. Ask to be put on mailing lists for free materials if you are interested in other materials they publish.
6. Use the readers' service postcards in magazines.
7. If materials are marked with restrictions such as "for teachers only," be sure to explain that your library serves teachers.
8. Ask for specific titles if there are particular ones you want. Word your request to include new titles on the same subject.
9. Be clear about the topics you are interested in if you are making a subject request.
10. Avoid vague requests such as "Send all of your publications." Ask for a catalog or list of publications if you need more information.

HOW TO FACILITATE MAILING

1. Check old addresses if you have not used them for some time. Organizations and businesses move frequently and the Postal Service will forward mail for only one year.

2. Consider a bulk-mailing permit. Check with the Postal Service for details, because there are specific requirements. Your institution may have a permit that you could use for certain groups of requests, for example, to embassies.

3. Use peelable return mailing labels on your postcards.

4. Have envelopes printed with your address if you have many requests for self-addressed, stamped envelopes (SASE).

HOW TO SIMPLIFY PAYMENT

Set up a deposit account for federal documents available from the U.S. Superintendent of Documents. Note that some government documents are available for sale only by the issuing agency.

Ask the publishers about blanket orders, annual subscriptions, or any other means of simplified billing. Remember that the cost of processing a purchase order increases the cost of the materials, especially in a large institution, where it can be as high as $75.

HOW TO KEEP TRACK OF ORDERS

Record-keeping for purchased materials will conform to the requirements dictated by the institution. In any case there should be some type of order card or form for each item ordered. Record-keeping for requests for free materials can vary widely. Actual practice ranges from keeping no records of requests to elaborate indexes by source and title.[1] Common sense will probably be your best guide. The following options may give you some ideas.

1. Mark the entries when ordering from a list of free materials (for example, write on your list or photocopy pages you order from. This is an easy way to keep a record of requests).

2. Record important requests (for example, for local history files).

3. Use a tickler file if you request certain publications on a regular basis (for example, annual reports).

4. Use a check-in card for regularly issued items (for example, college catalogs). You can easily record an order notation.

5. Keep a source file if you order frequently from a source (for example, combine requests and order every two months).

6. Use your computer if it simplifies record-keeping for you (for example, record the date of request, source, address, items, cost, date of receipt, and comments). Set up your computer file so you can sort by title (item), source, subject, or anything else that is important to you.

Remember that the more time you spend on each item, the more expensive it becomes.

YOUR ORDERING ALTERNATIVES

An option in the ordering process is to use a pamphlet jobber, service, or agent.[2] The advantages are simplified bookkeeping, reduction of correspondence, and a higher percentage of filled orders. Disadvantages are slower service and added expense. One example is Accents Publications Service, Inc., a distributor of U.S. government publications and association publications for trade and professional associations; scientific, technical, and scholarly societies; and public policy and intergovernmental organizations. They also provide a document retrieval service for reports and journal articles and supply scientific, technical, and scholarly books — all this for a fee, of course.

Supplementary materials are not ordered in the same way that book and periodical orders are handled. There are a number of options related to ordering supplementary materials. Each librarian will choose the means that works best for the situation.

SUMMARY RECOMMENDATIONS

- Keep the ordering process simple.
- Order groups of materials when appropriate.

NOTES

[1]Geraldine H. Gould and Ithmer Wolfe, *How to Organize and Maintain the Library Picture/Pamphlet File* (New York: Oceana Publications, Inc., 1968 out of print). The authors recommend a system of controlling requests based on a three-section file for (1) sources requested, (2) sources received, and (3) subject cards listing sources.

[2]Library Reference Service, though not a pamphlet jobber in the true sense of the word, offers some shortcuts in making available sets of pamphlets and articles by compiling sets of files on various topics. Social Issues Resources Series (SIRS) offers similar packages in loose-leaf notebooks. The Gold Files is a series of education topics offered by the Arizona Educational Information System on the campus of Arizona State University. Addresses, telephone numbers, and related information about these and other vendors are listed in the vendors section.

5
Initial Processing and Labeling

INITIAL PROCESSING

Very quickly after you send your first batch of requests you will begin getting mail. You need a system for processing materials when they arrive. It may seem like a lot of steps at first, but it will soon become routine. You may find that it is helpful to have a checklist posted where the materials are processed to ensure that everything gets done (see figure 5.1). The general routine is initial processing, assignment of a subject heading or classification, and then labeling. Occasionally notes are added during the labeling process.

Write on each item:

_____ Source including address

_____ Cost of the item

Stamp each item:

_____ Library name and address

_____ Date of receipt

_____ Name of file or collection

Sort for organization:

_____ By file or special collection

Fig. 5.1. Checklist for initial processing.

Following is a step-by-step guide to initial processing:

☐ Check to be sure that the name and address of the issuing body on the mailing envelope is repeated on the publication. Add the information by hand before you discard the envelope or packaging. Names and addresses are important for several reasons: to determine whether the information is authoritative, to alert the user to any slant or bias, to provide full bibliographic information, to provide information for ordering new editions for the library, and to provide information to the patron who might want to write for a personal copy.

☐ Mark the cost or free status of material. This information is useful to the librarian deciding on replacement or to the patron who wants to order a personal copy. If you don't keep acquisition records, this may be your only record of cost. Again, you should select a standard location. For pamphlets a recommended place is the top inner corner of the first inside page. You can use the same location for the source information when it needs to be recorded.[1]

☐ Stamp each item with the following: date of receipt, library name and address, and name of the file or special collection. It is important to write or stamp the date of receipt on all items, particularly if there is no date on the publication. The date of receipt will give an indication of the period when the item was being distributed and will indicate that the publication was the newest available at the time of receipt. This practice will also aid patrons who are not skilled at hunting for the publisher's date, which is often concealed in a code. In addition, stamping the date of receipt on items will speed the process of weeding. Use a date stamp on which the month, day, and year can be changed. Including the library name and address is important because people move frequently, and library materials may get returned if the patron has the address available. As indicated above, the ownership stamp and the dater can be combined into one stamp. Adding the name of the file or special collection as part of your stamp will facilitate refiling and avoid confusion. Date stamps, or "daters," that incorporate all of these items are available. Rubber-stamp firms are located in most cities, or stamps can be ordered from library supply catalogs.

☐ Stamp each piece of material in the same location. Determine an alternate place to stamp if the cover is too dark or too glossy to accept stamping.

☐ Rough sort materials by setting up boxes according to eventual disposition. Examples include college catalogs, pamphlets, maps, or pictures.

☐ Decide where the material will be placed in the collection based on your policy decisions and according to your organization system. Once that is done you are ready to continue the processing with the labeling of the item.

LABELING

Labeling is a very important step in the processing of supplementary materials. Labeling is the step in processing that marks the material with the identifying information for shelving and circulation. Labeling may or may not include the use of a separate label affixed to the item. The speed in finding and filing materials is directly related to the manner in which they are marked. The problems and options related to specific kinds of materials are discussed in later sections. The recommendations that follow are for the general vertical-file materials.

34 / 5—Initial Processing and Labeling

Make headings uniformly placed and instantly recognizable. Do not fall into the trap of underlining words in the cover titles of pamphlets or headlines of clippings. The time saved will be lost many times over in the filing process. If materials are to be filed upright in a box, the logical place for the heading is the upper left-hand corner. If the item is to be filed in a file folder, you can label it near the closed edge of the spine. Pamphlets should be filed so that the spine or closed edge is at the top. This practice of filing keeps small items from being slipped between the pages and makes it easier to distinguish where one pamphlet ends and the next one begins.

Hand print headings or use labels that are hand printed, typewritten, or computer printed. Many libraries hand print headings directly on the item. If you are hand printing, use a marking pen that is bold but fine enough to form clear letters in the space available (see figure 5.2). Try different points until you find one that pleases you. Some libraries use red ink for more permanent items and green ink for those with a shorter shelf life.

Typewritten or computer-printed labels are always uniform and look very nice, but the extra time required to make labels and match them with material is something you will want to consider carefully.

Use a pen if you hand print labels. The argument for using a pencil is that headings for supplementary resources change. The need for occasional revision does not justify using a pencil. Penciled headings are difficult to read, they fade and smudge, and they are messy looking.

Consider color-coding. You can facilitate access to certain resources and prevent mistakes in filing by color-coding. The use of colored labels is the most effective way to color-code items. Labels are available in solid colors or with colored bands. Colored ink can be used for coding but it is not as obvious as the color used in labels. Colored dots are another option for coding but are more likely to peel off. One problem with color-coding is that the system breaks down if you run out of the right color label or pen and begin to substitute.

Use a stamp to differentiate groups. An example would be "TRAVEL" stamped just above the heading.

Consider the adhesive for your label. You have many choices of adhesives for temporary or permanent labels. Labels are available in gummed, pressure sensitive, and now in Post-it materials. They can be found in a variety of sizes and shapes and in a rainbow of colors.

Supply information for the circulation of materials. For example, if there are multiple copies of a publication, there should be a notation of the copy number. If an accession number or bar code is used, it becomes a part of the labeling process if it was not applied before. If the material is for reference only, the reference sticker or stamp Not for Circulation or For Use in the Library Only should be used.

PUBLIC LAW 102-1—JAN. 14, 1991 105 STAT. 3

Public Law 102-1
102d Congress

Joint Resolution

To authorize the use of United States Armed Forces pursuant to United Nations Security Council Resolution 678.

Jan. 14, 1991
[H.J. Res. 77]

Whereas the Government of Iraq without provocation invaded and occupied the territory of Kuwait on August 2, 1990;

Whereas both the House of Representatives (in H.J. Res. 658 of the 101st Congress) and the Senate (in S. Con. Res. 147 of the 101st Congress) have condemned Iraq's invasion of Kuwait and declared their support for international action to reverse Iraq's aggression;

Whereas, Iraq's conventional, chemical, biological, and nuclear weapons and ballistic missile programs and its demonstrated willingness to use weapons of mass destruction pose a grave threat to world peace;

Whereas the international community has demanded that Iraq withdraw unconditionally and immediately from Kuwait and that Kuwait's independence and legitimate government be restored;

Whereas the United Nations Security Council repeatedly affirmed the inherent right of individual or collective self-defense in response to the armed attack by Iraq against Kuwait in accordance with Article 51 of the United Nations Charter;

Whereas, in the absence of full compliance by Iraq with its resolutions, the United Nations Security Council in Resolution 678 has authorized member states of the United Nations to use all necessary means, after January 15, 1991, to uphold and implement all relevant Security Council resolutions and to restore international peace and security in the area; and

Whereas Iraq has persisted in its illegal occupation of, and brutal aggression against Kuwait: Now, therefore, be it

50 USC 1541 note.

Resolved by the Senate and House of Representatives of the United States of America in Congress assembled,

SECTION 1. SHORT TITLE.

This joint resolution may be cited as the "Authorization for Use of Military Force Against Iraq Resolution".

SEC. 2. AUTHORIZATION FOR USE OF UNITED STATES ARMED FORCES.

(a) AUTHORIZATION.—The President is authorized, subject to subsection (b), to use United States Armed Forces pursuant to United Nations Security Council Resolution 678 (1990) in order to achieve implementation of Security Council Resolutions 660, 661, 662, 664, 665, 666, 667, 669, 670, 674, and 677.

Authorization for Use of Military Force Against Iraq Resolution.
Kuwait.
50 USC 1541 note.
President.
50 USC 1541 note.

Fig. 5.2. Example of hand printing directly on the item. The SuDocs (Superintendent of Documents) number has been printed directly on the slip law from a special collection of U.S. government documents.

NOTES TO FILES

Another issue that comes up in the discussion of labeling is adding notes. One note you may want to consider is for older materials that you have determined are important to keep in your file: *NOTE: This item is more than five years old, but it is still useful.* It is better to avoid labeling materials if possible, but there may be cases where you feel that an explanation is needed regarding particular points of view. You can make a note in your signage or in your handouts reminding users that you have attempted to include differing points of view, but you may also want to add a note to a particular file folder or envelope: *NOTE: There are differing points of view about this subject. The library has attempted to represent some of them in the material in this folder.* Computer labels can be generated for the two notes above. If a computer is not available, you can also use a copy machine to photocopy labels. Print enough to have on hand when they are needed.

Once a routine is established, the processing of materials can be done quickly. Students and volunteers can easily handle the initial processing and labeling. Ideally, the person who works with the files should be the one to assign subject headings or classification numbers to the items.

SUMMARY RECOMMENDATIONS

- Put name and address of the source and the cost on each item.

- Stamp each item with the name and address of the library, date received, and name of the file or special collection.

NOTES

[1] If you bar code vertical-file items, this may be the place to add it to your processing. Bar codes are labels containing machine-readable data (generally representing a number) in the form of vertical bars. Bar codes are used in automated circulation systems. The use of bar codes for vertical-file materials will be discussed in the section on organization by sequence/accession and also in the section on circulation.

6
Organization

The usefulness of supplementary materials is dependent to a large part on the way they are organized. Supplementary resources vary so much in format, subject, size, and use that it is impossible to wrap them up in one neat organizational package. There are three important elements in the topic of organization: the type of organization, subject headings, and indexes. These areas represent some of the most important decisions you will make regarding your supplementary materials collection.

TYPES OF ORGANIZATION

Here we discuss several options for generic approaches to the organization of supplementary materials for your vertical files. The easiest ways to organize information are based on the basic concepts of arranging materials either alphabetically, numerically in sequence, or a combination of the two in an alphanumeric system.

An example of a simple alphabetical arrangement of material would be to arrange by some obvious element of the work such as name or title. This is the arrangement used for most indexes and directories. Organization by numerical sequence can be a simple 1,2,3 arrangement or 00001, 00002, 00003. A variation of numerical arrangement is chronological, such as 1991, 1992, 1993; or 92-0001, 92-0002.

When organization is by subject, materials can be arranged alphabetically by subject or classified by subject using one of the standard classification systems. Most libraries use either the Dewey Decimal Classification system or the Library of Congress (LC) Classification system. Dewey has a numerical system for subject classification, and LC uses a combination of letters and numbers in its alphanumeric system.

Special collections of materials often have unique characteristics that provide logical ways to organize them. It is likely that you will have one or more special collections. Particular problems related to specific types of materials are addressed later. The important thing to remember in the decision for the arrangement of materials is to select the system of organization that works best for your collection. Use the system that you think will be best for your users but keep it as simple as possible.

Alphabetical by Subject — The Dictionary Arrangement

The widely used system of organization that employs an alphabetical arrangement of subject headings is sometimes called a dictionary arrangement. This arrangement is an efficient, economical way to cope with supplementary materials and is probably the most popular approach. This approach has a number of advantages. First, it is direct. There is no need to translate verbal ideas into an artificial code. Second, it is simple. The alphabetical arrangement is easy to understand and to manipulate. Patrons can be more independent in their use of the files. Third, it is detailed. A dictionary approach allows for the use of individualized and definitive terms, which speeds access to materials. Fourth, it is adjustable. New subjects are easily added to a dictionary arrangement. Refinements of old subjects are easy to incorporate. Fifth, it is easy to spot weaknesses because materials on the same subject (but not related subjects) are filed together. An empty file indicates a lack of materials. However, the dictionary arrangement has several disadvantages: related materials are not filed in proximity to each other, for example, lions and tigers; additional cross-references are necessary to ensure that materials are found; and outdated material is harder to weed than in a sequential system because you must look at each item in every file.

Classified by Subject — Dewey or Library of Congress (LC) Arrangement

The concept of classifying pamphlet material appears in the early literature of the profession, written when the few pamphlets permitted inside a library were given legitimacy by being classified and placed on the shelves with their more respectable cousins. Sometimes single pamphlets were allowed this distinction, but more often related pamphlets were bound together into what were called pamphlet volumes or into groups of associated pamphlets in boxes on the shelves with the books.

If you decide on classification for your supplementary materials, you will most likely use the same classification system used for your book collection. In theory, using Dewey or Library of Congress classification numbers for all library resources simplifies and correlates their use.[1]

The classification of pamphlets and other supplementary materials without full cataloging is done in some collections. Some librarians shelve pamphlet boxes with related books in the traditional manner; others set aside small rooms or areas where boxes of pamphlets stand in general classification order. Classified pamphlets and clippings are frequently housed in vertical filing cabinets.

A few attempts have been made at constructing special classification schemes for general vertical files. If the decision is made to classify materials, then the advantages and disadvantages should be considered carefully. Special collections of supplementary materials are another issue. Special collections often are better organized by a specialized system for the particular discipline or material. Advantages in using Dewey or LC systems include:

Ease of use of a ready-made scheme like Dewey or LC. Unless there is a special scheme that can be easily used for special types of materials such as the Superintendent of Documents (SuDocs) number or the Dictionary of Occupational Titles (DOT) system, then you have a good reason to invent your own system.

Logic of applying the same finding code to all library resources on the same subject. This concept of unifying all library resources is particularly appealing to school librarians who are eager to present a quick overview of all library holdings on a particular subject to teachers and students.

Helpfulness of having related subjects in close physical proximity. For example, the patron who is interested in pets may find it useful to have all pamphlets on dogs, cats, and hamsters within easy eye range rather than scattered through the file under widely separated headings. Physical closeness, made possible by the classified system, makes it more convenient to work one's way back to broader classes if information is not found under the specific topic.

Ease in surveying the library's holdings in the basic areas of knowledge in a classified system. Strengths and weaknesses in relation to the collection as a whole are readily apparent.

Some of the problems related to using a classified system include the following:

Generalized classification blurs the emphasis on specifics. The classification of supplementary materials does not work as well in practice as in theory because of an important characteristic of supplementary materials: Most of them concentrate on small areas of emphasis with very specific subjects. The result is use of a long, complex classification number or the burial of the item in a general class number that will not give a precise clue to its contents.

Generalized shelving also blurs the emphasis on specifics. Shelving pamphlets with related books presents the same problem of weakening the specific approach, though the addition of full cataloging helps somewhat.

Using Dewey or LC may not be expedient. One of the arguments for collecting supplementary materials is the availability of very current materials. When librarians are forced to make decisions regarding classification in addition to assigning subject headings, the processing of materials is likely to be slowed to the point of losing the edge of currency.

There is a lack of flexibility. New concepts are slow to appear in revisions and updates of classification tables.

Classification involves dependence on an index to the collection. The artificial symbol creates an additional barrier between the user and the information.

Sequential by Number—Accession Number Arrangement

Some libraries do not attempt to physically group their materials by subject; rather they simply arrange them by order of receipt. Materials are marked with a sequential code consisting usually of an accession number, e.g., 91-0001, 91-0002, 91-0003, but sometimes a combination of letters and numbers, e.g., P-00001, P-00002, P-00003, for pictures is used. Access is achieved through an index. The index can be a card file, a part of the card catalog, or a computer file. The code number is recorded under the appropriate subject or subjects. If author and title cards are used, the code number is recorded there also.

A sequence of bar codes can be assigned to the vertical files or to special collections of materials. If items are organized by bar-code number, it serves as an aid to both organization and circulation. Other options for the use of bar codes will be discussed in chapter 10, "Circulation."

Dale E. Shaffer incorporated a modified form of serial arrangement in his Sha-Frame system. His plan called for arranging pamphlets by size as well as by acquisition order. This system is no longer for sale, but there may be remnants of the system in some libraries, and the booklet is available on interlibrary loan.

The flaw of using a sequence or accession system is in retrieval. Retrieving only one pamphlet is no problem, but this system discourages the use of multiple pamphlets on the same subject. Browsing is not possible and the system depends upon materials being kept in precise order.

The use of a computer simplifies the record-keeping part of a sequential system. Difficulty in retrieval is still a concern; however, filing by accession number does facilitate the weeding process based on date. The system has been used successfully in personal information files for librarians and teachers.

SUBJECT HEADING ALTERNATIVES

You have several alternatives in your choice of an authority list for subject headings. You can use a subject-headings list written for vertical files; you can use the standard subject-headings list used for the book collection; you can select headings from various indexes and other guides; or you can make up your authority list by consulting a combination of available resources and using the headings most appropriate for your users.

Subject-Headings Lists Written for Vertical Files

There have been some lists of subject headings written specifically for vertical files, but they are soon out-of-date because of the nature of the materials that belong in information files. Subject-headings lists used in the past include the following out-of-print resources:

Ball, Miriam Ogden. *Subject Headings for the Information File*. 8th ed. New York: H. W. Wilson, 1956. This list was based on headings used in the Newark (New Jersey) Public Library.

Ireland, Norma Olin. *The Pamphlet File in School, College, and Public Libraries*. Rev. ed. Boston: F. W. Faxon Co., 1954.

Subject Headings for Vertical Files. 2d ed. Toronto, Canada: Toronto Public Libraries, 1971. The first edition was in 1964 and a third edition is expected in 1992. Based on *Sears List of Subject Headings*. Canadian emphasis.

Standard Subject Headings for the Book Collection

The use of standard subject-headings lists for the book collection, i.e., *Sears List of Subject Headings* (see figure 6.1) and *Library of Congress Subject Headings* (see figure 6.2), can be used for many topics. Adopting one of these standard lists has both advantages and disadvantages.[2]

> **Caste**   294.5; 305.5; 323.3
> *See also* **Social classes**
> *xx* **Brahmanism; Hinduism; Manners and customs**
> Casting.   *See*   **Founding; Plaster casts**
> **Castles** (May subdiv. geog.)   728.8
> *x* Chateaux
> *xx* **Architecture; Architecture, Medieval**
> Casts, Plaster.   *See*   **Plaster casts**
> **Casualty insurance**   368.5
> *See also* **Accident insurance**
> *x* Insurance, Casualty
> *xx* **Insurance**
> Cat.   *See*   **Cats**
> CAT (Computerized axial tomography).   *See* **Tomography**
> CAT scan.   *See*   **Tomography**
> **Catacombs**   393; 726
> *See also* **Church history**—30(ca.)-600, Early church
> *x* Burial
> *xx* **Cemeteries; Christian antiquities; Christian art and symbolism; Church history**—30(ca.)-600, Early church; **Tombs**

Fig. 6.1. Sample page from *Sears List of Subject Headings*.

The advantages of the *Sears* system are that (1) subjects can be coordinated with book and media subject headings; (2) it is easy to use as a subject authority by simply checking entries; (3) Dewey Decimal numbers are given that correlate with the collection; and (4) cross-references are given. The disadvantages of this system are that (1) it contains general subject headings; (2) it is designed for small collections; and (3) it is not widely used as a subject authority in data bases.

Castillo de Matamoros (Guatemala,
    Guatemala)
    [F1476.G9]
    UF Castillo de San Rafael de Matamoros
            (Guatemala, Guatemala)
        Fuerte de San Rafael de Matamoros
            (Guatemala, Guatemala)
        Matamoros Castle (Guatemala,
            Guatemala)
        San Rafael de Matamoros Castle
            (Guatemala, Guatemala)
    BT Castles—Guatemala
        Fortification—Guatemala
        Prisons—Guatemala
Castillo de Mesones de Isuela (Mesones de
    Isuela, Spain)
    UF Mesones de Isuela Castle (Mesones de
            Isuela, Spain)
    BT Castles—Spain
Castillo de Omoa (Omoa, Honduras)
    USE Fortaleza de San Fernando (Omoa,
            Honduras)
Castillo de Ponferrada (Ponferrada, Spain)
    UF Ponferrada Castle (Ponferrada, Spain)
    BT Castles—Spain
Castillo de San Juan de Ulúa (San Juan de
    Ulúa Island, Mexico)
    UF San Juan de Ulúa Castle (San Juan de
            Ulúa Island, Mexico)
    BT Castles—Mexico
        Fortification—Mexico
        Presidents—Mexico—Dwellings
        Prisons—Mexico

Casting directors *(May Subd Geog)*
    BT Motion picture producers and directors
        Theatrical producers and directors
Casting of motion pictures
    USE Motion pictures—Casting
Casting of plastics
    USE Plastics—Molding
Casting of plays
    USE Theater—Casting
Castings, Fossil
    USE Coprolites
Castings, Metal
    USE Metal castings
Castings, Molybdenum
    USE Molybdenum castings
Castings, Titanium
    USE Titanium castings
Castle (Chess)
    USE Rook (Chess)
Castle Amber (Imaginary place)
    BT Geographical myths
    RT Zelazny, Roger—Settings
Castle Clinton (New York, N.Y.)
    (Not Subd Geog)
    UF Clinton, Castle (New York, N.Y.)
        Fort Clinton (New York, N.Y.)
        West Battery (New York, N.Y.)
    BT Fortification—New York (State)
    RT Castle Clinton National Monument
            (New York, N.Y.)
Castle Garden (New York, N.Y.)

Fig. 6.2. Sample page from *Library of Congress Subject Headings*, 13th ed., 1990.

The advantages of the *Library of Congress* system are as follows: (1) subjects are easily coordinated with book headings; (2) it can be used as a subject authority by checking entries; (3) cross-references are given; (4) it is widely accepted as a standard subject authority; and (5) generally, entries are more specific than *Sears*. The disadvantages are that most new topics will not be entered and many awkward terms are used that are inappropriate for vertical files.

Subject Headings from Indexes and Guides

Some libraries use the headings from *Vertical File Index*, which provides a good source for the latest terms. The *Readers' Guide to Periodical Literature* is another standby resource giving detailed current headings that change with the times. Large libraries and special libraries can easily make use of the subject headings from specialized indexes in their collections.

There are many specialized periodical indexes in subject areas (for example, *Education Index* for education topics, *Art Index* for art topics, and *Index Medicus* or *Index to Nursing & Allied Health Literature* for medical and health subjects). A number of indexing services publish their list of subject headings sometime during the year as part of the subscription. For example, subscribers to *Index Medicus* receive an updated copy of *Medical Subject Headings* in January each year, but the list can also be purchased separately. *Index to Nursing & Allied Health Literature* lists all headings in the annual cumulation and can also be purchased separately. Another index that offers a subject-headings list as a separate publication is the Public Affairs Information Service (*PAIS Subject Headings*, 2d ed.).

Other guides such as printed thesauruses for on-line searching of the various specific databases may be helpful (for example, *Thesaurus of ERIC Descriptors* [12th ed. Phoenix, Arizona: Oryx Press, 1990] for education terms and *Thesaurus of Psychological Index Terms* [6th ed. Arlington, Virginia: American Psychological Association, 1991] for psychology).

Establishing Your Own Subject-Headings List

The best solution for providing subject headings is to choose an authority list for a guide but adapt it to meet your needs. You will always need a provision for assigning your own headings for the topics that are not covered in your authority list. Give the responsibility for assigning subject headings to one person if possible. Others should certainly have input and be consulted and informed of decisions, but one person can keep a better view of the entire collection. A few principles may help you with this challenging task:

Make subject headings specific. To make the file most useful for your patrons, try to imagine how they will be looking for something (for example: AIDS [Disease] rather than Acquired Immune Deficiency Syndrome). Usually they will want a specific subject.

Make subject headings simple and direct. Use the terminology your patrons will be using. For example, House Plans is better than Architecture, Domestic if what you actually have is house plans. Information on pen pals in other countries is much more likely to be found under Pen Pals than under International Correspondence, and Money would be more useful than Currency.

Avoid inverted subject headings if possible. People do not think in terms of inverted concepts, so the most user-friendly approach is simple and direct (for example, Jazz Music rather than Music, Jazz).

Use subdivisions carefully. You will need to use subdivisions, but be careful that you do not lose your browsers with too many subdivisions:

Education—Algeria	Education—Finance
Education—Bibliography	Education—France
Education—Canada	Education—Germany
Education—Congo	Education—Hawaii
Education—Congress	Education—Higher
Education—Cooperative	Education—History
Education—Denmark	Education—Iceland

Change headings as necessary. For example, government agencies are renamed, women marry, and new terminology emerges—or you may find a better heading and want to change your mind. Your system should allow for easy modification instead of relying on cross-references to new terms. If you have written or typed directly on the material, then you can just use a new label to reflect the change. For example, Blacks—South Africa—Segregation might be changed to Apartheid—South Africa.

Get a second copy. If an item fits two subject areas, get a second copy or photocopy portions to put under the second heading if copyright infringement is not an issue. (If you duplicate material under two headings, note on each item the location of the other copy.) Another option for dealing with dual subjects is to put a referral note in the related file.

Establish some scope notes. Clarify confusing topics by preparing scope notes to go with your subject heading. For example:

> Abused Children
> Victims of child abuse. Works on adults who
> were abused as children are entered under:
> Adult Child Abuse Victims.

Be generous in your use of cross-references. Use "see" references from terms that are not used and "see also" references from related terms. Beware of blind references, which refer the user to a topic where there is nothing filed. Cross-references are particularly important in a dictionary file. For example: Acquired Immune Deficiency Syndrome. *See* **AIDS (Disease)**; A.I.D.S. *See* **AIDS (Disease)**.

Your subject-headings list should change to reflect new topics for which you are receiving information. You will find the use of a computer very helpful, if for nothing more than to record your headings so that you can print a current copy frequently.

INDEX ALTERNATIVES

An index or guide is essential. The index provides access to the files with scope notes and "see" and "see also" references. Ideally, entries for your information files will be included in your card catalog or on-line catalog. If that is not possible, your collections may have a separate index or may be self-indexed. Self-indexing simply means that files themselves will serve as guides with scope notes and references written on the folders.

Catalog entry. You can have entries in your library catalog under the main subject with cross-references to related subjects ("see also") and terms that are not used as subject headings ("see"). It is sufficient to use a generic note like the following: "For information on this subject consult the Vertical File." Sample "see" and "see also" cross-reference cards or entries may read "For additional information on this subject consult the Vertical File: [give the subject or name of the file]"; or "For information on this subject consult the Vertical File: [give the subject or name of the file]." Sample reference cards may be found in figure 6.3. Give enough information to be helpful to the patron but keep it simple enough to be easy for you to manage. In some cases you may want to adapt the scope notes included in the LC and *Sears* subject-heading guides to provide additional information for your patron.

In addition to references to your vertical files and supplementary collections in your library catalog, a printout of headings and cross-references near the files will be helpful.[3] Some libraries also keep a shelf list for files. Shelf-list information kept on a personal computer would simply be a printout of files in the order in which they are filed (alphabetical, classified, or sequential) without scope notes or cross-references. You can use this as an inventory of files.

Computer index printout. A computer index is easy to update, and you can provide frequent updates near the files and at the reference desk. Copies can be duplicated for individuals or departments. Your index will be more helpful with numerous cross-references (see figure 6.4).

Card index. This type of index (3"x5" cards in a tray or rotary card file) is easy to update, and references can be listed on the back of the cards. It is time-consuming to prepare.

Typed list. A separate index or printed guide has the advantage of being compact, portable, easy to photocopy for duplication, and easy to use. The disadvantages are that it is difficult to change and that it can easily get lost.

Self-indexing

Self-indexing has the advantage of confining everything to the file cabinet. Extra folders are used for "see" references and "see also" references are written directly on the subject folders. It is very easy and it may save time. Some of the problems with self-indexing are that files must be kept in perfect order, every file must stay in the cabinet to maintain the index, and it is cumbersome to check in the cabinet instead of checking an authority list.

Decisions regarding organization, subject headings, and indexing must be made by each library. There is no correct answer for everyone. It is important to address each of these three elements in organization.

46 / 6 – Organization

For alphabetical vertical file.

CASTLES
   Additional material on this subject may be found in the vertical file under the above heading.

For classified vertical file.

CASTLES
   Additional material on this subject may be found in the vertical file under 728.8.

Generic reference card.

CASTLES
   Additional material may be found in the special collections below

   _____ vertical file   _____ picture file

   _____ map file   _____ local history file

   _____ travel file

Fig. 6.3. Sample index entries.

Vertical File Index

		Revised August 21, 1991
Abortion		
Abraham Lincoln Birthplace National Historic Site	See	Kentucky
Acadia National Park	See	Maine
Accidents		
Accounting		
Acid rain	See	Pollution
Adolescence	See also	Mental health
Adoption		
Adult education	See	Literacy
Aeronautics	See also	Airplanes--Piloting
Africa	See also	Individual countries
Agate Fossil Beds National Monument	See	Nebraska
Aged	See also	Credit
Aged	See also	Insurance
Agriculture	See also	Crops
AIDS (Disease)		
Air--Pollution	See also	Pollution
Airplanes	See also	Aeronautics
Alabama		
Alaska		
Alaska National Parklands	See	Alaska
Alberta		
Alcohol		
Alcoholism		
Allegheny Portage Railroad National Historic Site	See	Pennsylvania
Allergies		
Alligator	See	Animals
Alzheimer's disease	See	Brain (Diseases)
Ambergris		
American Revolution Bicentennial, 1776-1976		
American Samoa		
Americans--Foreign countries		
Anatomy		
Andersonville National Historic Site	See	Georgia
Anemia		
Animal behavior		
Animals		
Animals, Treatment of		
Anorexia nervosa	See	Mental health
Antarctica	See	Geology
Antelope	See	Animals
Antibiotics	See	Medicine
Apostle Islands National Lakeshore	See	Wisconsin
Appomattox Court House National Historical Park	See	Virginia
Aquarium fishes		
Arches National Park	See	Utah

Fig. 6.4. Sample computer index screen.

SUMMARY RECOMMENDATIONS

- Choose a plan for organization that is appropriate for your collection.
- Select an authority for subject headings with provision for modification.
- Provide an index for your users.

NOTES

[1] Full cataloging of supplementary material is a luxury not possible (or desirable) except for exceptional materials. The advantages of full cataloging are tighter control over the material, fuller indexing, and greater likelihood of permanency. Disadvantages of full cataloging include increased cost in time for processing, delays in availability of materials because of increased processing time, and reduced likelihood of materials being weeded when they are outdated. Permanency can be either an advantage or a disadvantage and in many cases will be the most important factor in your decision regarding full cataloging.

[2] *HCL Authority File* is a subject-headings list designed by the Hennepin County Library system (Minnetonka, Minnesota: Hennepin County Library. Quarterly microfiche for $7.50/year). The authority file is updated regularly by the *HCL Cataloging Bulletin* (Hennepin County Library. Bimonthly for $12/year). It is user oriented and provides an alternative authority list for subject headings.

[3] You should be able to input data once for your index and labels.

7
Preservation and Protection

The next step in the processing of supplementary materials is to consider some options to prevent wear and tear on the items. You may choose to do nothing additional. You will need to decide how much you are willing to spend on your items considering the time and materials required for protection. Clippings or pamphlets that will be in your files only for a short time may not be worth the extra step, but materials you collect for local history, materials that will be used heavily, and those you expect to keep for some time will last longer if you take the time in processing to provide some protection for them.

There are a number of printed aids that will serve as handy guides and will help you with additional information about the preservation and protection of materials:

Book Preservation and Repair. Madison, Wisconsin: Demco, 1989. $2.49. 36-page booklet. Includes a section on pamphlets.

Bookcraft: Protection, Maintenance and Repair of Library Materials. Syracuse, New York: Gaylord, 1987. $2.95. 32-page booklet.

Care & Repair: Book-Saving Techniques. Fort Atkinson, Wisconsin: The Highsmith Co., Inc., 1990. $2.75. 22-page booklet.

Nonbook Media: Collection Management and User Services. Chicago: American Library Association, 1987. $35. An excellent resource.

Options for preservation and protection will be discussed for flat, single items and for multiple pages. General guidelines will be given for the care, handling, and storage of film. Suggestions for the preservation and protection of specific kinds of materials are given in the particular discussions of those materials.[1]

FLAT, SINGLE ITEMS

Flat, single items are the most likely to be lost or damaged without protection. Clippings and other small items and odd-shaped materials will be more manageable if they are photocopied or placed in a standard size or shaped container. Options for providing protection for flat, single items include protective housing, mounting, laminating, encapsulation, and cloth-backing.[2]

Protective Housing

Plastic sleeves. One of the easiest options is to put the material in a plastic sleeve. Material can normally be used without removing it from the sleeve, so it has a great deal of protection. There is a variety of types available with openings on the top, side, or top and bottom. They come in several pocket sizes, although the standard overall size for file cabinets is 8½" x 11". Oversize sleeves are available for larger items. These sleeves are available from library suppliers, office supply companies, and photography suppliers.

Folders. Some libraries have used homemade folders to make a protective cover. Materials can be secured by paper fasteners or stitched on a sewing machine. Manila folders, both letter sized and legal sized, can be easily cut for a variety of sizes and shapes.

Envelopes. Separate envelopes for subtopics can be filed in folders, pockets, or boxes under the main topic. This does not really solve the problem of preservation for clippings because clippings still have to be handled, but it does help in the management of small items.

Tubes. Sometimes tubes can be used for large, flat materials that can be rolled, such as posters or maps. If materials are rolled with the print outside, they will lie flat for easier use. A press or a warm iron can be used to flatten materials for use after being rolled for storage.

Mounting

Mounting is recommended for newspaper clippings and some graphic materials such as pictures and portraits, and you may also want to consider mounting for charts, graphs, maps, and some other items. Mounting will protect the material, add to the attractiveness, and make it easier to use. On the negative side, mounting is expensive in time and materials; mounted materials take up more space; and use of colored mounting material limits variation in displays. You will want to consider this issue carefully. You may want to consider each item individually and mount only the things that need protection because of high use or because they are not easily replaced.

If you have decided to do at least some mounting, there are a great number of options for mounting materials. You may want to visit an art store to see some of the choices. (Construction paper is not recommended for permanent mounting because of its short life.) The following steps are suggested in mounting.

> Prepare the items for mounting by trimming them to fit to the shape of the mounting paper. Leave room at the top of the paper for the subject heading and also leave room for the library ownership stamp.

> Position the articles for mounting. If you think it is worth the extra staff time and want to save paper and space, group related articles on the same mounting paper. Save clippings until you have several to mount together or partially fill your mounts and check the file each time you have one to mount to see if it will fit one you have begun. Arrange your clippings chronologically within the subject. You may want to cut standard-sized mounting paper in half to accommodate small clippings. This becomes an optional

standard size for clippings that can be filed two abreast in the folders providing the advantages of individual circulation, conservation of space, and ease in mounting. Longer items that will not fit on a standard size will have to be cut and repositioned to be mounted or mounted on a larger sheet that can be folded.

Choose the right adhesive. You have a number of choices in adhesive materials including pastes and glues, rubber cement, spray adhesives, tape, and dry mounting.

Pastes and glues. There are many pastes and glues available from library suppliers and office supply companies. You may want to experiment by using a small container and trying different products for a while. Pastes and glues should be thin enough to spread evenly but not so much that they soak the clippings. Glue sticks are easier to use. The Library of Congress in its Preservation Leaflet No. 5, *Newsprint and Its Preservation*, does not recommend pastes or glues for use with materials you want to preserve indefinitely.

Rubber cement. Many librarians like rubber cement because it can be cleaned up by rubbing excess from the edges and because it makes a neat, smooth bond. Rubber cement can be applied so that it provides a temporary bond or a permanent bond. A temporary bond is provided when the rubber cement is applied to only one surface, the back of the clipping. A permanent bond is achieved by applying the rubber cement to both the mount and the clipping, allowing it to dry to the "tacky" stage, and then putting the surfaces together. Some brands of rubber cement may contain toxic chemicals that can be absorbed through the skin. Be aware of this when cleaning excess. Use only in a well-ventilated area. Rubber cement should be used selectively as an adhesive. The Library of Congress (Preservation Leaflet No. 5) does not recommend rubber cement for clippings that will be a part of your permanent collection because it hastens the deterioration, darkening, and brittleness of newsprint.

Spray adhesives. Artwork and display materials may require you to use spray adhesives. They provide a quick and easy means of mounting. Some of the problems with using spray adhesives for vertical-file materials include the fact that they are expensive, flammable, messy, and often not permanent. Use only in a well-ventilated area. In using any of the techniques involving paste, glue, rubber cement, or spray adhesives it is advisable to use a protective underlay such as old newspapers. Attach all outer edges, not just the corners, firmly against the mount for full protection. Use waxed paper between sheets of mounts until they dry. Press mounts using a liquid paste or glue in a pressing device or with weights (you can use large books) until dry to avoid curling.

Adhesive tape. If you are going to use tape, choose a good quality acetate-base tape such as 3M's Scotch Brand Magic Transparent Tape. The Magic Plus tape is removable and may be helpful for temporary mounts. Using double-sided tape improves the appearance of adhesive tape mounts but is difficult to use. Avoid cellophane tape, which becomes yellow and brittle with age. Using adhesive tape for mounting can be expensive and is not recommended for permanent items; however, it is neat, easy to use, and acceptable for items that will be in your files only a short time.

52 / 7—Preservation and Protection

Dry mounting. This mounting technique is achieved by bonding the item to the mount with heat, using mounting tissue that is coated with a thermosetting adhesive and that looks like waxed paper. The tissue is tacked to the item by a quick application of heat, trimmed with a paper cutter or scissors to the exact size of the clipping, positioned on the mount with another quick application of heat, then sealed in the dry-mount press. Seal presses are the most widely used equipment for dry mounting and laminating. For permanent dry mounting use MT5 mounting tissue. An alternative is Seal Fusion 4000 dry-mounting film, which is more expensive to use but can be reinserted in the press to reverse the mounting process. Dry-mounting supplies and equipment are available from library supply companies, school supply companies, and photography supply companies.

Some of the same mounting techniques can be used with a laundry iron and film, but to insure a smooth, neat, lasting bond, the larger surface of the dry-mount press is necessary. Many schools have dry-mount presses available for teachers.

Laminating

Heat-process lamination is another technique you can do with a dry-mount press. Seal-Lamin Film applied with a dry-mount press makes materials waterproof, smearproof, resistant to tearing and discoloration. Laminating film can be applied to the front of items or to both sides. It can be combined with the mounting process so that materials (pictures, charts, etc.) are laminated on the front and mounted to a board, or mounted and then the whole piece laminated. Techniques for laminating and dry mounting are described in the publications of the Seal Company and in various books and articles on the subject.

A cold lamination process can be achieved by using a plastic, transparent, self-adhesive film. You can apply the film to one side or to both sides. Materials are readily available and no equipment is needed except a pair of scissors, but application can be difficult. Film with a delayed-action adhesive doesn't set immediately and allows you to make adjustments.

Encapsulation

Encapsulation is really the best method for true preservation. This technique encases the item between two sheets of polyester film. Double-coated tape is used on all four edges to hold the layers of film together. The document is protected from air, dirt, and handling and remains in its original physical condition. It can be removed when needed.

MULTIPLE PAGES

Items that have multiple pages can be reinforced or placed in some type of protective housing such as slip cases, boxes, pamphlet binders, report covers, or three-ring notebooks.

Reinforcements

Taped spines. Two-inch or wider tape can be used to reinforce the spines of pamphlets. The tape will provide added protection for items that will have high use.

Pamphlet reinforcements. Additional protection can be given to pamphlets and other folded items by using a pamphlet reinforcement such as *Easy Hold* by Kapco (see figure 7.1). The reinforcement is placed on the top and the bottom of the item as shown.

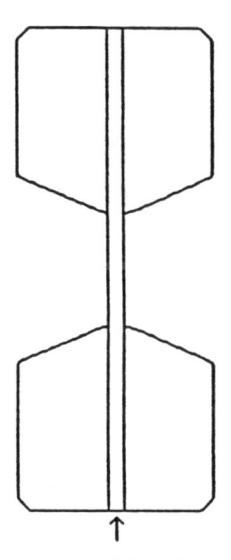

Reinforced Peel 'n Place® Strip

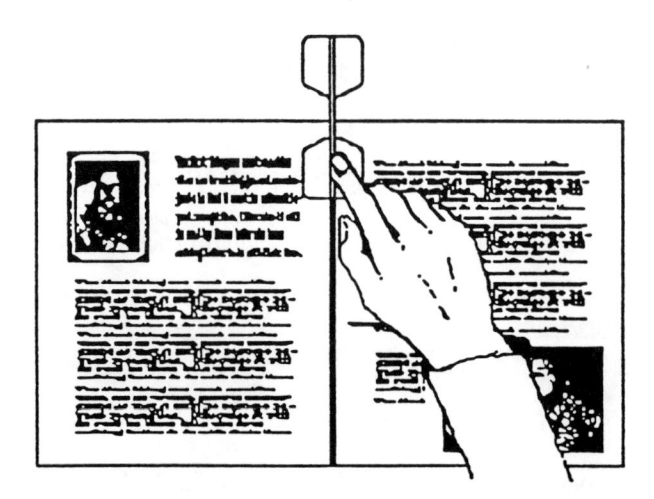

Fig. 7.1. *Easy Hold* pamphlet reinforcement. Reprinted with permission.

Protective Housing

Report covers. These come in many colors in both paper and plastic with clips, plastic "bone" grips, brads for punched material, and pockets. Transparent or opaque covers are available.

Three-ring notebooks. Prepare material using a standard three-hold punch and inserting in the notebook with or without page protectors. Hole reinforcements and dividers can also be used.

Pamphlet binders. Library supply companies have a variety of pamphlet binders of stiff pressboards in various types including single-stitched (with gummed center strip), double-stitched (for thicker publications), tie binders (for punched material), and staple-set binders (for use with a heavy-duty stapling machine). They come in a variety of sizes and materials. These are relatively economical and offer added protection to materials.

Punch and bind. Library supply companies and office supply companies have machines available for purchase that will bind with the plastic ring spines or with wire spines. If you have a lot of loose-leaf materials, you may want to consider this investment.

Thermal-adhesive binding system. The purchase of a thermal-adhesive binding system is another option for added protection of materials.

FILM MEDIA

All types of film media including filmstrips, microforms, motion pictures, slides, and transparencies should be stored in areas that are not subject to fluctuations in temperature of more than 20 degrees F (11 degrees C). The optimum storage temperature is 70 degrees. If film is subjected to a change in temperature, it should be returned to room temperature before showing. Humidity should be about 50 percent. Items should be stored in dust-proof containers free of acid, sulfur, or peroxide. Film should be handled only by the edges.

Preservation and protection adds expense in time and materials to supplementary resources. Some measures should be taken to protect items for which heavy use or a long shelf life is expected, but you should be careful to spend an appropriate amount of time and supplies on supplementary materials.[3]

SUMMARY OF RECOMMENDATIONS

- Consider preservation and protection when processing *new* items.

- Estimate the shelf life and use of an item to determine if protection is necessary.

NOTES

[1]See guides for specific kinds of materials such as Ralph E. Ehrenberg *Archives & Manuscripts: Maps and Architectural Drawings* (Chicago: Society of American Archivists, 1982).

[2]When using flat items on the bulletin board, use straight pins to display materials by holding them in place without putting pin holes in the items or try mounting for display with Post-it double-faced tape, which can be removed.

[3]General guidelines for media care and handling as well as suggestions for special kinds of materials are included in *Nonbook Media: Collection Management and User Services*. Chicago: American Library Association, 1987. $35.

8
Housing

Metal filing cabinets are the most popular way to house supplementary materials. There are a number of alternatives in file cabinet styles, colors, and configurations. This section will address the choices in housing and the internal filing devices for effective housing.[1]

EXTERNAL HOUSING UNITS

File cabinets. These standard external housing units should be made of heavy-gauge steel with a full suspension system in order to allow easy access to all materials in the drawers. Drawers should glide easily on roller bearings. Compressors to keep file folders erect should be easy to operate. Thumb-latch controls will insure safety. A lock is necessary only if there is some reason to lock the files; otherwise it will be an irritation because some people will instinctively lock the drawer after use.

The dimensions of files is a matter of personal choice. The first choice is between letter size and legal size. Legal files are slightly larger, so they are a little more expensive. Most pamphlet material is letter size, but many libraries prefer legal size simply to allow a bit more space in the files. Legal files are recommended if you have pictures or other large items integrated with standard-size materials.

The subject of height is another decision related to file cabinets. Four-drawer standard files are the most economical because they require less floor space, but for patron use, libraries should consider three-drawer units, which provide a counter-height top for examination of materials. These units do not block vision, so they offer a great deal of flexibility in placement. A single top can be made to tie all of the files together as one unit and the top can also serve as an area for special displays.

Lateral cabinets offer another option in the configuration of files. They can be put in places where standard files will not fit. Lateral files must be used from the side or arranged facing the opening. Other innovations in filing cabinets are now available, including revolving and circular files, double-sided cabinets, and others. Your local office supplier can advise you on the options. Choice depends on the space available for file placement.

File boxes. Pressboard boxes the approximate size of a file drawer can be purchased for files. Most are not permanent but can certainly substitute quite nicely for a short time or for small groups of files. Folders are filed directly into the boxes. Boxes can be placed on wide shelves or counters for patron use.

Pamphlet boxes. Materials may be stored in boxes on book shelves. Advantages are that the boxes take up less space and can be shelved closer to related books. It is likely that you may choose to shelve special groups of materials in pamphlet boxes on the shelves interfiled with books or in a separate section. Examples include such things as annual reports, mail-order catalogs, college catalogs, or any other group of materials you want to keep together. In any case there are a number of options in your choice of boxes.

Library supply companies such as Demco and Highsmith offer a selection of boxes of all sizes, shapes, and prices. Hard plastic boxes are the most expensive but also the most durable. Fiberboard boxes vary in price depending on the material and color. Colored boxes offer another means of distinguishing certain groups of materials. Metal label holders add a bit to the cost but create a more finished look. If adhesive labels are used, they should be placed in the same place on all boxes to ensure a uniform look.

Ordinary pamphlet or magazine boxes can be purchased closed except for the open back, closed with the opening on the front, and open-top with cut corners. Boxes are available that close on all four sides. The potential use should be kept in mind when buying boxes for a special group of materials. Visibility, accessibility, preservation, and security are other considerations.

INTERNAL FILING DEVICES

The accessories used within file drawers are very important in ensuring ease of use. Assume that your files will be used extensively and use good-quality materials. It is important to use a folder, envelope, pocket, or some file carrier with your supplementary files. Materials that are filed directly into the file without folders are more difficult to use and to maintain. In addition there will likely be more damage to materials that tend to slip to the bottom and become crushed, torn, and misplaced.

Frames. Frames can be inserted into any vertical or lateral file to hold folders that are suspended from the frame. Hanging folders slide back and forth on the frame. Because folders do not rest on the bottom of the drawer, they are easier to manage. Reinforced tabs are also very beneficial.

Hanging folders with internal folders, pockets, or envelopes. Some libraries simply use the hanging folders with tabs for their vertical files. Others use standard file folders, envelopes, pockets, or file carriers with their hanging folders (see figure 8.1). Pockets and envelopes are available with open or closed sides as well as open or closed tops. It is important to have a separate folder or envelope for each subject heading in your files. Closed envelopes make filing more difficult but they keep the files looking neater. In each case you should select them to match the size of the file drawers.

Most folders have scoring near the fold, which is helpful in housing large files. Pockets are available with expanded bases and some expandable envelopes are available. When a file is full there are several options: (1) A new folder can be added. Both folders should be marked to alert the patron to the multiple folders, for example, Folder 1 of 2; Folder 2 of 2. (2) Materials can be shifted to an expanding pocket that holds more than the folder. Choices in expanding pockets include those that have an open or closed top, tie closure, or elastic bands. (3) The information can be divided into several more specific subject files.

58 / 8—Housing

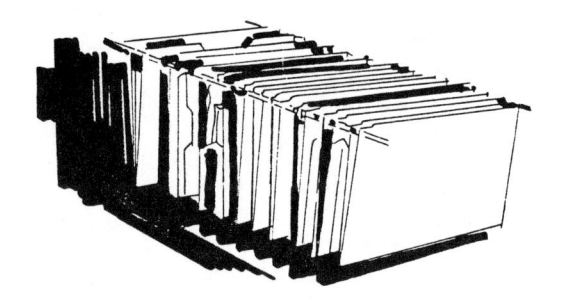

Fig. 8.1. Frames and hanging folders. Reprinted from "How to File and Find It" with permission from the Quill Corporation, 100 Schelter Road, Lincolnshire, IL 60069.

In selecting folders there are a number of choices. Manila folders have been used most widely, but now folders are available in a variety of colors in both paper and plastic materials. Colored folders may be slightly more expensive than manila ones, but ability to easily color-code certain files may be worth the extra investment. Likewise, plastic folders are more expensive than paper-based ones but will withstand more wear.

Tabs and file cuts. There are several choices regarding the size and position of tabs. Some librarians prefer to have the tab in the same position for all of their files. The advantage is that it is easy to scan the headings by looking in just one position. The disadvantage is that folders with very little material in them will not stand apart enough to be seen. Staggered tabs make it easier to spot headings. Folders are available in a choice of tab cuts (see figure 8.2). Third-cut, letter-sized folders are designed for 3½" labels and allow plenty of room for headings. Fifth-cut folders allow more staggering but may not give adequate space for headings.

File guides. File guides are used by libraries to indicate divisions, major subject headings, or cross-references. They may be purchased with regular or metal tabs or may be made from manila folders. File guides are sometimes used to indicate cross-references or scope notes, though some libraries use no file guides but simply record "see also" references on the folders themselves and "see" references in the index. Self-indexing systems should make some provision for "see" references. File guides sometimes are also used as substitutes for file folders, with guides staying in the drawer and items filed behind the guide not placed in a folder. This is generally not very satisfactory because materials can easily slide to the bottom and become crushed, torn, or misplaced.

"Out" guides are sometimes used to replace a folder that is being used. It also serves the purpose of expediting refiling. You cannot really depend on patrons to consistently use out guides.[2]

Your choices of housing materials and equipment will affect how your users respond to your filing system. The choice of quality file cabinets and the use of proper internal filing devices will aid your users in ease of access.

Popular Tab Cuts

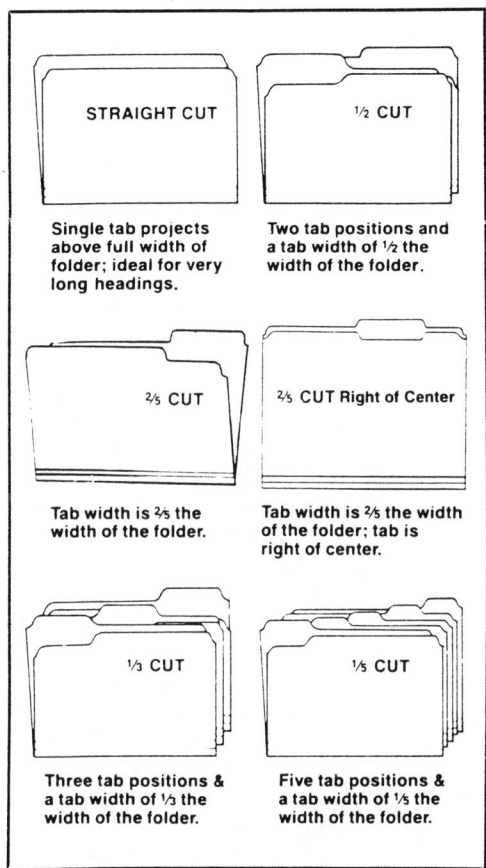

STRAIGHT CUT — Single tab projects above full width of folder; ideal for very long headings.

½ CUT — Two tab positions and a tab width of ½ the width of the folder.

⅖ CUT — Tab width is ⅖ the width of the folder.

⅖ CUT Right of Center — Tab width is ⅖ the width of the folder; tab is right of center.

⅓ CUT — Three tab positions & a tab width of ⅓ the width of the folder.

⅕ CUT — Five tab positions & a tab width of ⅕ the width of the folder.

Fig. 8.2. Examples of different tab cuts. Reprinted from "How to File and Find It" with permission from the Quill Corporation, 100 Schelter Road, Lincolnshire, IL 60069.

SUMMARY RECOMMENDATIONS

- Decide on the best height, width, color and style for your files and be consistent.

- Use appropriate internal devices.

- Use bold, large-print labels and guides.

NOTES

[1]Alternative ways to store vertical-file materials include microfilm, microfiche, and CD-ROM technology.

Vertical File on Microfilm (VFOM). As reported by Shirley Miller in *The Vertical File and Its Satellites* (Littleton, Colorado: Libraries Unlimited, 1979), Dr. Chester B. Stout conceived of the idea of offering an extensive collection of vertical-file materials, Vertical File on Microfilm (VFOM), in a limited space while he was director at the McKinley Library in Niles, Ohio. When the material was requested, a form letter was included that asked for copyright clearance to make microfilm reproductions and/or copies for users. The letter indicated a willingness to pay a copyright fee and instructed the source to send the material only if copyright clearance was available. Microfiche master jackets were prepared by the library and duplicate microfiche were made for the file used by the public which is arranged using a Cutter code. An extensive index facilitated use. Prints were available using a microfiche reader/printer.

The advantages of this system are that it saves space, the fiche are a consistent size, there is no damage to originals, there is an efficient retrieval through the index, magnification is possible through the lens variety, there is less problem with security, and the files can be duplicated for branches, patrons, or commercial sales. The disadvantages include the additional cost of microfilming equipment, the extra step of getting the copyright clearance, the loss of items to the collection because of lack of copyright clearance, the problem with color reproductions, the negative feeling some people have for microfiche, the loss of material for displays, and the fact that the items will probably never be weeded.

Commercial vendors who are putting vertical-file materials on microfiche or CD-ROM format include NewsBank and Chadwyek-Healey, Inc. NewsBank began a very successful newspaper clipping project in the 1970s. Clippings from newspapers from hundreds of U.S. cities were included in the service, which began with paper indexes and microfiche clippings. The service now uses CD-ROM technology and continues to thrive. Chadwyck-Healey, Inc., embarked on a recent project to put vertical files on microfiche from the *New York Public Library Artists File*. The clippings file of more than 1.5 million items of 76,000 painters, sculptors, architects, crafts people, jewelers, furniture and interior designers, commercial artists, fashion designers, collectors, connoisseurs, critics, and curators is now available on more than 10,000 microfiche. It is expensive ($20,000 — beyond most of our budgets), but it does provide a wonderful service by sharing that information and expertise in collecting the material. These examples are probably just the beginning of vertical-file resources available on microfiche or CD-ROM products. They are bargains when you think of the time, energy, and money involved.

Another project of related art resources includes *Artists Scrapbooks*, which covers 42 major artists from the Museum of Modern Art in New York (642 microfiche for $3,900) and the *New York Public Library Print File* on printmakers (in progress).

[2]If you use two tabs, one on the hanging folder and one on the folder, envelope, or pocket, you eliminate the need for out guides. In addition, refiling is easier when the entire folder has been removed. Computer-generated labels in a 14-point font printed on a laser printer are easy to read and look very nice.

9
Promotion

Once you have put together a file of supplementary materials, it is important to promote it to ensure that it is used. A number of suggestions are listed to provide some ideas for promoting your files.

Location. Materials must be in a good location. Put the vertical file in a prominent place, preferably near the reference desk. If you want your patrons to use the file, you must make it accessible to them.

Signage. Patrons must be able to find the area where the materials are located. Use attractive signage and make your lettering large enough to be seen from a distance.

Appeal. The area should be attractive and neat. If possible use file cabinets in the same color and size. Control the clutter and use uniform labels on drawers and file folders. Replace worn file folders before they look ragged and consider using color for file folders to brighten the files.

Access. Files must be easy to use. Enter references in your collection database (card catalog, fiche catalog, etc.). Prepare a handout for patrons giving a brief overview of the contents. If you have a small vertical file, you could put the entire index in the handout. Place a copy of the index near your collection and give instructions for locating materials. Clarify circulation policy and procedures and make the subject-headings lists available if possible.

Advertising. Tell patrons about your supplementary files. Use your newsletter to highlight new or interesting items. School libraries can use the school paper for feature articles or to highlight special collections. Prepare one-page handouts for patrons to pick up in the library. Post flyers in appropriate public places. Prepare pathfinders on special topics including vertical-file subject headings. Talk about vertical files and special collections in your orientation tours.

Acting as role model. Use it yourself. Select items for displays and exhibits and identify the source. Refer people to items in the vertical files and special collections. Believe in the value of the resource.

Be sure that you have something worth promoting. Good selection practices and prompt processing of materials will help ensure that your file is valuable to your patrons. Refile things promptly after use. Make sure that materials are up-to-date and useful.

SUMMARY RECOMMENDATIONS

- Make your files visually attractive.
- Make your collection easy to find and easy to use.
- Tell your users about your supplementary materials.

10
Circulation

Whether to circulate supplementary materials or keep them for library use only will depend on your own situation. Some libraries circulate materials, some restrict materials, and some libraries have even established two files: one for circulation and one for reference. You will likely reach a compromise, circulating most items but restricting certain items.

For those items that seem invaluable for reference use, you may want to consider ordering a duplicate copy or making a copy (with copyright clearance). Mark the original "Reference" or "Library Use Only" and allow the second copy to circulate. Or, you could provide a copy machine near the vertical files so that patrons can copy the parts of the materials that they need rather than checking them out.

There are a variety of ways in which you can manage the circulation of supplementary materials. There is not one best solution. You should choose your system carefully, keeping in mind your patrons, your collection, and your own staff time.

MANUAL CIRCULATION

Transaction form. Use a separate form for each item circulated. Items can be listed or you can simply indicate the total number. Forms can be duplicated on NCR (no carbon required) paper so that there is a duplicate copy for the transaction. One copy can be stapled to a manila envelope in which the items from the vertical file have been placed for circulation. The slip is removed from the envelope when items are returned, and envelopes can be reused. Slips for returned items are matched with checkout slips in the circulation file. Slips can be filed under the borrower's name, under the subject, or under the date due. See figure 10.1.

Sign-out sheets. Libraries that allow patrons to check out materials themselves may simply use a dated sheet of paper fastened to a clipboard near the files or at the circulation desk. This honor system of borrowing simplifies checkout. If the patrons check things out themselves, make the system simple or it may defeat itself by encouraging users to bypass it entirely.

Ledger book. Maintain a ledger book in which circulation is recorded with items crossed off when they are returned. This is a variation of the sign-out sheet.

```
┌─────────────────────────────────────┐
│                                     │
│        Vertical File Checkout       │
│                                     │
│   Subject _____  │
│                                     │
│   Item or Items _____  │
│                                     │
│   _____    │
│                                     │
│   _____    │
│                                     │
│   _____    │
│                                     │
│   _____    │
│                                     │
│   Name _____  │
│                                     │
│   ID _____  │
│                                     │
│   Date Due _____  │
│                                     │
└─────────────────────────────────────┘
```

Fig. 10.1. Sample transaction form.

Master card. The master-card system is another option in which the librarian maintains a master card for each subject in the file. The cards are kept at the circulation desk and circulation is recorded on line after line of the card. One advantage in this system is that it gives a very clear picture of circulation, which is helpful in weeding and developing the collection.

Check-out card. Attach a card and pocket to each piece for circulation. This would work best for collections such as annual reports, college catalogs, scripts, or reports. The process increases your investment in time and materials but it allows greater control. Libraries that use this system argue that the time invested in providing cards and pockets is balanced by time saved when pamphlets are circulated. This system also lets your patrons know that you value the material enough to spend the time processing it. If labels for cards and pockets can be created by computer, this is a more appealing system than hand-typing cards and

66 / 10 – Circulation

pockets. Color-coding of book cards can indicate special collections. Even with the use of volunteers, preparing check-out cards is a very labor-intensive job if you have a collection of substantial size. Another option is to attach a check-out card to each folder or envelope of material. This means that you would circulate the entire folder to one user. This is not a popular approach.

AUTOMATED CIRCULATION

Anything that has a bar code on it can be run through your automated circulation system; however, a bar code number will be of little use unless it is attached to an item record. You can bar code a set of envelopes for circulation and indicate by the range of numbers that they are for vertical-file items (see figure 10.2). When an envelope is lost, you will not have specific identification,

VERTICAL FILE

1. Place items in envelope.
2. Note the number of items on the envelope.
3. Check out as you would a book.

Z. J. Loussac Public Library
3600 Denali
Anchorage, AK 99503

Fig. 10.2. Circulation envelope including bar code.

but you will know that one vertical-file item was lost. Many libraries do not replace vertical-file materials, so the only information needed is the charge for lost materials. That can be facilitated by setting a flat rate for vertical-file items.

Bar-code numbers can serve as accession numbers when you have an automated system. If you are using sequence (or accession numbers) as a system for arranging materials, then you can easily assign a range of bar-code numbers to your vertical file and attach the bar-code number to your individual record. The sequence system requires an index with individual record information since it is arranged in the order of acquisition and not by subject. This system works well for special libraries or for special collections of materials.

CIRCULATION PROCEDURES

You can provide some protection and security for items by using a "carrier envelope" for circulation. The use of a carrier is to isolate each loan group, protect the materials, and perhaps offer a place for recording pertinent circulation information. The most popular type of carrier is a large paper envelope. You can use old mailing envelopes or buy envelopes especially constructed for circulation, which are made of sturdy kraft paper with reinforced edges. Office suppliers also offer envelopes with string ties.

Stamp or print the name and address of the library on the envelope to ensure returns. This will help the patron identify the envelope as library materials and will also encourage return if the materials are lost by the patron.

When old envelopes are used, circulation data can be put directly on the envelope. Libraries that use special envelopes they have purchased often attach a date-due slip or printed form to the front of the envelope. Often a copy of the transaction slip is attached. In any case the date due should be clear to the patron. Information to remind the patron of the number of items should also be included so that it is easy to see that all checkout materials are returned.

Some libraries do not use carriers. In that case the date due may be stamped on the back cover or on the inside of the back cover of the work. Although this can be quite messy, it does give an indication of the number of times an item has circulated.

In some libraries the entire file or box of materials may be checked out. Often there will be a card and pocket on which the number of items is noted. Patrons can then check out the entire collection of materials. Closed boxes or envelopes with flaps, ties, or rubber bands should be considered for situations with this type of circulation.

Regardless of your policies, your system, and your process for circulation, it is important to make it easy for your patrons to use the materials from your supplementary files.

SUMMARY RECOMMENDATIONS

- Establish circulation policies regarding: loan period and late or lost materials.

- Choose a simple circulation system which will be easy for the user and will provide you with the information you need.

11
Weeding

Weeding is a library term for removal of items from a collection. It is the final step in the cycle of library materials. Like a gardener, the librarian goes through the collection systematically removing dead growth, looking at everything and pulling out items that detract from the collection. As in the case of a beautiful garden, your vertical file will thrive with regular weeding.

PURPOSE OF WEEDING

Weed to insure the quality of your vertical file as a resource. It is critical that your collection, which should seek to have the most current materials in certain subjects, be kept up-to-date in order to provide your patrons with resources they can depend on being accurate and current.

Weed to make your collection more appealing. As in a garden, if you do not pull the weeds, your patrons cannot see the beauty. Your files will look better and people will be able to find what they seek more easily.

Weed to conserve space. Even if you do not need the space now, you will someday. It is much better to stay on top of it than to wait until you run out of space and have such a huge job it will never get done.

Weed to save time in searching and maintaining the collection. Patron time and staff time will be saved by keeping files up-to-date. They will not need to reject outdated materials found in the files.

Weed to keep a close check on the collection. Regular weeding will keep you more familiar with the collection. You will be able to encourage use and see that the management of the files is carried out in the most efficient manner.

Weed to provide feedback on the strengths and weaknesses of the collection. Going through the collection in a systematic way will keep you aware so that you are subconsciously tuned in to this valuable resource. You (or the person responsible for the files) will be the most critical link in the development and use of the collection.

NEGATIVE FACTORS TO CONSIDER WHEN WEEDING

There are several guides to help you in weeding library materials.[1] Many of the general factors for consideration also apply to vertical-file materials. Weeding is discussed in different terms, but the negative factors for consideration can be grouped in the following general categories.

Content. Is it accurate? Poor content or incorrect and misleading information is the most important factor in weeding. You *must* discard inaccurate information. Bad information is worse than no information at all.

Age. Age is a very important factor in vertical-file materials. Currency is one of the characteristics of supplementary materials. Ask yourself the following questions: Is the information more than five years old? Has the material been updated? Do you have a current address for the publisher? Age is easy enough to evaluate if it is printed on the item. The next best indication is the date that the item was added to the collection. You should be able to assume that the information was current when it was put into the file. Stamping the date received is important even when the date of publication is available so that you know that as of the date received it was considered current.

Need. Is this the only source of this kind of information? Need based on extra copies is an easy factor. The difficulty is when you have the information available in a different source. Ask yourself the same questions you did before you added the material: Is this information somewhere else in the library? or Is this information in another library in the area?

In the case of superseded information, there is probably no good reason to keep an old version of supplementary material when you get a new one. If you have questions about keeping older information, refer to the questions you asked yourself regarding the initial selection.

Is this information still needed? A number of items in your supplementary materials collection may seem trivial. The characteristics of supplementary materials include words like *unique, unusual*, and *small segment of knowledge*. There may be a fine line distinguishing *unique* from *trivial* in evaluating supplementary materials. You will have to answer that question for your own library.

Use. Is this material used? Is it used often? Circulation systems that leave a record of use make this an easy factor to evaluate. For example, the date due stamped on the back of the item, a check-out card for the item, or a bar code attached to the individual record would track the use. Another way to measure use is to put a small hash mark on the back of the item each time the item is filed (Example:̄T̄H̄L̄ ||||). It is not a foolproof system but it may give some indication of use. You will have to determine whether it is important for you to know.

Condition. Appearance is an easy factor to evaluate. When items become yellow, torn, dirty, or ragged, it is time to discard or replace them. If the material is valuable and you cannot replace the item, then you should consider making a photocopy. If you use some protective material or preservation techniques when you add items, you can avoid some of the appearance problems for materials that will receive heavy use.

To summarize, you need to consider the following in your evaluation of materials for weeding: Content, Age, Need, Use, Condition = CAN U C (**Can you see** any reason to keep these materials?).

WHEN TO WEED

Most librarians agree that weeding should be done once a year. It can be done as a large project all at once; you can do it continually; you can do spot weeding; or you can do a combination. Except for some special collections such as archives or local history, supplementary materials need to be weeded to give life to the collection.

Annual weeding. Many special collections are most efficiently weeded once each year. Dated items such as annual reports, newsletters, or college catalogs can be discarded at the end of the year, keeping only the current year, latest two years, or more, depending on your policy. If you know you will discard on a certain date, try using a bright colored dot with the discard date written on it to speed the weeding process.

To do an annual weeding as one large project, you might consider some of the following recommendations: (1) put weeding into your annual schedule to insure adequate time; (2) choose a slack time in the library, for example, near a holiday; (3) set up a system for weeding; and (4) put your files in order before weeding.

Continuous weeding. Continuous weeding involves setting up a system so that you are weeding some on a regular basis throughout the year. There are several ways to do continuous weeding. One way would be to schedule one subject area per month for systematic evaluation. Another might be to schedule a certain amount of time each week for weeding. You could do one file each day. You can establish your own schedule for a continuous weeding plan.

Spot weeding. Spot weeding means that you check some of the folders some of the time. Unless you combine it with another systematic weeding process, some folders will never be weeded. There are several suggestions for spot weeding. First, check each folder as new material is added. Do a quick check of materials in the folder to see whether (1) the new material updates an earlier edition, (2) older materials contain historical or background information that is omitted in recent works, (3) the new item adds a different dimension or restates what is already there (if it does not offer a fresh approach, determine whether it is needed anyway because of the popularity of the topic). Then determine whether there is a need for two copies. Pencil the date checked on the file when it has been examined. Second, check each folder as it circulates. Examine each folder and discard material that is (1) no longer useful, (2) inaccurate, (3) worn or in poor physical condition, or (4) superseded with newer versions. Change subject headings that need to be updated; divide the file into finer groupings if it is too full; discard material from overcrowded folders, boxes, and drawers; and regroup materials into broader headings if needed. Pencil the date checked symbol on the file when it has been weeded.

Weeding, like the other steps in the life cycle of resources, offers a number of options. The important thing is to do it and to continue the process by locating new resources, adding them to your files, maintaining them, and thus keeping the cycle alive.

SUMMARY RECOMMENDATIONS

- Establish a policy and procedure for weeding certain kinds of materials.

- Keep your files "lean and clean."

- Set up a plan for systematic weeding and schedule it into your work day, week, month, or year.

NOTES

[1]Stanley J. Slote's *Weeding Library Collections*, 3d ed. (Englewood, Colorado: Libraries Unlimited, 1989) is a standard reference for weeding book collections. Slote's factors for weeding materials include attention to appearance, duplication, content, age, and use. Joseph P. Segal (*Evaluating and Weeding Collections in Small and Medium-sized Public Libraries: The CREW Method*, Chicago: American Library Association, 1980) developed a system of weeding called CREW, which stands for Continuous Review, Evaluation, and Weeding. The system is based on the date of the material, time since it circulated, and whether or not the material is "MUSTY":

> **M** - misleading or factually inaccurate
> **U** - ugly
> **S** - superseded by newer information
> **T** - trivial
> **Y** - your collection has no use for the material or material is irrelevant to your patrons

The formula may not be applicable to your files, but the MUSTY factors are important to consider in weeding any collection. Using the negative factors as a guide gives you a basis for evaluating materials.

Part II
Supplementary Materials and Special Collections

There are many different kinds of materials that can go into supplementary collections. Each institution will determine whether it will collect certain types of materials and if so, how they will be handled. Some materials will go into vertical files, some will be cataloged as part of the collection, others will be kept in boxes, shelves, closets, or cupboards.

This section includes examples of many kinds of supplementary materials that may be found in libraries and classrooms. Most materials will be collected for patron use, but others may be retained for the personal use of librarians and teachers. For discussion, the supplementary materials are divided into four chapters: "Supplementary Materials for Information Files," "Other Free and Inexpensive Supplementary Materials," "Supplementary Materials for Personal Files of Librarians and Teachers," and "Special Collections of Supplementary Materials." The groupings and suggestions are not intended to be restrictive in any way.

A great deal of imagination was used in compiling a list of materials that could go into vertical files and supplementary collections. There are even more items that could be added. This broad listing of materials by type is intended to give some specific direction to people who are beginning work with vertical files. This approach was also taken to emphasize the many kinds of things that are possible additions in order to encourage readers to be open-minded in the consideration of information resources for collections. Hopefully, librarians, teachers, and others working with supplementary materials will think of many options for using supplementary information sources in their particular libraries and classrooms.

Each entry includes a brief discussion of the type of supplementary material, followed by suggestions for the acquisition, processing, and management of the information. Recommendations made in part 1 apply to all supplementary materials and should be kept in mind. In part 2 the emphasis is on suggestions particular to each format. For example, in the suggestions for weeding, all of the guidelines in part 1 should be considered, but the weeding notes in part 2 highlight particular criteria for consideration. See the notes at the end of the chapter for alternatives for consideration by libraries with larger budgets and sources for further reading on the topic.

The items are arranged alphabetically within the sections. It is hoped that by browsing through the list the reader will be introduced to new resources for libraries and learning, ideas for finding them, and suggestions for managing them. The world is full of exciting resources if you keep an open mind as you browse.

12
Supplementary Materials for Information Files

ANNUAL REPORTS

Annual reports from business, industry, foundations, and agencies can be an important resource for many types of libraries. Public libraries will want to keep copies of the annual reports of businesses in their area or even in the state. They may also want to keep copies of annual reports of businesses and associations that are of particular interest to patrons. University libraries may need samples of annual reports of major corporations and/or agencies for students in business or in particular subject areas. Faculty and students should know that this can be an important resource and should give direction to the acquisitions department with specific recommendations. School libraries will provide annual reports for the use of economics classes that focus on mock stock-market portfolios. Special libraries will collect annual reports of businesses and organizations that relate to their focus.

Acquisition

Sources. Individual annual reports can usually be acquired by writing to the source of the report.[1] Patrons may give you annual reports if you let your interest be known.

Selection. Choose local and state-related companies; consider the largest 50 or 100 companies and select those with patron interest in mind.

Ordering. Try to get on mailing lists or set up a tickler file to remind you when to order annual reports. Consider doing a bulk mailing once or twice a year. Large orders can be processed by a vendor.

Processing

Initial processing and labeling. Stamp, label, and indicate the source. Check in as a serial if you receive the particular annual report on a regular basis. Use a Discard After [Date] label for reports to be weeded on a regular basis.

Organization. Arrange by name, subject, or year, or set up a special collection of annual reports arranged by name and then year, or by year and then name. Other alternatives:

- Handle like a monograph and classify for the shelf.
- Handle like a serial and shelve with periodicals.
- File in the vertical file as part of the pamphlet collection.
- Keep as a separate collection in the vertical file or on a shelf.
- Consider local annual reports for your local history section.

Preservation and protection. Use pamphlet reinforcements, tape the spines, put in pamphlet binders or bind commercially. You can bind several years of reports together or bind reports individually.

Housing. Store annual reports in filing cabinets, on shelves, or in pamphlet boxes.

Management

Promotion. Include reports from local and state groups with your promotional materials for local history. Promote sample annual reports to students of business or students in related subject majors. Annual reports from foundations will be helpful to people applying for grants. Display groups of annual reports focusing on either business or graphic features. Include annual reports in the appropriate displays of subject material. Prepare a bibliography of annual reports you receive from various groups and companies.

Circulation. Circulate individual reports as you would other vertical-file materials. Other options for circulation include treatment as a serial or circulation as a monograph, depending on how you have treated the material.

Weeding. Establish a policy for weeding when you decide to collect annual reports, such as only keep latest year, keep all, keep three years, etc. Write the discard date on the cover or use Discard After [Date] labels when you do initial processing to speed weeding. If you have a special collection of annual reports, weeding is very easy.

ART REPRODUCTIONS

Reproductions of paintings and drawings come in many forms. Many are used for study, but they can also provide enjoyment to your patrons. They are available as postcards, slides, individual pictures, posters, flash cards, and games. Many are inexpensive and can add interest to your collection with very little investment.

Acquisition

Sources. You can usually depend on quality reproductions from museum, education, and art suppliers. Art reproductions are available on slides, videotapes, and laser discs, which can be borrowed, rented, or purchased. Following are some commercial resources.

Haddad's Fine Arts offers more than 2,100 art reproductions and posters in their 400-page catalog. Prices seem to range from $1.50 to $30. The catalog is $25.

Each issue of the Metropolitan Museum of Art's *Metropolitan Museum of Art Bulletin* (quarterly, $18/year) focuses on something from the collection in the museum. Some back issues are available.

The National Gallery of Art is one of the best sources of art reproductions of all types. Many works are available in several sizes, from postcard size to large framed reproductions. Items are reasonably priced, with discounts available for educational and religious institutions. (Slides are available for purchase or loan. Videotapes and 16mm films are available for loan.)

The National Gallery of Canada offers reproductions in the form of postcards, posters, reproductions, and assorted sidelines. Prices are competitive with other sources.

University Prints is a "visual archive of 7,500 basic art history subjects for college-level teaching." All prints are 5½"x8" and are priced at 6 cents each in black-and-white and 12 cents each for color prints. Prints are available individually or in various sets. Instructors can select prints for classes, with student sets collated and custom bound for a small charge. The 246-page catalog is $3. Prints are available bound or loose.

Art & Man, a periodical from Scholastic, includes four-color reproductions and articles about great artists, notes on traveling exhibitions, and a pullout poster in each 16-page issue. There are six issues each school year. It is aimed at grades 7-12, but the interest level is much higher. Sample issues are available.

Selection. Request samples to compare quality and cost before purchasing large sets of art reproductions. You will probably need to make some decisions about the scope of your holdings in this area because there are a great number to choose from.[2]

Ordering. You will order direct from most sources. Purchase museum and gallery reproductions when you visit the individual museum or gallery.

Processing

Initial processing and labeling. Stamp and label the back of reproductions but check to be sure that the ink does not show through the paper.

Organization. Consider the approach your patrons will be taking: artist, medium, or style. If your collection is very large, you need to make a decision whether to establish a special collection. Special classifications for large collections may provide an approach by period, country, school, or art or alphabetical by artist. You may want to use the vendor's catalog as an index to the collection or cut up a catalog to make a card file of reproductions in order to provide easier access by patrons.

Preservation and protection. Mount or laminate if you expect heavy use. Page protectors can be used for circulation. You may want to rotate some in an area of framed prints.

Housing. You can use pocket envelopes, notebooks with page protectors, or boxes for large sets.

Management

Promotion. Inform your art teachers, students, and those interested in art. Use appropriate art reproductions in subject displays and indicate that the prints came from the art print file or the vertical file. Teachers can use art reproductions to stimulate writing. Art can complement studies in subjects such as history, literature, or social issues.

Circulation. You may want to extend the circulation time if people are checking out these reproductions to hang on their walls. Libraries may circulate framed art reproductions for several months at a time.

Weeding. Weed only worn items.

ASSOCIATION INFORMATION

Small public libraries, special libraries, and school libraries might want to collect information about associations, organizations, or clubs as a service to their patrons.[3] Association information may include such things as membership flyers, pamphlets, membership directories, newsletters and conference announcements, programs, papers, and reports.

Acquisition

Sources. There are several aids for finding materials including the following.

The Encyclopedia of Associations from Gale lists addresses for national associations. It is expensive at $305 per year. Regional, state, and local chapters will be covered in the companion set (5 volumes for $450 or $95 each) *Encyclopedia of Associations: Regional, State & Local Organizations.* There is no overlap between the sets except for some regional and state organizations that have national significance. These tools are found in many large public and academic libraries where you may consult them for addresses. Some state and local chapters can be located through the local telephone directory. You may want to provide a file of local groups without trying to collect additional materials. Addresses for many national associations and organizations are listed in almanacs.

Association information can be managed easily by establishing a database and updating it on a regular basis. Some libraries keep their community file on a computer database with dial-up access.[4]

Selection. Choose only local or state groups unless you have a special group of patrons who need other information. It is difficult to keep information on local groups current because officers change frequently and such groups rarely have a permanent address.

Information on upcoming national conferences may be of interest to possible attendees. This information may be better posted on a bulletin board in the library.

Ordering. Write or call the group. Watch local newspapers, which often have a regular listing of meetings and people to contact for information. Information should be updated once a year. Send a form postcard or letter to local groups once a year in January. Put a reminder to yourself in a tickler file.

Processing

Initial processing and labeling. Be sure to date everything you receive and place an address on material if it is not included. Use a Discard After [Date] label if you know the expected time of usefulness.

Organization. If you have only a list, you can put it in one folder in the vertical file. Association information will be easier to weed and to update if you keep it together, so you may want to consider an organization section subarranged alphabetically. You might have an association notebook with dividers for each group. Another option is to file materials alphabetically by the name of the group in the vertical file.

Preservation and protection. You can use page protectors and report covers or laminate items that will be heavily used.

Housing. Use file folders, theme binders, notebooks, and periodicals boxes to house material about associations, organizations, and clubs.

Management

Promotion. Current association material can be valuable to your patrons. Inform clubs and groups that you will keep the files current; encourage their use of the files and enlist their help in seeing that you have needed information. During the fall when many groups have membership meetings, you might have a display of their organizations.

Circulation. Do not circulate basic information. Most patrons will have no reason to check it out. Conference tapes and papers should circulate like other vertical-file materials.

Weeding. Weed once a year unless you are keeping materials for local history or archives collections. Throw out old membership information when you get new flyers; keep newsletters only for current year or current year plus one. Conference papers (or tapes) may be relevant for a few years. Students or volunteers can pull Discard After [Date] items with an expired date.

BIBLIOGRAPHIES

Most libraries have a collection of bibliographies, and teachers and librarians may collect specific kinds of bibliographies. Annotated bibliographies will be the best for your collection and are the most valuable to your patrons. If you have an automated system from which you can pull bibliographical citations, you can tailor bibliographies of your holdings to fit your patrons' specific needs and prepare them as needed.

Acquisition

Sources. Bibliographies are available in library literature, as reprints and handouts from meetings, as exchanges from other libraries, and as the ones you put together yourself. If you do on-line searching or have CD-ROM searching available in your library, you can save useful search printouts for your bibliography files[5] or download information that you can reformat for your own bibliographies.

The American Library Association (ALA) publishes a number of good bibliographies in leaflet format, including such titles as the *Newbery Medal Books, Caldecott Medal Books, Best Books for Young Adults,* and *Notable Books,* all revised annually. The series of bibliographies of outstanding books for the college bound, including topics of biography, fiction, theater, nonfiction, and fine arts, is revised periodically with 1991 being the latest current date. You may want to order multiple copies to give to patrons. Some ALA bibliographies are available with camera-ready pages for your own duplication.

There are a number of kinds of bibliographies available from the U.S. Government. The U.S. Government Printing Office's *Subject Bibliographies* are available from the Superintendent of Documents on many topics. There is a *Subject Bibliography Index* from which you can select titles for your collection. Most of the bibliographies are revised regularly. Each bibliography lists other government documents along with the stock number and price for ordering. The Library of Congress Tracer Bullets bibliography series should be checked. *U.S. Government Books* is available three times a year at no charge. This is an annotated list of new materials in 24 subject areas.

Vance Bibliographies, Inc. is a commercial source of individual bibliographies with most titles priced under $10. Vance offers a 40 percent discount for standing orders, which are available for subject areas. Vance Bibliographies are heavily indexed in *PAIS International in Print.*

Other resources include *Bulletin of Bibliography,* "Bibliography" in *Magazines for Libraries* from Bowker, and "Bibliography" in Adeline Smith's *Free Magazines for Libraries* from McFarland.

Selection. Save only bibliographies that you cannot find or duplicate easily. Annotated bibliographies in special subject areas are useful to keep.

Ordering. Consider a deposit account with the Superintendent of Documents if you order many government documents.

Processing

Initial processing and labeling. The source and date are most important. Most bibliographies go out-of-date fairly quickly, so adding the date is essential.

Organization. You may want to keep all bibliographies together in a file or notebook arranged by subject or you may file them by subject. If you have many, you will need to make decisions about arrangement. It may be helpful to have two copies—one for the bibliography file and one for the subject file.

Preservation and protection. Short bibliographies that are heavily used can be laminated or put into page protectors.

Housing. Library copies can be kept in notebooks, files, or boxes. Bibliographies you are giving away to patrons can be displayed in racks and labeled as free materials or stacked near a related exhibit of materials.

Management

Promotion. Prepared bibliographies can be used as buying guides, as starting points for exhibits or minidisplays, as topics for book-talks, or as tools to promote reading with various groups. The bibliographies you prepare can be great public relations tools to use with faculty, parents, students, and other groups of patrons. They can play a large part in your public relations materials, so the ones you use for handouts should be done as nicely as possible. You can create some great little promotional bibliographies with a brief list of materials, a little clip art, colored paper, and a photocopy machine. If you use generic bibliographies, it is helpful to your patrons to indicate your holdings.

Circulation. Do not circulate. Provide a photocopy machine or provide free copies.

Weeding. Remove most bibliographies from the public files that are more than two or three years old but keep them in your personal files if you expect to use them as a starting point for building a subject bibliography. For example, a list of stories about horses or a bibliography about your state or region should be kept. Put your own bibliographies on a computer so that you can update them frequently and easily.

BIOGRAPHICAL SKETCHES AND OBITUARIES

Biographical sketches are available in a variety of formats. You may have articles or clippings from periodicals and newspapers. Publishers often distribute sketches of their authors in leaflet or pamphlet form, or you may clip dust-jacket information. Calendars somtimes focus on individuals. Libraries that do not have a large variety of biographical tools will be most interested in collecting individual biographies.[6] Teachers will be interested in collecting biographical sketches of historical or prominent people in their subject area to help students considering a career in the field.[7]

Obituaries may be clipped for your local history file or for people in the news who will be of interest to your users. There is no need to clip obituaries available in indexed newspapers that you have available on microfilm or microfiche unless you expect a great deal of interest in the individual.

Acquisition

Sources. This is an area for clipping and gleaning from all sorts of sources. Schools often need more biographical information than they can easily provide when whole classes or grades are doing biographical reports. If that is your problem, you might even consider ripping apart withdrawn encyclopedias for biographical articles that will not become dated.

One excellent source for libraries is a periodical that focuses on individuals: *Images of Excellence* (Images of Excellence Foundation, P.O. Box 1131, Boiling Springs, North Carolina 28017). It is published six times per year for $5 and is designed for grades 5-8, but the interest level is higher. Each issue highlights a different historical or contemporary figure from world culture.

Current Biography from H. W. Wilson is an excellent source of articles (with portraits) for people currently in the news. It is issued monthly with a bound volume each year including all entries from the monthly issues. You can clip monthly issues for the vertical file after the annual volume is issued. *Biography Index*, also from H. W. Wilson, can be used to find articles on specific individuals.

Portraits for Classroom Bulletin Boards series, available from Dale Seymour Publications, includes nine sets of 15 profiles each in the following areas: mathematicians, women mathematicians, scientists, authors, poets, women writers, artists, and women artists. Each set has a one-page biography of the individual along with a black-and-white line-drawn portrait. The material is designed to be copied. Each set sells for $6.95.

Selection. Choose carefully the people you want to include in your file, keeping in mind your patrons' needs. Select only items that you think will be used. Short articles and multiple copies of clippings can be a great help when you continually have runs on certain people.

Ordering. Watch for information available through library conferences, periodicals lists, catalogs, and publishers' representatives. They often provide information about getting biographical material from publishers. Publishers often provide flyers containing pictures and biographical information about their authors including information about their books. Information from publishers is particularly important regarding new authors, who may not be covered in biographical reference books. Write to the publishers or call customer service on the toll-free numbers that are listed in the publishers' volume of *Books in Print* or in the *Bowker Annual*.

Processing

Initial processing and labeling. Be sure to indicate source and date on the material. Be consistent in your form of the name by establishing an authority file for names. This will avoid confusion in filing.

Organization. File alphabetically by last name unless you have some reason to group people or unless the "subject" is more important than the individual. You may want to have a separate biographical file.

Preservation and protection. Laminate or use page protectors for heavily used subjects. Remember that many of these materials will stay in your files for a long time. Photocopy or mount obituaries to standardize the size for your files.

Housing. File biographies and obituaries in folders, pockets, or envelopes.

Management

Promotion. Promote with the study of people in literature, history, or other subject areas. These files can supplement your book collection by providing additional sources.

Circulation. Circulate as you do regular vertical-file materials.

Weeding. Most of your biographical material will require very little weeding. If you have files no longer being requested, you may want to eliminate them. Do not keep material that is duplicated in encyclopedias unless you need it for easy circulation or as an additional resource.

82 / 12 – Supplementary Materials for Information Files

CALENDARS

Calendars of all kinds can enhance your collections. They come with all kinds of subject emphases, from pets to literature and sports. Many are available with a great deal of information about the specific subject. Calendars also come in a variety of formats, such as the "page-a-day" (which seems to be very popular now), the page-a-month with a nice picture for each month, and the kind that has special events written on each day. You may want to compile a community or school calendar if one is not available from your institution.

Acquisition

Sources. Book wholesalers, local bookstores, department stores, card shops, associations, and agencies are just a few of the many sources. Everyone seems to distribute calendars. If you are getting them for the pictures or information rather than the dates, you can often buy them at a very reduced price a few months into the year.

Selection. Choose subjects that are of interest to your patrons and that you might use for bulletin boards or displays. Keep a large, clean copy of a perpetual calendar in your file for patron use.

Ordering. Order calendars early in the fall from jobbers or associations. Bargains will be available off the shelf in bookstores or card shops in the spring.

Processing

Initial processing and labeling. Process only the calendars you plan to keep intact, e.g., the ones with events filled in for each day. Others you may cut apart for individual picture mounting. Stamp and label each picture if it is likely to be separated from the group. Page-a-day calendars will probably be discarded after use, though they can be recycled into trivia games.

Organization. Those with a subject focus will probably be most useful if filed by subjects either as separate pictures or in groups of pictures. General calendars can be filed under the general heading Calendars if there is any reason to keep them. Individual pictures or monthly dates may be better placed in holiday files.

Preservation and protection. Pictures clipped from calendars can be mounted or laminated.

Housing. Place calendars in files or envelopes in the vertical-file cabinets.

Management

Promotion. Calendars are wonderful for displays; a theme calendar plus a few books on the subject makes a very easy exhibit. Example: A calendar of quilts provides 12 coordinated pictures showing a variety of quilt patterns; add a few quilt books and a quilt or quilt paraphernalia, and you have an instant miniexhibit. Page-a-day calendars add interest at circulation desk, reference desk, and other parts of the library. Other calendars can be hung throughout the library near related subject areas or in places where they add to the decor.

Circulation. Do not circulate.

Weeding. Keep only the current year unless the pictures or the information is valuable for your vertical file. Keep informational calendars as long as you have an interest in the topic.

CARTOONS

Cartoons may be found in the vertical file in various forms such as clippings from newspapers and periodicals, overhead transparencies for use in presentations, or copies from books and other sources. Political or social cartoons may be important for studies of popular culture.

Acquisition

Sources. Cartoons for your vertical files are available as clippings from newspapers, periodicals, and journals in particular subject areas. You may even want to buy inexpensive paperback books of cartoons and pull them apart for your subject files.

Selection. Libraries that have developed collections of materials on popular culture will be interested in clipping cartoons to support that collection. You should establish a policy regarding the clipping of cartoons. Clipping requires a commitment of time. Your choice of cartoons to clip may focus on social or political issues, on humor or satire, on the art of cartooning or drawing, or on the work of the individual artist. You should have a clear idea of the need for clipping cartoons before you begin collecting them.

Ordering. Clip cartoons or comics from newspapers or periodicals. Some sets are available for purchase from school supply companies and can be used in a variety of ways. For example, a set of political cartoons from World War II would make an interesting addition to a display of books and materials on the period or to a classroom bulletin board. A number of cartoonists have published their own books, and there have been collections of cartoons from periodicals such as the *New Yorker*.

Processing

Initial processing and labeling. Identify the source and be sure to date every item.

Organization. Items can be arranged by subject, by artist, or grouped into a cartoon file as examples.

Preservation and protection. Clippings of cartoons can be mounted, laminated, photocopied, or put into page protectors.

Housing. Files, envelopes, or notebooks are recommended for cartoons.

Management

Promotion. Appropriate cartoons are helpful to speakers, teachers, artists and students of satire and humor.

Circulation. Circulate as you would other clippings.

Weeding. Weed every two years or when items are worn and/or interest has dropped off.

CHARTS AND DRAWINGS

Charts of one type or another are bound to be a part of your collection. There are a number of inexpensive charts and some that are free. They come in all sizes including large wall charts, posters, or notebook size. They may be a part of a series, a set, or individual charts. They may be designed for bulletin boards, flip charts, projections, or handout material. Most charts convey a single concept and are very effective tools for communication and education.

Drawings are another way to present a concept graphically. Some libraries have collections of drawings of decks, storage buildings, house plans, and other projects for do-it-yourself patrons. Technical drawings may be in the form of a plan, an elevation, cross-section, diagram, or perspective. They should be drawn to scale. Drawings may be on tracing paper, blueprint, or some other material. Unless you are in a special library, you will probably not actively collect many technical drawings, but you may have some that you are expected to maintain.

Acquisition

Sources. Charts are available from many sources including associations, manufacturers, the federal government, and educational supply companies. Most educational charts will have to be purchased, although many are inexpensive.[8]

Selection. Choose the topics in which your patrons will have an interest. Select items that convey the intended information clearly.

Ordering. Order charts when you request or requisition other materials from the same source.

Processing

Initial processing and labeling. Stamp and label the back of the chart if possible.

Organization. Charts can be organized by subject or accessioned by number. Size and storage will contribute to your decision regarding organization.

Preservation and protection. Charts can be laminated or cloth-backed for added protection.

Housing. Small charts can be folded and put in the vertical file. Large charts are a problem to store. Options for storage include stacking them flat in map cases or rolling them to put in tubes placed in a frame.

Management

Promotion. Charts are wonderful teaching aids and make nice backdrops for displays.

Circulation. Circulate as needed.

Weeding. Weed when tattered, faded, or when the information is out-of-date.

CLIPPINGS

Clippings are articles torn or cut from current newspapers, periodicals, discarded reference books, or other sources. Traditionally they have been filed in vertical-file cabinets with pamphlets; for many libraries clippings and pamphlets have been the only things in the vertical file. Many people think immediately of clippings when the topic of vertical files comes up.

Many, many hours have been spent by librarians and aides in clipping. Clippings files can eat up a great deal of time and effort, so it is very important to establish a clear policy on clipping to insure that you spend an appropriate amount of time.

Acquisitions

Sources. Newspapers will provide the most up-to-date information on topics. Unindexed periodicals may be clipped for the information they contain. House organs published by various businesses, industries, agencies, and associations can be clipped. Corporate newsletters offer relevant items for clipping. Indexed periodicals may be worth clipping for certain types of materials.

Selection. You need to be very selective in your clipping. In most cases you will not duplicate what you can retrieve easily through newspaper or periodical indexes. Examples of situations in which clipping indexed periodicals is justified include the following:

- Information is needed on new developments, awards, political appointments, informational oddities, special columns, feature articles, items of local interest, local biographies and obituaries, poems in advice columns that your patrons may request.

- There is a need for duplication: for example, if your periodicals do not circulate and your users need additional resources to be checked out.

- The material is not available otherwise, such as when a library only keeps a few years of back issues.

- The format is desirable: for example, if you keep indexed periodicals in a black-and-white microform format and the colored pictures are important to the information.

Ordering. You may receive gift copies of magazines or newspapers you want to clip such as *National Geographic*. Extra copies of newspapers or certain magazines may be secured just for clipping. (If titles are not indexed, then clipping is the only way they will be valuable to your collection, except for browsing.) You may order some free periodicals for the sole purpose of clipping. You can clip your own newspapers and periodicals when you are ready to discard them. Be sure to take your name off mailing lists if you no longer want to receive publications.

Processing

Initial processing and labeling. You must remember to identify clipped items! Unidentified articles are worthless as references. Sources of clipped articles must be identified on the item immediately upon clipping so that there is no confusion. Do not bother with labels but identify the item immediately.

Newspaper clippings must have the name and date of the newspaper and preferably the page number as well. An easy way to handle clippings (if you have a copy machine conveniently located) is to rip the article (including the name and date at the top of the page) with a metal ruler, then photocopy the article with the identifying information. File the photocopy and toss the clipping. This keeps all clippings in a standard size and format.

Periodical articles must have the name and date of the periodical with page numbers added if you do not clip the whole page. Clip whole pages when possible. Staple pages together if it is an article you do not expect to keep more than five years. (Staple twice for additional strength.) If it is an article of lasting importance, you may want to slip the article into a plastic sleeve to keep the pages together.

Organization. Most clippings will be organized by subject.

Preservation and protection. Loose or small clippings from newspapers are fragile and will not last long if you do not do something to preserve or protect them. Single clippings can be laminated, mounted, photocopied, or put in plastic sleeves. Multiple-page clippings from periodicals will probably be fine with no added protection. Plastic sleeves can be used for added protection.

Resist the temptation to use inexpensive scrapbooks and rubber cement for clipping collections, because the materials will deteriorate. If you want to use a scrapbook approach for certain kinds of clippings, consider using three-ring notebooks and plastic page protectors. Library suppliers have varieties of materials that can be used. Look through the archival supplies for appropriate materials.

Housing. Clippings can be filed in folders or envelopes, which in turn may be placed in files, boxes, or notebooks.

Management

Promotion. Advertise clippings as you do other materials. Clippings relating to the history of your school or library will be of interest on anniversaries, reunions, and retirements.

Circulation. Circulate as needed. You can encourage photocopying by providing equipment in a convenient location.

Weeding. Weed, weed, weed. This is the type of information that needs to be weeded ruthlessly. Except for local history, biography, and other topics of lasting importance, your clippings should probably not stay in your file more than three years.

COLLEGE CATALOGS

The individual catalogs from various colleges and universities that describe the programs and courses of the institution in detail are needed in a number of libraries. College catalogs are available in hard copy or in microfiche sets. If you decide not to collect individual college catalogs, you can provide reference sources with addresses so patrons can write for personal copies. College catalog collections will be found in school and academic libraries, special college collections in school counseling offices, special collections in school districts, and more limited collections in public libraries.

Acquisition

Sources. Addresses for colleges are available from a number of sources including the *College Blue Book*. You may want some hard-copy catalogs with a microfiche set to supplement gaps in your collection. College seniors or other patrons will sometimes donate extra catalogs after they have made their choice of schools.[9]

Selection. If you collect college catalogs, you will want all local and state catalogs and the out-of-state catalogs that are requested frequently. International catalogs and vocational catalogs should be collected as needed. Keep class schedules of local colleges for reference or distribution to patrons.

Ordering. Write to the individual colleges for copies of their catalogs and get on their mailing lists to receive new catalogs automatically if possible. Most institutions issue their catalogs on a regular basis in the summer or winter, either annually or biennially. Facilitate ordering by keeping your file on computer so you can generate mailing labels and keep track of your holdings as well as the publishing schedule for the institution. If a computer is not available for this, then you can photocopy sets of mailing labels for catalogs you request regularly. Send a self-addressed mailing label with your request if needed. Some institutions charge for catalogs or provide catalogs on an exchange basis for other universities and colleges.

Processing

Initial processing and labeling. Manage your collection with a computer or use a serial check-in card. Consider making a computer printout or a Kardex file available for patron use. Be sure to stamp the date of receipt on the catalog. Label catalogs to facilitate finding and shelving.

Organization. If you have a large collection, the easiest way to organize it is (1) by state and then alphabetically by institution or (2) alphabetically by name of the university or college. If you have only a few, you may want them on your ready-reference shelves, in your vertical file under Universities and Colleges, or under the name of the college.

Preservation and protection. Probably nothing extra is needed unless you feel the need to tape the spine of frequently used catalogs or use some of the simple pamphlet protection techniques suggested earlier.

Housing. Magazine boxes or Princeton files for each state can be used for easy sorting. If you have periodical shelving with metal dividers, you can skip the boxes, but you will want shelf labels to facilitate use.

Management

Promotion. If your catalogs are in a separate section, you need a good sign. You can advertise your collection in newspaper articles or flyers during periods such as spring and summer when people are thinking about colleges. Career centers, counselors, and registrars should know what you have in your collection.

Circulation. Heavily used collections should be for reference only; in other collections you may want to circulate items for one week. In some cases you may want to have multiple copies of catalogs and circulate all but one reference copy. High-school students will want to check out catalogs so parents can read them too.

Weeding. Keep only the latest edition of each catalog in most cases. Microfiche collections with older catalogs are useful in colleges and universities where students need to verify course descriptions for classes taken at other institutions.

COLORING BOOKS

Coloring books must be selected with care. Generally coloring books have received strong criticism by many librarians and teachers; however, many are really books of good line drawings that can be adapted for educational purposes. Coloring books are generally aimed at the young child, and there are a number of them available from associations, corporations, and government agencies. School and public libraries and individual teachers will find the most use for coloring books in their files. An example of an educational coloring book is the National Aeronautics and Space Administration's *Discover Aeronautics and Space—A Coloring Book for Elementary Students* (1990), which provides copyright-free drawings adaptable for clip art or as a master for self-produced overhead transparencies.

Acquisition

Sources. Associations, corporations, and government agencies list coloring books when they are available. Educators Progress Series and Carol Smallwood's guides to free materials list coloring books from special groups. Dover Publications offers dozens of coloring books on nature, history, costume, and design for under $3 each.

Selection. Establish a policy regarding coloring books before you begin collecting them. Distinguish between those that can be adapted for educational purposes, those for clip art, and those that are simply for entertainment. Consider each one that is available on the basis of the information it provides and whether you need that kind of information.

Ordering. Order direct from the association, corporation, or government agency or U.S. Superintendent of Documents when you place orders for other vertical-file materials.

Processing

Initial processing and labeling. Include the source, address, cost, and date of receipt on each item in case patrons want to order personal copies.

Organization. Arrange by subject in the supplementary file.

Preservation and protection. Add the label Do Not Color to each coloring book. Print a supply of labels by photocopy or computer so that this is an easy step. Pamphlet reinforcements or tape can be used for added protection.

Housing. Use file folders or envelopes for arranging coloring books in the vertical file.

Management

Promotion. Many of the association, corporation, and government coloring books are copyright-free and can be duplicated for handouts. You can promote them with teachers for transparency masters. Copyright-free materials can be used as they are or adapted.

Circulation. Consider library-use-only status for these materials, but provide a photocopy machine.

Weeding. Weed when the information is outdated or when the material is worn.

COMIC BOOKS

You will find comic books for instruction as well as for entertainment. If you choose to include comic books in your collection, you need to make a distinction in your established policy statement regarding the type of comic book you collect. Most likely you will consider good instructional comic books of an educational nature but exclude comic books for entertainment.[10] Instructional comics can be powerful educational tools that will reach some students who need the aid of the illustrations for understanding or for whom you need an attention-getting gimmick. Libraries that serve children and youth will be most interested in including comic books in their supplementary materials collections.

Acquisition

Sources. A number of organizations and associations use the comic-book format to present factual information about their product. For example, the National Committee for Prevention of Child Abuse uses The Amazing Spider-Man for a comic-book approach to communicating with children about emotional, sexual, and physical abuse.

Selection. Choose items because of their content, format, quality, and relevance for your collection. Many comics are printed on newsprint, so they will not withstand heavy use, but a number of them are well done and simply use the comic form of illustration. Beware of comics that are pure advertising or propagandistic in nature.

Ordering. Order from associations as you see comic books available. Sets of comics such as *Illustrated Classics* may be ordered from jobbers. Pendulum Press offers series in fiction, Shakespeare, American history, biography, and Spanish language.

Processing

Initial processing and labeling. Process as you would any vertical-file materials. Be sure that the date is indicated on educational comics that contain factual information that may become outdated.

Organizations. Nonfiction comics should be filed with the subject. Fiction may be kept together in a box or file of comics. You may want to make the box available in a casual reading corner of your library or classroom. You may also want to keep a list of nonfiction comic books for teachers or patrons to use with special groups of students.

Preservation and protection. Tape the spines or use pamphlet reinforcements. These materials are not designed to last long.

Housing. Store comics in boxes or files.

Management

Promotion. Use with reluctant readers, ESL (English as a second language) students, special students, or students with learning disabilities.

Circulation. Comic-book formats are fragile, but you can circulate as needed.

Weeding. Replace when they are worn or discard when they are outdated.

COURT CASES

Students will often ask for specific court cases, and you may find it helpful to have photocopies of some cases as they appear in the legal reporter if you do not have the *Supreme Court Reporter* or other primary sources in your library. You may also want to include other vertical-file materials about the cases. There are a number of books, articles, videos, and other related forms of information on landmark cases.

Acquisition

Sources. You can get photocopies of reports of cases by visiting a library in your area that has the legal resources and making your own copies. If you are responding as you have requests, you can, of course, request materials on interlibrary loan.

Selection. Begin by limiting your selections to landmark cases that students will be encountering in their studies. For cases of important local or state significance, you may want to include clippings as well as the actual case.

You may want to consider some of the following Supreme Court decisions: *Marbury v. Madison* (1803), *McCullock v. Maryland* (1819), *Trustees of Dartmouth College v. Woodward* (1819), *Dred Scott v. Sanford* (1857), *Munn v. Illinois* (1877), *U.S. v. E.C. Knight Co.* (1895), *Plessy v. Ferguson* (1896), *Northern Securities Co. v. U.S.* (1904), *Muller v. Oregon* (1908), *Standard Oil Co. of New Jersey Et Al. v. U.S.* (1911), *Schenck v. U.S.* (1919), *Schechter v. U.S.* (1935), *Dennis Et Al. v. U.S.* (1951), *Brown v. Board of Education of Topeka* (1954), *Roth v. U.S.* (1957), *Mapp v. Ohio* (1961), *Baker v. Carr* (1962), *Miranda v. Arizona* (1966), *Furman v. Georgia* (1972), *Roe v. Wade* (1973), *University of California v. Bakke* (1978) and *Bowers v. Hardwick* (1986).

Ordering. The easiest way to get these cases is to visit your area library that has the *Supreme Court Reporter* or other legal decision reporting services and make your own copies.

Processing

Initial processing and labeling. Be sure to include the citation in the correct legal form.

Organization. File under the specific case if you have a number of cases or if you are including information about the cases in your files. You may also file under the subject. You can make cross-references or duplicate the case. You can group the cases into a general file, Court Cases, if you have only a few.

Preservation and protection. Laminate or use page protectors to protect your copy.

Housing. Use file folders or envelopes in the vertical file for court cases.

Management

Promotion. A bibliography of important cases with related information sources would be very popular with students and adults.

Circulation. Do not circulate but encourage photocopying.

Weeding. Weed files of cases of passing interest. Keep files for landmark cases but photocopy or replace worn items as needed.

DIRECTORIES

There are a number of directories you will consider for your files. Many will be locally produced, such as members of the chamber of commerce, friends of the library, groups, faculty directory, a directory of libraries in your city, a membership list for your state or regional library association. You will of course have the telephone book for your own city, but directories for other cities in your state and for other major cities in which your patrons have an interest may be useful. You can buy hard-copy telephone directories or you can get sets of telephone books on microfiche.

92 / 12—Supplementary Materials for Information Files

Acquisition

Sources. Most of the local-interest directories will come to you directly from the groups producing them. You can contact your local telephone office to get information on ordering telephone directories for your state or area. Commercial vendors such as World Wide Directory Product Sellers Inc. sell directories.[11]

Selection. Choose directories your patrons need. Consider telephone directories for neighboring communities and major cities in your state. You may put membership directories for organizations or clubs in your association files. Club and organization membership lists should only be included with permission from the group and with the understanding that they will be in a public file.

Ordering. Plan to request information on an annual basis unless you can get on the mailing list of the group. Telephone directories may be purchased at the local office in some cities, but in other communities you may need to order them.

Processing

Initial processing and labeling. Be sure to stamp with the ownership stamp and the date you received the directory. Revisions are done at various times, so you may need a tickler file to aid in your replacement of old issues. Use Discard After [Date] labels if you can anticipate the date for weeding.

Organization. Special directories may be in the file under the name of the group. You may have a Directories box or file for those you frequently consult. Telephone directories for cities can be arranged alphabetically by city or alphabetically by state and then subarranged by city if you have a large collection.

Preservation and protection. Consider permanent binding or using some kind of directory cover.

Housing. Small collections can be housed in your vertical file cabinets. Larger collections can be arranged on shelves or in periodical boxes on the shelves either with or without full cataloging.

Management

Promotion. Use good signs to indicate the location. This will be a popular collection in most libraries.

Circulation. Do not circulate. You can put telephone books in your reference collection so that they are near your reference desk.

Weeding. Discard when you get a new edition. You may want to keep a copy of your local directory in your local history collection.

DOCUMENTS (FACSIMILE)

Reproductions of certain documents will be important to have in your library, and it is likely that in many institutions they will be housed in the vertical file. Copies of historical documents such as the United States Constitution and the Bill of Rights are probably first on the list for most collections but there are many others to choose from. Social studies, speech, and journalism teachers may also want to keep copies of certain documents in their personal files.

Acquisition

Sources. You will find a number of sources for reproductions of the most popular documents. You can keep several if it is important to be able to offer a variety of sizes and formats; otherwise discard extra copies. Sets of certain types of documents are available.[12]

The National Archives offers a number of documents. The ongoing series of booklets focusing on milestone documents in U.S. history include such topics as Washington's Inaugural Address of 1789, The Emancipation Proclamation, F. D. Roosevelt's "Day of Infamy" address in 1941, and John F. Kennedy's Inaugural Address of 1961. Booklets in the series are about 25 pages long and include historical introduction with facsimile and transcriptions in each. Booklets follow an 8½"-x-11" format and sell for $2.50.

Parchment reproductions of landmark documents are also available from the National Archives for 75 cents each for the following: Declaration of Independence, Constitution, Bill of Rights, Louisiana Purchase, Monroe Doctrine, Magna Carta, Emancipation Proclamation, Statue of Liberty Deed of Gift, George Washington's Inaugural Address, John F. Kennedy's Inaugural Address and the Articles of Confederation.

Selection. Choose topics related to your patrons' interests and needs. Remember to consider relevant state documents.

Ordering. Most sources will need direct orders.

Processing

Initial processing and labeling. Process as sets when possible. Label and mark items on the back.

Organization. Organize by subject in the vertical-file or poster section. If you are using an accession system, be sure to index adequately.

Preservation and protection. Mount or laminate for protection and/or store in cardboard folders.

Housing. Store in flat cases or bins. You may want to frame special documents for permanent display.

Management

Promotion. Display when possible and indicate that documents are available for circulation.

Circulation. Circulate as needed. Documents in the public domain can be reproduced freely, so you may want to encourage patrons to copy those documents rather than borrow them.

Weeding. Weed only when items are worn or material is irrelevant.

ELECTION ISSUES

Election materials will be available in nonpartisan form or with a political viewpoint. You will have access to local, state, and national election materials. You may limit your materials to issues only or may include individual races for political positions. Public libraries will have a particular interest in making available voting information and materials on election issues.

Acquisition

Sources. League of Women Voters membership may facilitate getting material from that group. The league promotes political responsibility, distributes information on candidates and issues, and encourages voting. It does not support or oppose candidates or political parties.

It is possible to obtain election materials from candidates and from groups interested in specific issues. You can likely get as much election information as you request.

Selection. Begin with general information such as League of Women Voters publications or newspaper reprints of issues, candidate profiles, sample ballots, and other nonpartisan publications. If you do have candidate information, you should be sure to have each one represented. Small communities and local history collections will be able to handle a broader range of materials.

Ordering. A telephone call to your local newspaper or to party or individual campaign headquarters will get you information. Membership with the League of Women Voters will put you on their mailing list.

Processing

Initial processing and labeling. No processing is necessary unless you are keeping information for a local history collection or file.

Organization. Arrange on a display table before elections. Material you are keeping for your files can be filed by candidate name or grouped in one file labeled by type of election, such as, City Elections 1992.

Preservation and protection. Laminate or use page protectors for items that will be heavily used, but remember that much of the election material will be discarded after the election. Preserve and store items of historical value.

Housing. File materials you are keeping in the vertical file in envelopes.

Management

Promotion. During pre-election periods you may want to set up an election corner or table for materials.

Circulation. Most materials may be distributed free rather than worrying about circulation. If you do not have extra copies for distribution keep a display copy or desk copy for reference.

Weeding. Most election materials will be discarded after the election except for materials you want to keep for local history files.

EXHIBITION CATALOGS

Catalogs are often prepared for special exhibits in institutions such as art, history, and natural history museums as well as in libraries. A great deal of information is presented in exhibit catalogs since they usually represent a large number of items pulled together for display. They are often the product of research and are high-quality publications. Art and history libraries as well as some university and public libraries will have a particular interest in exhibition catalogs. Small public and school libraries may be interested in specific relevant topics.

Acquisition

Sources. Museums, galleries, and libraries in your state will be good sources of exhibit catalogs for local or traveling exhibits. Catalogs and guides such as the Smithsonian Institution's *Generations: The Study Guide* are frequently available. Examples of other notable institutions producing catalogs are the New York Gallery of Art and The National Gallery of Canada. The National Gallery of Canada offers many catalogs for under $5 featuring items from their own special collections.

A number of catalogs are published in association with a university or commercial publishing company such as the University of Washington Press. Kraus International Publications has announced a bibliography of art exhibition catalogs due in 1992.

Selection. Collect catalogs for exhibits from your city and other catalogs as they fit your collection.

Ordering. Order direct from the institution or buy with petty cash when you visit exhibits.

Processing

Initial processing and labeling. Include the source and dates of the exhibit if they are not included on the catalog.

Organization. File by subject or by institution depending on the way your patrons will be looking for materials. Make cross-references. Some titles may be classified for your circulating collection.

Preservation and protection. Exhibit catalogs cannot be replaced, so consider binding important catalogs. You can use pamphlet binders, pamphlet reinforcements, or tape for other catalogs.

Housing. Use file folders or envelopes for vertical-file storage or classify for the general collection.

Management

Promotion. Promote your exhibit catalogs with the subject matter. Use them in displays when preparing your own book exhibits.

Circulation. Circulate as you would other vertical-file materials.

Weeding. Weed when worn or interest is past.

96 / 12 – Supplementary Materials for Information Files

FORMS

People come to libraries in search of all kinds of forms, including genealogy, home inventory, health-related and budget and expense forms. You may be asked for IRS forms, legal forms, sample job application forms, sample resume forms, living will forms, power of attorney forms, business forms, and many other miscellaneous kinds of forms. In addition, you will find forms helpful in managing your library or collection. Some forms may be copied, but many will be adapted to serve a specific purpose.

Acquisition

Sources. There are books of forms to supply some of this kind of information, but you may want to supplement that selection.[13] You can get copies of U.S. tax forms from the IRS or your local post office. Contact the company or agency if there are other items your users request.

Selection. Choose forms that serve as examples for business classes or those that your patrons frequently request. Be selective in the forms you provide that patrons might use for legal or business purposes without seeking the appropriate professional advice.

Ordering. Order from publishers, jobbers, your state agencies, and the U.S. Government Printing Office.

Processing

Initial processing and labeling. Identify the source clearly.

Organization. File forms under the subject or in a section on forms. Frequently requested forms should be on your ready-reference shelf.

Preservation and protection. Use page protectors or lamination for some heavily used forms.

Housing. Use files or notebooks with protective page protectors.

Management

Promotion. Promote as you would other vertical-file materials. Be very careful not to offer advice on the use of forms.

Circulation. Do not circulate. Provide a copy machine for photoduplication.

Weeding. Discard when outdated.

GOVERNMENT DOCUMENTS

The U.S. federal government is the largest publisher in the world, so you can be sure that there is a wealth of material of all kinds available. Nearly every agency, bureau, and department issues a large number of publications including booklets, posters, educational guides, and audiovisual materials. Nearly every library will have an interest in some documents from the federal government. In addition there are municipal documents, state documents, United Nations documents, and documents from other nations.

Government Documents / 97

Acquisition

Sources. Two free catalogs, *Government Books for You* and *New Books: Publications for Sale*, by the Government Printing Office will keep you informed of most of the publications you will want to order. Other recommended references include Carol Smallwood's *Guide to Selected Federal Agency Programs* (as well as some of her other books that include federal sources) and Leticia Ekhaml and Alice Wittig's *U.S. Government Publications for the School Library Media Center*. Both titles are published by Libraries Unlimited. Another guide from Michael Spencer, *Free Publications from U.S. Government Agencies*, discusses various agencies and the types of materials they have available. Many agencies and departments issue their own catalogs.

The Monthly Catalog is a more comprehensive list of publications but requires a paid subscription. The microfiche PRF file is the *Books in Print* for U.S. government documents and lists stock number and price. Watch for the annual list of notable documents for the previous year of publication. (The eighth annual list was in *Library Journal*, May 15, 1991.)

Selection. Select materials that will be useful to your patrons. There are plenty of materials available for very little cost, but you should be selective or you will have more than you can possibly keep up with. A collection of state constitutions, for example, would be of interest. Some of the best U.S. government document series for the vertical file include the following: Background Notes, information about countries; Subject Bibliographies, lists of resources; and Occupational Outlook Handbook Reprints, brief articles about different careers.

Ordering. Open a deposit account with the U.S. Superintendent of Documents to facilitate ordering and bookkeeping. Order specific publications from the Superintendent of Documents or from the individual agency. Your state and U.S. representatives may be able to provide you with publications related to the committee work they are assigned. State, federal, or United Nations[14] documents must be ordered direct.

Processing

Initial processing and labeling. Indicate the source and cost of the item. Patrons may want to order copies, or you may want to order a new edition at a later date.

Organization. Small collections of government documents can be treated like other pamphlet material and arranged by subject in your vertical file. You may choose to establish a special collection of documents if you have a large collection, in which case you will probably arrange by Superintendent of Documents (SuDocs) number. This keeps materials together by issuing agency.

Preservation and protection. Standard pamphlet preservation techniques can be used if necessary.

Housing. Use manila folders or boxes for regular vertical-file materials and shelves for large collections.

Management

Promotion. Include items in your catalog. Provide a copy of *Monthly Catalog* for indexing and additional information about government documents. Use signs to promote a special collection.
   Circulation. Circulate as needed.
   Weeding. Weed government documents when they are no longer useful.

GUIDES

Guides to types of library materials, special collections, general subject areas, or individual items in the collection will be found in many libraries. Library guides, often called *pathfinders*, will usually lead the patron through various resources in a particular subject area such as biographical materials. Other types of guides give directions and aids to use of various items or types of materials. Some of your guides may also come under the general discussion of handouts in chapter 14.

You may have pathfinders or guides to specific kinds of information in your city or area. For example, the Anchorage Library Information NetworK (LINK) has prepared a series of guides to certain kinds of information such as U.S. Government Documents and legal information located in the various libraries in the city.

Acquisition

Sources. Guides from other libraries can be picked up when you visit, but you will want to write your own guides to reflect your collection.
   Selection. Prepare guides that are needed the most by your patrons. Buy useful guides you find available.
   Ordering. Establish a standard format for your own guides. Design a standard heading or order an appropriate letterhead that can be used for all guides to make them look unified. Duplicate the guides for distribution.

Processing

Initial processing and labeling. Put an identifying mark on the guide to indicate the date, author, and source of the guide.
   Organization. Keep your masters in a file or notebook. File other guides in your personal or general vertical files.
   Housing. Put copies out on a literature rack if possible. Extra copies can be housed in the vertical file.
   Preservation and protection. Keep your master on computer with a backup disk or in a nonpublic file.

Management

Promotion. Place a good sign over the literature rack to promote items you have for users to take. Other guides can be promoted with subject or general vertical-file materials.
Circulation. Give away extra copies of your own guides. Encourage photocopying guides that you have for reference; circulate other guides from your files as needed.
Weeding. Revise your guides when needed. Weed commercially prepared or other generic guides when they are outdated or no longer useful.

HOLIDAY ITEMS

Many libraries participate in holiday programs, but even if you do not, your patrons may be looking for materials for their own holiday activities. Holiday materials include such things as decorations, poetry, plays, recipes, games, costumes, and crafts.

Acquisition

Sources. Books, magazines, school supply companies, card shops, and many other sources will provide ideas for your holiday collections.
Selection. Choose the types of things that your patrons request, such as poetry, plays, customs, games, and recipes. A file of universally requested items that can be duplicated instantly might provide for last-minute requests. An example is Frank P. Church's editorial "Yes, Virginia, There Is a Santa Claus" in *The New York Sun*, September 21, 1897.
Ordering. Some holiday items such as decorations can be purchased, but many of these things will be clipped from holiday magazines and greeting cards or collected from a variety of sources.

Processing

Initial processing and labeling. Stamp and label the backs of items if possible or mark in an unobtrusive place.
Organization. File by specific holiday. You may also want to consider filing by season.
Preservation and protection. Copy or laminate heavily used paper items.
Housing. If you have many miscellaneous sizes and shapes, you may want to use a cardboard file box to keep the materials for each holiday together.

Management

Promotion. Use items in library displays or special library events programming, with notes that additional holiday materials are available for check out.
Circulation. Encourage duplication of some items if you do not have enough to supply all of your requests.
Weeding. Weed when worn.

INSTRUCTIONS

Many library patrons request information on how to do many different things, from how to make a poinsettia bloom to how to read an annual report. These may be called how to's, directions, or simply instructions. Most are very concise and outlined step-by-step so that the reader can follow the procedure. The subject matter varies from library to library, but the type of information is the same.

Acquisition

Sources. Directions are available from associations, organizations, and businesses as well as in magazines and newspapers. Be alert to well-written, clear, concise instructions that your users may request. Several years ago there was a popular series of magazine advertisements that provided how-to directions for such things as reading poetry and interpreting annual reports. Dover Publications has a number of inexpensive booklets of instructions for arts and crafts.

Selection. Choose topics that will be of interest to your patrons.

Ordering. Collect instructions as they become available. Many will be found in newspapers, periodicals, and lists of free and inexpensive materials.

Processing

Initial processing and labeling. Stamp and label as you would any other vertical-file material.

Organization. In most instances these will simply be a part of your file on the particular subject.

Preservation and protection. Page protectors or lamination is recommended for heavily used instructions.

Housing. Use file folders. An alternative method might be a 4"x6" card file where instructions are listed or clippings are posted.

Management

Promotion. You might want to list some of your popular how-to guides in a separate bibliography to call attention to the many kinds of directions you have available. You could feature some instructions along with how-to books in a special display. Always identify the way to find items you are using from the vertical file.

Circulation. Provide a copy machine and encourage photocopying for brief instructions. Circulate instructions as you see necessary.

Weeding. Weed when no longer useful.

INTERVIEWS

Interviews may be published in magazines or newspapers or recorded on audio- or videocassettes. They may be commercially produced, professionally done, or locally prepared.

Acquisition

Sources. Interviews are available from a number of sources including commercial vendors, periodical and newspaper articles, and individual interviews that may be a part of an oral history project in the community or school.

Selection. Choose all available interviews with notable authors, artists, and other significant personalities from your community and state which are relevant to your locale. Select others as they enhance your biography section.

Ordering. Tapes of famous individuals are available from commercial sources, but local-interest interviews are often available only from local sources. You will have to be alert to get copies when they are available.

Processing

Initial processing and labeling. Be sure that the date of the interview as well as the date of receipt are attached. Dates should be clearly distinguished. The place of the interview, the occasion, and the name of the interviewer should also be included.

Organization. In most cases you will include interviews as a part of your biography file under the name of the individual.

Preservation and protection. No particular preservation is required; page protectors can be used if you expect heavy use. Consider backup copies for unique items that cannot be replaced.

Housing. Keep paper transcripts of interviews in file folders or pockets or with a tape of the interview. Reprints of interviews from periodicals or newspaper reports can be filed in folders in vertical file cabinets.

Management

Promotion. Promote with biographical and career materials where appropriate. Ties can also be made with history and the subject for which the individual is noted. Interviews can add a personal interest to the study of many areas.

Circulation. Circulate as needed. Make backup copies if needed.

Weeding. Very little weeding is needed unless interest lapses and the material is available elsewhere.

LESSON PLANS AND CURRICULUM GUIDES

Lesson plans are simply outlines or guides to teaching a particular topic. You will find these in personal files, school libraries, school-district professional collections, or education libraries on university campuses. Many coordinate with the specific curriculum guide for the discipline. In addition, many lesson plans are available with commercially prepared supplementary materials, and free and inexpensive materials are offered by special groups and companies. It is this latter group that the library may be interested in acquiring.

School districts write curriculum guides for each subject area. Public and university libraries may find it useful to have copies of the curriculum guides for the local school district. University libraries with active teacher-education programs may want to invest in curriculum guides.[15] Individual schools will most likely have a set of district curriculum guides in the library. Guides are revised every few years, so you may want to give them the vertical-file treatment in your collection unless you have a historical collection.

Acquisition

Sources. Many agencies, organizations, and companies have education departments that write materials for teachers to use in the classroom. Many of these resources are excellent. The *Elementary Teachers Guide to Free Curriculum Materials* from Educators Progress Service lists a number of the materials they have evaluated. Other lesson plans and guides can be located by writing to the education department of the individual group. The Educational Resources Information Center (ERIC) provides many lesson plans and curriculum guides in *Resources in Education*, a document collection on microfiche. You can call ACCESS ERIC at 1-800-USE ERIC to find the nearest collection.

Selection. Choose subjects that relate to the curriculum of the institution you represent or that of the students you serve. Include topics that may be of interest to special study groups including youth organizations and women's clubs and civic groups and that cover hobbies or special interests of adults.

Ordering. Order direct, but to simplify your request, use a form postcard or form letter with a place to insert the specific title you are requesting.

Processing

Initial processing and labeling. Be sure that the source and date of receipt are on the materials. It is important to include the date of the materials if it is available.

Organization. Organize by subject or discipline. If you have a large collection of lesson plans, you may want to establish a special collection. Consider setting up a subject heading or subheading for lesson plans.

Preservation and protection. Page protectors may be helpful if you expect heavy use.

Housing. Use file folders or report covers for most lesson plans and guides. Pamphlet binders, notebooks, or boxes can be used for some materials. You may put curriculum guides in your vertical file cabinets, but if they are too lengthy, they can be shelved in boxes or binders on the shelves.

Management

Promotion. Advertise to appropriate teachers, youth leaders, and other educators. If you can generate a computer list by heading, you can easily update your list of lesson plans available. Parents and education students will be interested in curriculum guides.

Circulation. You can be flexible in your circulation of these materials by allowing teachers to use them as long as necessary.

Weeding. Weed annually. Anything used for education should be as up-to-date as possible. Much of the material has a maximum shelf life of seven years.

LIBRETTOS

The libretto is the book or written story that accompanies a presentation of a musical comedy, opera, or operetta. The libretto ties together the story, integrating the dialogue, music, lyrics, and dancing. Librettos may be found in public, academic, and school libraries.

Acquisition

Sources. Commercial vendors such as Dover Publications supply some librettos. Local productions will often make librettos available before the performance.

Selection. Select titles that are being performed in your community and those for which there is interest among your patrons. Consider titles that are in the news or are movie or television related.

Ordering. Order with general library requests. Consider ordering the recorded music or video to use with the libretto.

Processing

Initial processing and labeling. Stamp and label as you do other library materials.

Organization. Many libraries will include librettos as a part of their book collection or as a supplement to the audio or video of the work. A special collection of librettos arranged in the vertical file or on the shelf may be considered if you have a large selection.

Preservation and protection. Tape the spines or use pamphlet reinforcements if you expect light use. Bind your librettos if you want to keep them permanently.

Housing. Use binders or folders when filing in vertical-file cabinets. Librettos can also be shelved in pamphlet boxes or on bookshelves.

Management

Promotion. Display librettos along with videos and other related materials when you have a musical production in your community.

Circulation. Circulate librettos as needed.

Weeding. Weed only when worn. Librettos will not become dated.

MAGAZINES (FREE)

There is a lot of good information available in free periodicals, but you must be selective. You can clip free magazines, treat them as you do your other periodicals, or file the whole issue under the appropriate subject.

Acquisition

Sources. Information about free magazines is available from a number of excellent sources.

Magazines for Libraries by Bill Katz and Linda Sternberg Katz published by Bowker (the sixth edition came out in 1989) has several good sections: "Index to Free Periodicals" (p. 23) and "Index to U.S. Government Periodicals" (p. 24) as well as "Free Magazines" and "House Organs." House organs are magazines published by organizations and companies that promote the interests of the group. Many house organs are free for the asking.

Free Magazines for Libraries by Adeline Mercer Smith and Diane Rovena Jones, a McFarland publication, is in its third edition (1989). It includes approximately 500 entries in 66 categories. The appendix includes several helpful lists including "Basic List of Magazines for Small to Medium Libraries," "Magazines Outstanding for Their Illustrations," "Magazines Useful for Career and Vocational Guidance," and "Magazines Indexed in Periodical Indexes and Abstracts." There is one index including titles and detailed subjects.

Selection. Be aware that free publications from companies and organizations may present the biases and views of the group. There are a number of very good resources available, often including beautiful illustrations. Select only the titles that will be used by your patrons. One example of an excellent free magazine is *Art to Zoo* from the Smithsonian Institution.

Ordering. Write directly to the company or organization on letterhead to request a sample issue or subscription. Remember to ask to have your name removed from the list when you are no longer interested in receiving the publication.

Processing

Initial processing and labeling. You have a number of options for handling free magazines. You can check in, label, and process them as you do purchased periodicals; you can just clip the items you want; or you can file the entire issue without keeping up with records for receiving issues. Consider Discard After [Date] labels for magazines you are keeping together for a certain period, such as the current year and one preceding year.

Organization. Treat the free magazine as a regular periodical if the title is indexed. If no indexing is available, you may want to file directly into your vertical file under the subject. Issues can be clipped to save only the relevant articles.

Preservation and protection. Use the same preservation techniques you use for regular periodicals. Consider microfiche or binding for selected titles.

Housing. Keep these magazines in pamphlet boxes if you treat the material as you do periodicals. Store in file cabinets with subject matter if you are clipping or filing the issue.

Management

Promotion. Provide *Index to Free Periodicals* with other indexes if you have a majority of the titles included. Promote with related materials on the subject.

Circulation. Circulation policy should conform to periodical circulation or to vertical-file items, depending on where you have put the magazines.

Weeding. Establish a policy for the title when you start the subscription to facilitate weeding. You might consider keeping only the current year and one preceding year, especially if the title is not indexed. Withdrawn issues can be clipped if they have valuable articles.

MAGAZINES (SAMPLE)

It is impossible to subscribe to every magazine, so in some cases you may want to provide a collection of sample magazines for your patrons. Sample magazines can provide a service to your users who are considering subscriptions in areas such as children's magazines. The opportunity to examine sample issues would be useful to parents, grandparents, and teachers who are considering the purchase of children's titles.

Sample magazines can also serve as reference material on subject-specific or hobby-related topics when you cannot justify a subscription but would like to provide at least one issue of a magazine for reference. Magazines devoted to specific kinds of pets, sports, or collectibles are examples.

Acquisition

Sources. You can get samples of magazines by buying them from the newsstand, by writing directly to the publisher on official stationery, or in some cases by submitting a list to your periodicals jobber. Library users will often donate magazines to be used in the files.

Excellent information about magazines is available in Bill Katz and Linda Sternberg Katz's *Magazines for Libraries*, published by Bowker. Entries for the 6,500+ titles selected from more than 70,000 possibilities include the title, date founded, frequency, price, editor, publisher, address, illustrations, index, advertising, circulation, indication of whether samples are available, date the volume ends, whether the articles are refereed, microform availability, reprint information, on-line access, where it is indexed, number of book reviews per issue, and audience plus an evaluative 100- to 150-word annotation. The entries are arranged by broad subject categories and indexed by title and detailed subjects. Subject categories also include special topic entries such as Abstracts and Indexes, Archives and Manuscripts, Bibliography, Children, Free Magazines, Large Print, Media and AV, Museum Publications, Newspapers. There is a companion volume, *Magazines for Young People.*

106 / 12 – Supplementary Materials for Information Files

The International Reading Association (IRA) and the Educational Press Association of America have an annotated list of more than 100 titles in their *Magazines for Children, 1990*. The list is arranged alphabetically and indexed by subject and grade level.

Selection. Select titles to reflect your users' interests and choose titles you are considering for purchase.

Ordering. Order as needed or once a year on a regular basis if you want sample magazines available for teacher or parent examination.

Processing

Initial processing and labeling. Date and label Sample so patrons do not expect to find other issues. You can keep all sample magazines together in a box marked Sample Magazines available for patrons or in your workroom. Indicate the date for discard if possible.

Organization. There are several options for organization, such as arranging titles alphabetically in your sample box, grouping magazines by subject for teacher or parent examination, or filing by subject in your information files for very specific topics.

Preservation and protection. Sample magazines will not be kept long, so no preservation is necessary. Two years is probably the maximum you will keep items of this kind.

Housing. Store sample magazines in pamphlet boxes or in file cabinets.

Management

Promotion. School librarians may want to order new samples in the spring for teachers to examine for consideration of classroom sets. School orders for fall are usually complete before June, so March is a good month to write for samples. Some companies will send them to you or the department as advertisement. Examination copies can be promoted to parents in the spring as an idea for summer reading.

If your school or community sponsors a magazine sale, you may want samples available then. Parents begin thinking about educational items in August when they are thinking about other back-to-school materials. Library users may be interested in a pre-Christmas examination period.

Circulation. Do not circulate sample magazines. This group of materials will most often be used in the library by teachers or parents. If there is some reason to take the samples out of the library, you can be flexible about circulation periods.

Weeding. Discard or replace sample magazines after a year or so. Discard After [Date] labels will facilitate weeding.

MAIL-ORDER CATALOGS

Catalogs will be of interest to many patrons, particularly those who live a distance from a large city. School supplies, education materials, clothes, gifts, flowers, seeds, gadgets, hunting and fishing equipment, automobile parts, and food of all kinds are just a few of the kinds of things people can order. In many communities a public library collection of mail-order catalogs will get heavy use.

Acquisition

Sources. Newspapers and magazines often have cards you can mark to order catalogs. Once you get on several mailing lists, you will have no problem getting catalogs.

Selection. Choose catalogs that interest your patrons and remove your name from the mailing list of those you no longer need. Large general merchandise catalogs such as Sears, J. C. Penney, and Montgomery Ward may be classified and shelved in the general collection to provide a history of fad, fashion, merchandise, and economics.

Ordering. Fill out a few cards in magazines or Sunday supplements to the newspaper, and the vendors will come to you. You will need to order large merchandise catalogs direct from the company or from your jobber.

Processing

Initial processing and labeling. Keep it simple. Do not bother checking in catalogs or trying to keep up with them. Establish a simple procedure such as a large colored dot or a colored label with the date received stamped on it. Change colors every six months and toss out all of the old catalogs. You can add an initial letter for the company if you want to try to sort alphabetically into smaller groups.

Organization. Put all mail-order catalogs together. Sort or alphabetize by company if you have more than 25.

Preservation and protection. Do not do anything. This is a bonus service, and it should be as simple as possible. Popular catalogs can be processed with a security device if you have a library security system and believe that it is necessary. Many libraries add large merchandise catalogs to their permanent collection. Consider binding catalogs if they are added to your permanent collection.

Housing. Make it easy on yourself. Toss all catalogs into a cardboard box. If you want to be a little more organized, you can use several magazine boxes with letters so you can sort by smaller groups.

Management

Promotion. Put a big sign on the box and leave it out where patrons can find it themselves. Encourage them to return catalogs to the box.

Circulation. Do not circulate.

Weeding. Throw away or give away old catalogs when new ones come or when a catalog is six months old. Colored dots or Discard After [Date] labels will help you keep the collection current.

MANUALS

You will likely have requests for different kinds of manuals: drivers' manuals, citizenship manuals, copyright guides, and perhaps even Scout manuals. These are, of course, available from other sources, but many people depend on their public or school library to provide everything informational.

Acquisition

Sources. You can pick up extra copies of drivers' manuals at the local examination center. You may want to have several copies to circulate and one for reference. High schools will have a big demand for drivers' manuals.

Selection. Select manuals that people have requested. Consider manuals for new adult readers if you have a literacy program in your community.

Ordering. Many of these are free items you just need to pick up or request from the right office. Find out about the schedule for revision and get on the mailing list or make yourself a tickler file entry to get the new editions when they are available.

Processing

Initial processing and labeling. Stamp, label, and mark with copy numbers if you have several. Do not worry too much about security or preservation. Use Discard After [Date] labels if you know the date of revision.

Organization. Shelve manuals where they are handy if you have a number of requests. Take care that they do not get buried in the vertical file and are never seen.

Preservation and protection. Do not worry about preservation. Throw them away when they wear out.

Housing. You can shelve manuals in a pamphlet box on the ready-reference shelf and/or in your information file.

Management

Promotion. Making manuals available to users is a great service, so let patrons know you have them. If you are able to get a good supply, you can let users keep copies.

Circulation. You can be lenient with circulation.

Weeding. Be sure to keep up with new editions. Throw away old issues when new ones are available.

NEWSLETTERS

Newsletters of one kind or another will be found in most libraries. Many are free or inexpensive and provide good, timely information. The treatment of newsletters varies, as does their importance, but there may be some that you will find valuable for your collection.

Acquisition

Sources. Newsletters are available from many groups and associations. Gale Research Company publishes an entire book on newsletters, *Newsletters in Print*. It is expensive if you do not need it for your reference collection, but it is an excellent resource for you to check when you visit a larger library.

Selection. Be selective in your choice of newsletters. Choose titles and topics for which you see a need.

Ordering. In most cases you will have to contact the sponsoring group to ask to be placed on the mailing list. Write for a sample copy before you get on the mailing list of free newsletters or try the title for a year. Remember to have your name removed from the list of those you do not want to receive. You can prepare a form postcard or a form letter to make your requests for newsletters.

Processing

Initial processing and labeling. Simplify this as much as possible by checking in newsletters on a periodical card and stamping. Use Discard After [Date] labels if you have established a policy regarding the shelf life of newsletters.

Organization. The easiest way to organize newsletters is alphabetically by the name of the newsletter or by the name of the group. Add cross-references as needed.

Preservation and protection. It is not necessary to preserve most newsletters.

Housing. Newsletters are usually only a few pages long, so you can punch them for a loose-leaf notebook or binder, file them in folders in the vertical file, or store them in boxes.

Management

Promotion. Inform faculty, members of the sponsoring group, or interested patrons of the newsletters. You might print a list of newsletters you receive, which could be posted near the files.

Circulation. Generally you can treat newsletters as you do periodicals. Do not circulate them in most cases.

Weeding. You will probably keep only the current year and one or two preceding years. Newsletters kept together by title or in a special collection can be weeded quickly. Discard After [Date] labels will facilitate weeding.

NOTEBOOK INSERTS

Notebook inserts are those 8½"x11" plastic or cardboard guides that contain summary information on various subjects organized for easy reference. They may list core facts (for example, punctuation, world history), important vocabulary (such as economics, music terminology), formulas (as in algebra), diagrams (such as human anatomy), or hints for use (such as computer shortcuts).

Acquisition

Sources. Notebook inserts are often available in bookstores, particularly on or near college campuses. These guides can also be ordered direct from the manufacturer.

Data-Guide is a supplier that has more than 60 titles in its Quick Chart series for $2.50 each. Each title is a self-contained summary of facts printed on an 8½"x11" loose-leaf plastic sheet. Sample topics include basic punctuation, bookkeeping, principles of psychology, essentials of algebra, and vocabularies for specific fields.

Avery Easy-Reference System has a *Quick Speller's Guide* to 5,000 frequently misspelled words, with tabbed sheets.

Selection. Choose topics that relate to your users' studies or to general interests such as parliamentary procedure, chess, or bridge.

Ordering. Buy notebook inserts at your local bookstore or office supply outlet or order direct.

Processing

Initial processing and labeling. The plastic surface may not accept ink from your ownership stamp. Stamp a blank label to indicate ownership or use a permanent felt tip marker.

Organization. File by subject.

Preservation and protection. No preservation is necessary for plastic inserts. Paper or cardboard may need to be laminated.

Housing. Use standard file folders or envelopes and store in your file cabinet.

Management

Promotion. Promote with your other study aids.

Circulation. Circulate as you would other vertical-file materials.

Weeding. Discard or replace notebook inserts when information is outdated.

ORAL HISTORY

Oral history can be a part of your local history collection or a separate collection in itself. Oral history is a record of what a person says about an event or events. The product is generally a cassette tape recording or a video recording. Oral histories are primary sources that supplement documentary history. They can add a great deal of interest and insight to historical events and can preserve a unique part of history for your community.

Acquisition

Sources. You may have a state or local historical association or a nearby university active in recording oral histories of people in your area. If some have been done, you may be able to obtain copies for your library for simply the cost of providing a tape. If no one is doing or has done oral histories in your area, you may want to encourage a group of volunteers to begin an oral history project. You can contact your state or local historical association for guidance and training.

Famous people outside your community may have been interviewed for a particular reason. Tapes may be available through your state historical association or from commercial vendors. Your state library or state historical museum may have information to assist you. Much has been written about oral history projects. Read, talk with historians, and plan before you begin a project.

Selection. Select individuals who have an important story or perspective to share related to your community. Choose others who would be of interest to your patrons.

Ordering. Order as items become available. Keep a cassette recorder and a supply of blank tapes available. Video recorders are an added bonus for oral history recordings, but they complicate the process and may distract the speaker. Keep it simple.

Processing

Initial processing and labeling. Be sure to identify the speaker and the interviewer, the date, location, and circumstances of the interview. Provide a written transcript of the interview along with the recorded format.

Organization. File items of oral history by subject or by name, but provide plenty of cross-references.

Preservation and protection. Make a copy of both tape and transcript to circulate. Attach a copy of the release form to the transcript.

Housing. Keep tapes in protective boxes. Provide a written transcript of the interview.

Management

Promotion. History teachers and students will appreciate oral history that relates to state and local events. You can do special displays and promotions during "frontier days," special birthdays, or at the time of the state fair.

Circulation. Circulate copies only.

Weeding. Weed infrequently.

PAMPHLETS

Pamphlet-type material will make up a large part of your vertical files. Reports, catalogs, reprints, newsletters, leaflets, brochures, flyers, and some serials are all part of the pamphlet family. A number of the special types are discussed in separate topics. Here we will discuss single pamphlets and pamphlet series.

Acquisition

Sources. There are a number of excellent pamphlet series you should consider for your library as a part of the vertical file, a special collection, or the general collection.[16]

Editorial Research Reports from Congressional Quarterly are weekly reports on a variety of topics related to U.S. interests in social, scientific, political, and economic issues. Reports are issued in a 16-page format and are punched for three-ring notebooks. They are very well done, with charts and graphs, illustrations, a bibliography, and a recommended reading list. Semiannual bound volumes with indexes ensure permanent reference. Once a bound volume is available, the back issues can be filed in the vertical file by subject. Reports are indexed in *Vertical File Index* and are available individually for $7 each.

Opposing Viewpoints Pamphlets by Greenhaven Press, Inc., is a set of 227 pamphlets on the topics of government and economics, health, social issues, and values. Each pamphlet is actually a chapter from one of the opposing viewpoints books. Schools and libraries that need concise information will appreciate the alternate format. Each pamphlet contains four to eight balanced viewpoints, a critical-thinking activity, and a bibliography. Each title is $2.95 and can be purchased individually or in sets.

For the younger reader (7th-9th grade reading level), Greenhaven's *World History Program* features 64 booklets of 32 pages each and contains 20 to 30 references to primary sources in topics that are designed to support classroom studies. The general areas covered include historical biography, great revolutions, enduring issues (population, law, religion, language, education), great civilizations, and political and social movements. Pamphlets can be filed in the vertical file or kept as a group on the shelf. Booklets are $2.45 each.

A series of pamphlets for university, college, and school libraries is the Phi Delta Kappa Fastback Series. Pamphlets are less than $1 each; there are about 16 new titles each year. Topics relate to education, and the small format is appealing to both teachers and students. The 4"x5" format is not the most desirable for vertical files, but the information is well worth the investment. There are generally very high-quality articles with bibliographies and some illustrations. Items can be fully cataloged, treated as a serial, or filed in the vertical file.

Selection. Choose series that best fit your needs and your budget. Consider input from faculty members.

Ordering. If your institution will permit standing orders, it will take the pressure off remembering to submit a request.

Processing

Initial processing and labeling. Stamp and label according to your regular routine.

Organization. You may choose to add some of these titles to your cataloged collection. The serials may be treated as serials, you may put them in the reference section in their subject classification, or you may keep them together as a set.

Preservation and protection. Heavily used articles can be reinforced with gummed or pressure-sensitive rings or taped and repunched. If you have a security system, you may want to bug your best pamphlets.

Housing. Pamphlets can be housed in boxes, files, or notebooks.

Management

Promotion. If you are in an academic setting, you can promote pamphlets through the classes and teachers most likely to use them. Point them out in your orientation tours and add them to your questions in your library exercises.

Circulation. Circulate as you do other vertical-file materials. Provide a copy machine if circulation is restricted.

Weeding. Weed with care.

PATTERNS, STENCILS, AND TEMPLETS

Patterns, stencils, and templets produce the same result but through different means. They can be made of paper, plastic, wood, or tin. Providing a few basic patterns in your vertical file is something you can do with very little effort and little or no cost. Patterns are available for many things from costumes and crafts to various shapes and designs. School and public libraries may have requests for patterns.

Acquisition

Sources. Home and craft magazines often include basic patterns for hobbies, crafts, gifts, and costumes. Commercial publishers such as Dover Publications have booklets of stencils and patterns. In addition, you may receive gifts of patterns for things that may be helpful to your patrons. Office, library, and school suppliers usually have an assortment of stencils for purchase. College bookstores have plastic templets and stencils for such things as lettering, flow chart symbols, architecture, and house planning.

Selection. Collect patterns for forms that you or your library users may need. Consider a policy to collect no clothing patterns. If you are in a position to receive clothing patterns, you might keep a pattern exchange box as a service to patrons. Choose stencils that will be used by your patrons. Select templets for creating outlines for posters, white- or blackboards, or for cut-outs.

Ordering. You might want to order a few collections of basic patterns or shapes for the files. School supply companies have patterns that may be useful in schools. Purchases can be kept to a minimum in this area.

Processing

Initial processing and labeling. Stamp and label the package of the pattern.

Organization. Arrange by subject unless you have a special section for patterns. Patterns related to crafts or holidays can be filed in that way.

Preservation and protection. Heavily used patterns can be laminated or reproduced on kraft paper. Outlines of patterns can be traced on cardboard, posterboard, or wood to make a templet. Patrons can be encouraged to copy with tissue paper.

Housing. Envelopes are better for files if you have multiple pieces. Plastic sleeves or envelopes are even better than manila envelopes.

Management

Promotion. Promote your patterns with holiday, craft, or subject materials. Teachers will use templets for white- or blackboard outlines of frequently produced shapes such as geometric figures, your state, the United States.
Circulation. Circulate or provide tissue paper for patrons to copy the patterns.
Weeding. Weed or replace when worn out.

PHOTOGRAPHS

Photographs can reproduce details of graphic information that are very important in the learning process. They can be used by individuals or groups. They can be reproduced easily and are relatively inexpensive. You can take photographs yourself, you may purchase them, or you may receive them as gifts. Many of the actual photographs in your collection will likely relate to the history of your institution or locale. There are also picture sets made from photographs. In such areas as history, biography, and science there are sets of photographic pictures available for purchase that are much easier to take care of than actual photographs and would be treated like any other picture or study print set in your files. These study photos are frequently found in school libraries.

Acquisition

Sources. Commercially produced pictures of various subjects are available from a number of sources. Dover Publications has more than 100 books of early and modern masters of photography, with most volumes priced from $4 to $6. Actual photographs are not found as frequently. You will probably want to keep some photos that relate to the history of your institution or area. Discarded photos from yearbooks or newspapers may be available from the journalism staff in schools. Photographs are often given to museums and libraries by people in the community. Often these gifts are more appropriately directed to museums or large libraries where they can be properly managed. Photographic pictures for study are available from school supply companies such as Social Studies School Service and SIRS.[17]
Selection. Select photographs that have some relevance to your collection. They should be clear and accurate. Be very selective. Study prints are more appropriate for most library uses if they will serve the same purpose.
Ordering. Order copies of photographs from school supply companies. Local photographs may be available only from the photographer.

Processing

Initial processing and labeling. You can number the photographs in the set and prepare a separate list of descriptive notes identifying people and places in the photographs. Record date, location, and people in photographs; prepare the list of information on a separate sheet of paper; and then include it with the set of photographs.

Organization. Sets of photographs will likely be stored together.

Preservation and protection. Photographs will require additional care and handling. Photographs should be stored in acid-free paper envelopes. "Avoid sulphur-based products: cardboard, wooden boxes, rubber bands, wooden frames and cheap photo albums."[18] Avoid writing directly on the photograph. Consider copying photographs for circulation (within copyright guidelines). Consider mounting photographs.

Housing. Store in individual envelopes in files or boxes.

Management

Promotion. Use photographs for displays or teaching.

Circulation. Circulate as needed. Circulate in protective bags or envelopes.

Weeding. Archival photographs should not be weeded; other photographs should be weeded when no longer useful.

PICTURES

Pictures of all kinds are important to most vertical files. You may have a special collection of pictures. Pictures are available in black-and-white or color, in many sizes and subjects, in sets or singles.

Acquisition

Sources. Specific types of pictures including art reproductions, cartoons, calendars, clip art, photographs, portraits, postcards, and posters are discussed elsewhere. Many pictures are available by clipping discarded or duplicate magazines.

Selection. You can be selective in your choice of pictures you clip for your files. Remember that black-and-white drawings or pictures with a lot of contrast reproduce best for student projects. Choose illustrations that relate to curriculum areas or topics you want to highlight in miniexhibits of books and materials.

You may want to keep a box of magazines with good illustrations for students to clip to use in collage projects or class reports. Replace magazines for student clippings as they become messy.

Ordering. If you have money available, it will be much easier to order special study prints or sets of related materials from school supply companies. See also the discussion of photographs. Order direct from the vendor.

Processing

Initial processing and labeling. Mark and label pictures on the back of the item if possible. Process groups as sets when it is appropriate and number the order if pictures are in a sequence.

Organization. In most cases you will arrange by subject.

Preservation and protection. Mount if time permits, laminate, or use page protectors. Consider storing in portfolios. Pictures will be easier to manage if you mount them so that they are near the same size.

Housing. Use file folders, pocket envelopes, or portfolios in vertical file cabinets or boxes to house pictures. Oversize files, map cases, or deep shelving may be used for large pictures.

Management

Promotion. Young students and people who work with them will use pictures in formal and informal teaching.

Circulation. Pictures that have been clipped for your files will probably be circulated with a simple note such as "3 pictures—elephants." There is really no way to replace clipped pictures, so there is no need to keep up with the specific reference. Sets that you purchase are another story, and you may want to attach a card and pocket to them for circulation or a bar code if you have an automated circulation system.

Weeding. Weed when worn or irrelevant.

PORTRAITS

A portrait is simply a picture of a person. Portraits can enhance your collection of materials about people. Pictures of famous people can be found in reference books, but an 8½"x11" or larger portrait that you can put on a bulletin board or send home or to class with a patron who is studying an individual can add a great deal to their appreciation of that person.

Acquisition

Sources. Portraits are available from a number of sources. Some examples of inexpensive sources include the following.

Dale Seymour Publications has nine sets of booklets of portraits (15 in each set) for classrooms and bulletin boards. Each person has a one-page biographical sketch with a black-and-white, line-drawn portrait. The material is designed to be copied. Each set is $6.95.

Giant Photos, Inc., has three sets of 64 portraits each in its Personalities in History series for only $4.99 per set. Each set contains black-and-white paper copies of photographs and engravings from the National Archives. The sets include famous people from the United States and around the world, though most are American.

There are a number of sets of portraits of famous women from the National Women's History Project in poster and postcard formats. Items are reasonably priced. U.S. Department of the Treasury Bureau of Engraving and Printing offers several series of portraits of the presidents and chief justices in various sizes.

Selection. Choose sets of portraits that have meaning for your patrons. Try to get portraits with enough contrast to photocopy well for students to use in their reports.[19]

Ordering. Order in sets if possible to simplify the process.

Processing

Initial processing and labeling. Record all information on the back of the portrait.
Organization. You can process sets together or break them up into individual files. Large sets should stay together to simplify processing, but cross-references for names and/or subjects will increase access to the collection.
Preservation and protection. Mount or laminate fragile portraits.
Housing. Use file folders or envelopes in vertical files or file boxes.

Management

Promotion. Portraits can be copied, framed, displayed on bulletin boards, or used with an opaque projector. Use in displays of material for authors, artists, musicians, or any kind of resource where biographical information would be relevant.
Circulation. Encourage patrons to make copies if you do not want portraits to circulate; otherwise circulate as you do other vertical-file materials.
Weeding. Replace when portraits are worn.

POSTCARDS

Postcards are an inexpensive way to build a graphics collection. You or your patrons can buy postcards when you travel, and with the use of an opaque projector you can have pictures as good as slides. Art reproductions are available in postcard size. Local scenes; state attractions; state flags, flowers, and birds; map drawings; jokes and cartoons; photographs and original artwork—all are available in postcard format.

Acquisition

Sources. Postcards can be collected as you find them. State visitor centers often have a good supply of postcards for your state. Your local galleries and museums have postcards of their features, and many art-reproduction postcards are available from national gallery shops (see the entry under Art Reproductions [page 75]). Postcard books are becoming popular. Running Press has a series of postcard books, each containing 30 postcards on a specific subject. Subjects include dinosaurs, big cats, birds, space, fighter planes, art and artists, and a variety of other topics at $6.95 to $7.95. Argus Posters offers some posters in postcard format. Sets of postcards are sometimes offered as a bonus for a poster order. Dover Publications also offers a number of postcard books.
Selection. Select items with good-quality color, without a lot of small details, for best results if you are planning to show pictures with an opaque projector. Projected images may look a little fuzzy.
Ordering. You can write for samples of many reproductions.

Processing

Initial processing and labeling. Label picture postcards on the back of the card.

Organization. Organize most travel postcards by locale. Attraction postcards can be organized by the state or city or by the name of the attraction. Provide cross-references. You can put together your own sets of postcards.

Preservation and protection. The card-stock quality should make preservation techniques unnecessary.

Housing. You may want to use plastic sleeves that are designed for photographs.

Management

Promotion. Use in groups for bulletin boards, for projected showing, or to pass around a classroom. Art reproductions can be grouped together in minidisplays. Postcards can be projected with an opaque projector and serve the same purpose as slides.[20]

Circulation. Circulate postcards as needed.

Weeding. Weed infrequently.

POSTERS

Everybody likes posters. There are a lot of wonderful free and inexpensive posters available for libraries and schools. Posters are available in many sizes and on many topics. They provide an excellent means of getting a message across to people in a very subtle, pleasant way.

Acquisition

Sources. Posters are available from commercial companies, book publishers, government agencies, associations, and special groups. There are many, many sources of posters; some examples include the following. Argus Communications offers a selection of inspirational and fun posters for $2.50 each with discounts for quantity orders. Garfield, Peanuts, Ziggy, cars, dogs, cats, and still lifes are some of the latest ones offered. Posters are 13"x19" and are very popular with students and adults. Giant Photos, Inc., offers many posters, photographs, portraits, and prints in various sizes with a choice of plain paper or laminated copies for many items. Prices are very low. There are specialized sources for specific areas such as theater showcard posters and keyboard and guitar posters, which are available from the Music Stand. The U.S. government, associations, and travel agencies are also important sources of posters.

Selections. Choose appropriate posters for library use and for circulation. If you are providing posters for classroom use, consider a fairly large collection for teachers to choose from.

Ordering. Order posters direct or collect them at conferences.

Processing

Initial processing and labeling. Stamp ownership information on the back of each poster.

Organization. You will likely have a separate collection for posters because they are difficult to house with other materials. You can organize by subject or accession number. Good indexing will make your collection more usable.

Some companies (such as Argus) assign a number to each poster that can be used with a general source number for Argus. You may find it helpful to mark your catalogs or make a card file of posters using a picture cut out of the catalog so that patrons can make selections without handling the posters themselves. Giant Photos has a set of 144 stickers representing most of their posters.

Preservation and protection. You can get plastic protectors in various sizes to slip posters into for shelving; mounting on posterboard or lamination will also help to preserve paper posters. You will probably find it worth the extra cost to buy laminated posters if that is an option.

If you have oversize items, you can apply a cloth backing such as Chartex with a dry-mount press. Items can then be rolled for storage. Large rolled items can have a sheet of paper or fabric rolled on the outside for additional protection. Identification should be clearly marked on the outside of rolled items so it is not necessary to unroll each item for identification.

Housing. Steel map cases are good for posters. Fiberboard cases will work and are much less costly. Bins for upright shelving or flat shelves will also house posters nicely. Large items can be rolled around a stick or cylinder and stored upright in a storage unit designed for that purpose.

Management

Promotion. Because posters are stored out of sight, it is important to include all materials of this type in your catalog with adequate indexing. Rotate your posters in the library and indicate that they came from the poster collection available for circulation. If you are in a school library, the circulation of posters for classroom use will be a very popular service. Make it easy for teachers to check them out.

Circulation. Encourage frequent rotation, but you can be flexible with your circulation policy, except with educational posters that are needed by a number of users.

Weeding. Replace posters when they are worn or topics are irrelevant.

PROGRAMS, PLAYBILLS, AND REVIEWS

You may want to keep some local (school and community) programs, playbills, and reviews for your local history collection. Performing arts students may be interested in programs from other productions as well. The popularity of your materials may depend upon the activity level of your users in the area of theater and drama.

Acquisition

Sources. A collection of programs and playbills will grow on its own if you make it known that you are collecting them. Friends and members of the performing arts groups will see that you receive copies. Clip only important reviews for productions of local interest or lasting importance.

Selection. Save programs from local plays and selected plays from large cities. Do not bother clipping reviews that can be found in indexed resources that you have on microfilm or microfiche. Consider programs for special events such as graduations, ground-breakings, openings, dedications, and anniversaries.

Ordering. You can request a set of playbills from various groups, but the best way to collect programs and playbills is to gather them yourself or ask a patron to get them for you.

Processing

Initial processing and labeling. Indicate the source, the date, time, and place of the production if it is not on the playbill.

Organization. Keep in a file of playbills arranged by title, or in some cases you may file local plays under the performing group. A separate file under each title or author is another option.

Preservation and protection. No particular preservation techniques are needed unless you plan to keep programs and playbills indefinitely for your local history collection.

Housing. File in file folders, envelopes, or pocket envelopes in the vertical file cabinet. Use pamphlet boxes for larger groups of materials.

Management

Promotion. Promote with drama materials such as scripts, costumes, theater paraphernalia, scenery, posters, and theater memorabilia.

Circulation. Circulate as requested.

Weeding. Weed if there is no interest.

REFERENCE MATERIALS (DISCARDED)

Discarded reference material may have some good information you can clip for your vertical file if you are in great need of material and your funds are limited; otherwise it probably is not worth your time.

Acquisition

Sources. Outdated encyclopedias make the best sources of basic articles for your file. You must be very careful to select only articles that are not dated. Monthly issues of *Current Biography* are excellent for clipping after the annual volume has been received. *Editorial Research Reports* individual titles can be filed under separate subjects after the cumulative volume is received.

Selection. Clip only when you have a high demand for the articles and/or the format is desirable for patrons to check out. This can be done when you are short of materials on subjects such as presidents, authors, or artists.

Ordering. Sometimes libraries advertise exchange lists of things they are weeding; otherwise you are limited to your own discards. Anytime you get a list of available materials from a library, it is essential to check it immediately and respond with your requests because the best things are requested first and others are soon discarded.

Processing

Initial processing and labeling. Be sure that the source is clearly indicated on the article. You will probably just staple the pages together. To be safe you can use two staples close together. (Do not use staples in clippings you expect to be permanent in your collection.)

Organization. File into subject folders.

Preservation and protection. No special preservation or protection is necessary for most discarded reference materials. You cannot afford to spend much in time or materials in this area. Use plastic page protectors if you feel something is needed for protection.

Housing. Use manila folders or envelopes and store in the information file.

Management

Promotion. This practice should be done only if you have a demand from teachers or users and need additional information resources for circulation.

Circulation. There need be no particular restrictions. You will circulate these materials as you do other items from your file.

Weeding. Weed when materials are worn, outdated, or no longer needed.

REPORTS

Reports may be important considerations for academic and special libraries and occasionally for public and school libraries. Reports vary in length from a few pages to hundreds of pages. These materials sometimes come under the general heading of gray literature. They are available on nearly all subjects. Many reports are a part of a series.

Acquisition

Sources. Many reports are published by the U.S. government and are available from the U.S. Superintendent of Documents or from the individual agency or department. Sometimes reports are a part of a series and may be ordered on subscription or a standing order. A number of associations and organizations produce reports that are often available free or at little cost as a service to their membership. The Public Affairs Information Service (PAIS) includes some reports and even indicates the cost or free status of materials. *Vertical File Index* includes some reports.

Selection. Select the reports or series that will be used. Choose only items that fit your needs.

Ordering. Order direct on a standing order if you want all reports; otherwise check the catalog and order by specific title.

Processing

Initial processing and labeling. Standard processing and labeling will be used for reports unless you choose to give them full cataloging.

Organization. File reports by subject. If you have a large reports series you may want to set up a special collection arranged by report number. Important reports you intend to keep should be cataloged as monographs.

Preservation and protection. Binders, folders, or notebooks will help to protect the reports. Permanent binding may be justified for some reports.

Housing. Long reports may be put on the shelf in binders, notebooks, or boxes. Shorter reports may be put in vertical file cabinets.

Management

Promotion. Advertise your report collections to appropriate faculty, patrons, or students.

Circulation. Circulate as you would similar materials.

Weeding. Weed when the information is irrelevant and no longer needed.

REPRINTS

Reprints, also called offprints, will come primarily from periodical or magazine articles, encyclopedia articles, newspapers, and special reports. They are generally publisher-produced copies of articles. You can get reprints from original publishers or from a number of companies that specialize in reprints. Reprints will sometimes be entered in *Vertical File Index.*

Acquisition

Sources. There are a number of magazines that advertise reprints including these examples: *Reader's Digest, U.S. News and World Report,* and *Wall Street Journal.* W. H. Freeman Company supplies reprints from *Scientific American*; the American Association for the Advancement of Science sells reprints from *Science.*

Reprints of encyclopedia articles, which are usually free to libraries, are available from most companies including the publishers of *World Book Encyclopedia* and *Compton's Encyclopedia.* Your local encyclopedia representative should be able to give you information on reprints available from their encyclopedias.

Selection. Choose reprints to supply additional copies of material needed because of high demand. Anticipate interest in articles such as the annual feature in *U.S. News and World Report* on America's best colleges. Select reprints that will enhance your collection by providing material you do not have including, for example, reprints from *Science.* Add reprints if the format extends your service by allowing patrons to check out materials when your periodicals do not circulate.[21]

Ordering. Many magazines give the address for reprints in each issue. Request encyclopedia reprints from your local encyclopedia representative. Order direct from reprint companies if you know the titles they distribute.

Processing

Initial processing and labeling. Stamp, date, and be sure that the source is indicated on the reprint.

Organization. Organize reprints by subject in your vertical file unless you keep sets of reprints together such as SIRS.

Preservation and protection. You can tape the spine if you expect heavy use; otherwise no particular preservation is necessary.

Housing. Use folders or envelopes for reprints.

Management

Promotion. If it is a popular item, put up a sign. Promote most reprints as you would any other vertical-file item.

Circulation. Circulate like other vertical-file materials.

Weeding. Weed once a year.

SCHEDULES

There are some schedules you will want to keep on your ready-reference shelf or in a place where you offer handouts to patrons. Some of the possible schedules include transportation schedules and class schedules for community college, university, arts, crafts, first aid, and other classes. You may have questions about dates for local school registration, graduation, holidays, or sports schedules. Schedules for community exhibits, special events, theater performances, and concerts may be requested.

If you have a bus system, it likely stops near your school or library. Your patrons may ask for schedules for the buses that they would be taking to and from the library. Train schedules and airline schedules may also be in demand.

Acquisition

Sources. Most schedules will be free for the asking, but others may need to be picked up or purchased. Some schedules will be printed in the newspaper.

Selection. Be aware of publication dates for various schedules. Put an entry in your tickler file to remind you to check on schedules when changes are expected.

124 / 12—Supplementary Materials for Information Files

Ordering. Local schedules can often be ordered by telephone, especially if the material is free. Many of the offices will deliver schedules if you are willing to make them available.

Processing

Initial processing and labeling. No processing is necessary for schedules you are passing out. Be sure to indicate the date of receipt on your desk copy.

Organization. Put them in a handy place on your ready-reference shelf. You may want to post copies if they are requested frequently.

Preservation and protection. Most schedules will be out-of-date in a short time.

Housing. You can put heavily used schedules in a magazine cover.

Management

Promotion. Put copies of your handouts with free materials.

Circulation. Do not circulate. This information will be needed for ready reference.

Weeding. Discard promptly when the material is outdated.

SCRIPTS

Play scripts can supplement your subject and holiday collections of materials as well as the literature section. Individual scripts can be classified and put on the shelves in the literature section, but some libraries prefer to keep them separate because of their small size.

Acquisition

Sources. Scripts for individual plays are usually available from the publisher for less than $5 each. The catalogs themselves are good reference tools and some libraries put the catalogs in their reference collections. Dramatist Play Service and Samuel French, Inc., are two good sources for scripts. Contact them for catalogs.

Plays for young people are included in *Plays*, a magazine that includes royalty-free scripts of plays, skits, and dramatized classics (7 issues per year for $24.75). In addition many magazines for teachers will include occasional plays. Holiday scripts are often available in monthly magazines.

Selection. Select classic titles and those your patrons will be interested in reading.[22] Check the ALA bibliography *Outstanding Theater for the College Bound* (1991) for classic titles. Ask for recommendations from faculty members or theater groups in the community.

Ordering. Order scripts direct from the publisher.

Processing

Initial processing and labeling. Stamp and label appropriately for the vertical file, pamphlet boxes, or a circulating book collection.

Organization. A simple way to handle play scripts if you do not fully catalog them is to provide pamphlet boxes, with a box (or more) for each letter of the alphabet. Arrange the plays by author or title and facilitate shelving by placing a large colored dot with the letter under which it should be filed. In most cases you will organize alphabetically by the author in the file or special collection. Provide an index by title and author. Often the vendor's catalog will provide an excellent resource for authors, titles, and subjects of plays published. If you have the majority of scripts from a publisher, consider keeping the catalog as an added index.

Preservation and protection. Spines can be taped if you expect heavy use. Pamphlet reinforcement will help protect from wear.

Housing. Princeton files may be useful for housing large groups of scripts.

Management

Promotion. With a small collection you could compile a complete bibliography of your scripts for use with faculty, students, and other patrons; you could update this bibliography occasionally on your computer. For a larger collection you might compile a selective bibliography and note that there are many more in the collection. Holiday and subject emphasis scripts can be promoted with the special topics they represent. Patrons should be aware of copyright restrictions and royalty obligations if plays are to be performed.

Circulation. Circulate as needed. Bar codes or cards can be used for circulation.

Weeding. Weed sparingly except when items are falling apart.

SHEET MUSIC AND SONG SHEETS

You may have a sheet music collection in your library or books of music classified on your shelves, but if you have only a few popular songs, you may just file them in your vertical file. You may also have song sheets with words for popular tunes that people know. Your library may serve as a depository for collections of sheet music for musical groups in the city.

Acquisition

Sources. Local music stores provide the easiest source of copies of individual pieces of music.

Selection. Select titles you know will be used. Consider state songs, school songs, or songs about your community or region.

Ordering. Order direct or buy from local music stores.

Processing

Initial processing and labeling. Be sure to stamp sheet music with the ownership stamp.

Organization. Your options include filing by the popular title, by the composes, or by the subject (especially if it is a holiday song).

Preservation and protection. Use file folders for single items. Consider attaching loose sheets or pages to cover sheets.

Housing. File single titles in the vertical file and put sets in boxes.

Management

Promotion. Promote with holiday materials, musicians, movie tie-ins, television programs.

Circulation. Be generous in your circulation time. Remind patrons that it is a violation of copyright to photocopy sheet music that is still protected under the law.

Weeding. Replace music when it is worn.

SPEECHES

You will be asked for famous speeches just as you are asked for notable court cases and popular poems. You may find it helpful to have a series of reprints or facsimiles of famous speeches or at least a copy available for photocopying. You will also have books of speeches available in your library and perhaps video- or audiotapes of the person or an actor giving the speech.

Acquisition

Sources. Facsimile documents are sometimes available from the U.S. Government Printing Office. The National Archives offers a series of booklets on milestone documents including a number of famous speeches (25-page booklets for $2.50 each). *Vital Speeches* is a source for current speeches.

Selection. Identify a dozen or so famous speeches and search for suitable copies that can be available for display or reference. Some speeches for consideration include Washington's inaugural address of 1789; Abraham Lincoln's Emancipation Proclamation; F. D. Roosevelt's "Date That Will Live in Infamy" address in 1941; John F. Kennedy's inaugural address of 1961; and Martin Luther King's "I Have a Dream" speech.

Ordering. Order appropriate speeches as you find them available. Short speeches such as the Gettysburg Address are sometimes available on bookmarks or cards that can be used as handouts.

Processing

Initial processing and labeling. Reprints, facsimiles, reproductions, and other visual or print materials should be stamped and labeled on the back of the speech.

Organization. You may group them into a collection of speeches or file in folders by the author of the speech.
Preservation and protection. Use page protectors and mount or laminate heavily used items.
Housing. File in the vertical file cabinet in file folders or envelopes.

Management

Promotion. You might have a special or permanent display of famous speeches somewhere in your library. People learn by frequent exposure to information, so displaying framed documents can be both interesting and educational. If you have reprints of speeches, you may want to list them in a bibliography.
Circulation. Make it easy for patrons to have their own copy.
Weeding. Replace speeches when they are worn.

STUDY GUIDES AND WORKSHEETS

It is likely that many of your patrons will come to your library to study. You may choose to provide some study guides or worksheets. There are generic guides to help people learn how to study and there are guides to studying specific topics or works. There are many booklets, flyers, and other brief guides to help your patrons in addition to the books and videos you may also offer.

Acquisition

Sources. Study guides are frequently available for public television series, novels, and other literary and historical works. You will see them advertised on television, in professional journals, and in some of the catalogs you receive from vendors. Contact your public television station for guides to productions they air as well as restrictions on use.

More than 200 titles in the Cliffs Notes series of booklets[23] are available for many literary works as well as for some general topics. Most individual titles are under $4. Browsing through a large bookstore will help you discover a variety of study guides you may want to add to your collection.

World Book has a reprinted article that is a guide to research, *A Student Guide to Better Writing, Speaking, and Research Skills*. Other types of study guides discussed separately include charts, guides, lesson plans, manuals, notebook inserts, and tests.

Worksheets frequently come with free and inexpensive curriculum materials or from teachers. The Perfection Form Company catalog for language arts offers study worksheets and guides for a number of literary works. Several general guides to studying from the same company include the following titles: *Making the Grade* (SQ3R study system), 60 pages, $3.25 each; *Strategies for Study*, 80 pages, $3.25; *The Short Report*, 48 pages, $3.25; and *Write in Style*, $3.50.

Selection. Provide support in the subject areas needed by your users.

128 / 12 – Supplementary Materials for Information Files

Ordering. Order study guides from the publisher or producer or buy them where you find them available. Teachers may place worksheets in the library for students.

Processing

Initial processing and labeling. Stamp and label as you would any other vertical-file material.
Organization. Group general guides together but consider putting specific guides with the subject.
Preservation and protection. Reinforce with tape or pamphlet reinforcements.
Housing. Store study guides in files or pamphlet boxes. Discard television production guides after the production or file with the subject if you expect permission to use the video at a later date. Be sure to comply with copyright laws regarding taping from television.

Management

Promotion. It should be emphasized to students that Cliffs Notes and other summary or digest-type materials are aids to study and not substitutes for reading complete works.
Circulation. Circulate materials as needed.
Weeding. Weed items when worn.

TESTS

You may have requests for information on a variety of tests your patrons take. Application booklets with information regarding test schedules for the academic year are available in counseling offices on most campuses. In addition you can get inexpensive books of sample questions for many of the tests. Providing practice test books is a very popular service in many libraries. The following are among the most frequently requested tests:

ACT (American College Testing) – for college entrance; high school seniors

AP (Advanced Placement) – for college credit in various subjects

GED (General Educational Development) – high-school equivalency test

GMAT (Graduate Management Admission Test) – business & management

GRE (Graduate Record Examination) – graduate-school entrance

LSAT (Law School Admission Test) – law-school admission

MCAT (Medical College Admissions Test) – medical-school admission

PSAT (Pre-Scholastic Aptitude Test) — practice SAT test for juniors

SAT (Scholastic Aptitude Test) — college entrance; high-school seniors

TEEP (Teacher Educational Examination Program) — education students

TOEFL (Test of English as a Foreign Language) — non-English-speaking students

Other professional and military tests may also be requested. You may have questions about standardized personality, IQ, or other educational tests. There are restrictions on the availability of many of these tests, so be sure that you are aware of them if you happen to have any in your collection. Most standardized tests cannot be photocopied.

One type of test you can have in your collection with no worry is practice tests for classes that your high-school or college teachers provide. These may be put on reserve for students to use or may be in a file or on a computer for drill and practice. This may be a good way for you to encourage a faculty member to use the library.

Acquisition

Sources. Annual booklets describing the tests with application information and a schedule of test dates are available in counseling offices. Ask the counselors to send you a set for reference when they receive their shipment. Commercially prepared practice books for standard tests are available in bookstores or from your book jobber. Patrons can be directed to bookstores if there are titles you do not supply that you know are available in the local stores. Personal tests will be supplied by the individual teachers.

Selection. Provide information appropriate to the level of your users. Be selective in your choices of practice books. There are many titles that change frequently. Encourage students to look for new editions at the bookstore.

Ordering. Buy practice books from your local bookstore, order from your jobber, or order from the publisher of the test.

Processing

Initial processing and labeling. Stamp, label, date, and put in your test section. Use Discard After [Date] labels for materials with expiration dates.

Organization. File by test name, by subject, or keep all test information together in a box or file for tests.

Preservation and protection. People should be encouraged to write on paper rather than filling in the blanks in the books or booklets. These titles will wear out quickly, so do not expect to keep them long. Replace titles frequently.

Housing. If your collection is large, you may want to keep materials in pamphlet boxes with a box for each type of test. For limited collections a single box or file may suffice.

Management

Promotion. Consider a descriptive handout if you have many test materials. Use special signs, flyers, or advertise during peak interest times. Word will get out and you will have a run on them when it is nearly time for the test.

Circulation. You may want to be flexible in your circulation policy to meet user needs.

Weeding. Discard test booklet information at the end of the academic year when it has expired or when you receive a new booklet for the current year. Practice books will wear out before they are outdated. Weed when they look bad. Weed professors' tests after a year or so.

TIME LINES

Time lines provide a visual way to put things in perspective. They are valuable teaching and learning tools. Libraries of all types should consider time lines in some form. There are posters, books of time lines, and computer programs to generate custom time lines. Time lines often accompany encyclopedia articles or other books.

Acquisition

Sources. Companies such as Social Studies School Service that sell educational supplementary materials often have time lines. A number of time lines are available as posters, murals, or "muralettes." In addition, there are books of general time lines that you may want for your reference collection as well as computer programs to help you design your own time lines.

Selection. Choose time lines that will visually highlight materials you have in your collection. Ask faculty members for recommendations.[24] If your library serves elementary students, you will have a demand for a time line for all of the geologic eras.

Ordering. Order direct from the publisher or from a jobber. Some time lines will be available with related subject materials.

Processing

Initial processing and labeling. Process as you would any book, graphic, or vertical-file material. Be sure to include the date of publication.

Organization. File under the subject if it is focused on one subject, but cross reference under Time Lines in your index if it is an important access point for your collection.

Preservation and protection. Laminate or cloth-back time lines if they are fragile. Use page protectors or plastic sleeves if the material fits.

Housing. Store in file folders or three-ring notebooks.

Management

Promotion. Display time lines in your library either permanently or on a rotating schedule. Put near the subject in an area where patrons have space to study the time line without blocking the flow of traffic. Promote time lines to faculty members as valuable teaching tools.

Circulation. Circulate as needed.

Weeding. Watch the cut-off date for current events. Try to keep updated time lines but realize that older time lines can be valuable.

TRANSCRIPTS

Transcripts are written or recorded copies of a program or presentation. They are available for a number of television programs and presentations including news, documentary, and public policy broadcasts.

Acquisition

Sources. Transcipts that are available for television programs are usually advertised at the end of the programs. News or interview programs such as "60 Minutes" (available for $4 each), "20-20," and other news or interview programs are frequently offered. Journal Graphics (267 Broadway, New York, New York 10007) provides a number of titles with costs ranging from $3 to $5.

Selection. Choose transcripts for issues that will be used in your files (transcripts should also be made for oral history interviews). Reading transcripts has a limited appeal, so be selective in your choice.

Ordering. The topics are usually very timely issues, so you should not wait long before ordering transcripts for your files.

Processing

Initial processing and labeling. Be sure to indicate the source, date of broadcast, name of the program, and participants.

Organization. File under the appropriate subject.

Preservation and protection. The transcript can be put in a plastic sleeve for protection if needed. Most transcripts will have a limited time for use.

Housing. File in folders or envelopes in your information file cabinet.

Management

Promotion. Promote with the subject. Transcripts from various programs can be displayed together for interest if you are preparing a media exhibit or one on interviews.

Circulation. Circulate as needed or provide a photocopy machine.

Weeding. Discard transcripts when the information is no longer timely.

132 / 12 – Supplementary Materials for Information Files

TRAVEL BROCHURES

Travel is big business and the travel information available reflects the interest and the advertising dollars that go into the industry. Travel brochures, posters, guidebooks, booklets, and other miscellaneous items can be a large part of your vertical file. Though material is designed to sell the reader on visiting the area, travel information also provides the library with a way to provide pictorial and descriptive information about areas all over the world.

Acquisition

Sources. Each state and country has an office or agency that handles travel information. Related information is often available from embassies. Travel industries such as travel agencies, airlines, and car rental companies may also have information. Your patrons may bring you their extra travel information after their trips.

The *World Chamber of Commerce Directory* is a good source of addresses for chamber of commerce offices, state boards of tourism, embassies, and related offices. This directory is revised annually in June and costs $24.

Selection. Choose areas in which your users have an interest. Carefully screen material as it is received to avoid filling your files with materials you do not need.

Ordering. Some travel magazines have cards for you to circle information numbers and return. That will simplify orders. You may also order direct from the agency or office. This is an area where you may consider doing a bulk mailing to your selected list of sources. You may put travel information on a rotating schedule so that you update information every few years.

Processing

Initial processing and labeling. Be sure to indicate the date of receipt along with the source. Patrons may want to order their own copies of some items. Use Discard After [Date] labels where appropriate.

Organization. You can file by country, state, city, name of the attraction (park, lake), or event (such as Rose Bowl Parade, Super Bowl game). Establish a policy regarding your system for organizing travel information. You may want to combine it with your map files. Use cross-references to help your patrons.

Preservation and protection. No particular preservation steps are necessary if you intend to replace the materials frequently.

Housing. You can use folders, envelopes, or boxes to store travel materials.

Management

Promotion. Promote travel brochures with travel books and maps when people are planning vacations. Geography, history, and social studies classes can use the material when studying that culture or country. Language teachers will appreciate travel information from countries representing the languages they teach.

Circulation. Circulate as you do other vertical-file materials.

Weeding. Some materials will not go out-of-date, but others that include admission prices, hours, or other information that is likely to change should be replaced more frequently if there is a demand for them.

WHEELS AND OTHER MANIPULATIVES

Wheels, measuring devices, slide gadgets, and other unique forms of presenting information, showing conversions, or indicating relationships will be very useful additions to your vertical files. In some cases the information may be identical to pamphlet or book information you have in other sources, but the unique format is the key element. These alternate methods of presenting factual material provide another way to reach some learners.

Acquisition

Sources. There is no one source for supplementary materials of this type, but you will run across them in your search for additions to your vertical files. Get several copies when you can because they will be used by children and youth as well as adults.

Giant Photos, Inc., has two wheels available for $3.99 each. One is "Presidents of the United States Profile Wheel" (through George Bush) and the other is "United States Geographer Wheel," which has information on the 50 states.

Color wheels showing basic color relationships are available from many art supply dealers. Dale Seymour has one available with a pocket guide to mixing colors for $5.75.

Selection. Choose items that effectively combine print and visual material into a piece that involves some type of manipulation by the user. Notice how individuals are involved in the process so that their attention is directed to the topic. This kind of participation in learning is desirable for some students who are less responsive to traditional formats.

Ordering. Order direct as you find such items and collect them when attending conferences, local fairs, and other settings where they may be distributed.

Processing

Initial processing and labeling. Mark and label as you would any other vertical-file material.

Organization. File manipulative materials under the specific subject. Most items will fit in a file folder or file pocket.

Preservation and protection. Use no particular preservation for plastic items. Cardboard items can be reinforced with tape.

Housing. Interfile with other vertical-file materials in envelopes or files in your filing cabinets.

Management

Promotion. Promote with the subject. Items will be particularly helpful to slow learners and reluctant readers.

Circulation. Circulate as needed.

Weeding. Weed when worn or broken. Much of this material is classic, but watch for dated information on such things as drugs or other contemporary topics.

NOTES

[1] Commercial vendors of corporation annual reports include Disclosure, Inc., and Q-Data Corporation. They supply paper, microfiche, and CD-ROM products. Individual report prices are moderate, but there are minimum charges. R. R. Bowker also has annual reports and 10K filings for 2,000 companies.

[2] Some libraries circulate special collections of framed reproductions. For additional information a good chapter to read is Billie Grace Herring's "Art Reproductions," in *Nonbook Media* (Chicago: American Library Association, 1987), 1-19.

[3] Large public and academic libraries will probably skip this type of material (except for local clubs and groups) and buy the *Encyclopedia of Associations*.

[4] Pikes Peak Library District (PPLD) in Colorado Springs has had an automated community information system including local clubs and a community calendar since 1976. See Nina Alexis Malyshev, "Concept and Reality: Managing Pikes Peak Library District's Community Resource and Information System," *Reference Services Review* 16 (4) (1988): 7-12.

[5] The Spencer S. Eccles Health Sciences Library at the University of Utah in Salt Lake City uses SilverPlatter MEDLINE on CD-ROM to enhance their vertical files. See Maureen O. Carleton and Catherine G. Cheves, "The Vertical File Enters the Electronic Age," *Medical Reference Service Quarterly* 8(4) Winter 1989: 1-10.

[6] Libraries with larger budgets may want to consider the *Faces of America I* and *II* (Facts on File American Historical Images on File series) collection of loose-leaf portraits of Americans with capsule biographies. Three hundred copyright-free, black-and-white illustrations are offered for $165.

[7] *Vocational Biographies* is a career information source that personalizes specific careers by writing about real people who work in specific jobs. It is biographical, but it is more appropriate for your career collection.

[8] Facts on File has a loose-leaf series of "on-file" topics that contain hundreds of copyright-free charts. Most titles contain about 300 charts for approximately $150.

[9] Large microfiche collections of catalogs are available in different sets from several vendors including Career Guidance Foundation.

[10] There are libraries that have a serious interest in developing comic-book collections as a part of their popular culture materials. Randall W. Scott's *Comics Librarianship: A Handbook* (McFarland, 1990) ($32) lists 48 libraries with specialized collections of comics and cartoons. See also Keith DeCandido's "Get the Picture? A Serious Look at Comics in Libraries," *Library Journal* (May 1, 1990).

[11] *PhoneFiche* are available from University Microfilms International for communities on the Bell system. Large public and university libraries may purchase PhoneFiche collections and keep only a few hard-copy telephone books.

[12] SIRS (Social Issues Resources Series). Some of the most popular documents found in the National Archives are offered in sets of reproductions by SIRS. There are eight unit sets of about 50 reproductions each including documents, charts, photographs, letters, drawings, and posters. This resource is designed for classroom use, but it can be a very valuable addition to other collections. Units are $40 each and include the following titles: *Constitution, Civil War, Progressive Years (1898-1917), World War I, The 1920s, The Great Depression and New Deal, World War II*, and *The Truman Years*.

[13] Examples of resources for forms include the following. *Book of Business Forms* and *Book of Personal Forms* from Facts on File will provide masters for many forms. They are available in loose-leaf notebooks and are copyright-free. In addition, each year the Internal Revenue Service (IRS) of the U.S. Department of the Treasury produces a loose-leaf notebook of reproducible tax forms. ($31) Copies of the popular forms can be distributed by the library for the convenience of patrons. Contact your nearest IRS office for information about ordering forms. After tax season you can put sample forms in your vertical file. People do continue to look for older IRS forms to file late or amended returns. See also Ruth Toor and Hilda K. Weisburg, *Complete Book of Forms for Managing the School Library* (West Nyack, New York: Center for Applied Research in Education, 1982). This book of forms may be very helpful for your own library management. Finally, consult Elizabeth Futas's *Library Forms Illustrated Handbook* (New York: Neal-Schuman, 1984). This book of forms is easy to use in the loose-leaf format.

[14] A bibliography of access tools for specialized agencies of the United Nations is available in Willis F. Cunningham's "A Reference/Documents Librarian's Treasure Map," *RQ* 30(2) (Winter 1990): 249-60.

[15] Kraus International Publications (One Water Street, White Plains, New York 10601) issues an annual collection of about 300 curriculum guides in microfiche. It is published in cooperation with the Association for Supervision and Curriculum Development and priced at $1,500 per year.

[16]Related materials include the following:

Opposing Viewpoints: Sources by Greenhaven Press, Inc., is a series of anthologies of materials from a variety of periodicals, books, position papers, pamphlets, and government documents on nine subjects including Soviet-American debate, America's Economy, Criminal Justice, Science and Technology, Nuclear Arms, Foreign Policy, Human Sexuality, Male/Female Roles, and Death/Dying. Each sourcebook title contains 100 pro/con debates. In 1991 this series was replaced by Current Controversies, a new series. Articles are designed for easy photocopying.

Social Issues Resources Series (SIRS), begun in the 1970s, offers a series of 32 social topics in loose-leaf notebook format. Articles are reprints from periodicals, newspapers, and special reports and include other information the editorial board of SIRS has selected. Topics are updated annually with 20 new items. Each notebook holds 100 reprints. Some topics are into the fifth volume. Replacement articles can be ordered for lost items but the recently added feature of microfiche backup has helped deal with the problem of missing numbers.

SIRS Digests Series is based on some of the topics of the Social Issues Series but instead of full-text articles the notebook contains summaries of several articles. The intended user is a younger reader or a new reader.

SIRS Science Series offers a similar format. Annual notebooks include 70 articles each.

SIRS Critical Issues Series is intended to be a means of providing information on issues that will not necessarily continue. The two topics available in this series to date are *AIDS* and *Atmosphere*. Each contains two notebooks of information.

[17]Another series was introduced in 1990 from Social Issues Resources Series. Each SIRS Photo Essay comes with a study guide and contains units with seven photographs and a map or graphic that can be used on a bulletin board or wall.

[18]Clara L. DiFelice, "Photographs," in *Nonbook Media* (Chicago: ALA, 1987), 162-73. Sources for photographs include *Free Stock Photography Directory* (New York: Infosource Business Publications, 1978- annual) and *World Photography Sources* (New York: Bowker, 1981- annual).

[19]Facts on File's *Faces of America* from the American Historical Images on File series includes portraits. They are copyright free and easy to reproduce. Each set includes about 300 illustrations for $125.

[20]Kathleen Beattie, "Post Cards as Learning Tools," *Learning* (November/December 1988): 106.

[21]Social Issues Resources Series (SIRS) sells sets of reprints. Their reprints are primarily from periodical and newspapers but also include special reports and other information not always readily available to small libraries.

[22] CoreFiche are available for a number of classic titles.

[23] The booklets are available at many bookstores or direct from Cliffs Notes. Cliffs Notes are also available in 24 hardbound volumes with a comprehensive index from Moonbeam Publications, Inc.

[24] Facts on File's *Book of Time Lines* is full of reproducible time lines. They are done in black line drawings, printed on card stock, housed in a notebook and are copyright free so that they can be copied for classroom or personal use. There are 300 pages in a loose-leaf notebook for $145.

13
Other Free and Inexpensive Supplementary Materials

There are many free and inexpensive supplementary materials that do not fit into your information file cabinets but may also receive vertical-file treatment. Most of these come under the heading of audiovisual or miscellaneous items. These materials, like more traditional supplementary items, will complement your collections of purchased materials. Examples of other kinds of free and inexpensive materials include cassette tapes, computer programs, films, filmstrips and videotapes, flags, flash cards, games, microforms, puppets, puzzles, and slides. There are others that could be included as well.

The materials will be discussed, like other supplementary materials, in terms of acquisition, processing, and management. Many libraries will incorporate these free and inexpensive materials into their audiovisual or special collections and will process all materials, whether free or purchased, in the same way.

Each librarian or teacher will collect only the kinds of materials that have relevance to his or her collection. The broad range of materials is introduced to spark the imagination and to suggest materials that may not otherwise be considered.

CASSETTE TAPES

Audiocassettes of all kinds will be a part of many collections. You may have, for example, classical or popular music, short stories, poetry, speeches, full-length novels, motivational tapes, how-to tapes, recordings of meetings, and oral history. Some sources offer recordings of authors reading their own works. You may have recordings you have purchased, received free, or some that you have recorded yourself. Cassette tapes may come in a kit with related materials, they may be part of a large collection, or they may stand alone.

The cassette tapes that are considered for the vertical file or vertical-file treatment are the free and inexpensive ones or the tapes you make. Tapes you have purchased will be a part of your cataloged collection. You may have audiotapes of meetings you have attended, which have only a limited shelf life. The vertical-file treatment is ideal for tapes of this nature.

Acquisition

Sources. There are a number of places to get tapes. Many free educational tapes are available from associations, special interest groups, and businesses. In many cases you will be sent a tape that you are free to duplicate. *Educators Guide to Free Audio and Video Materials* lists free-loan tapes.

Selection. Choose tapes that fit your collection guidelines. Screen possible propaganda or promotional materials. Look for materials of local interest such as taped speeches of local officials, local plays, and oral history.

Ordering. Order free tapes direct from the organization, association, government agency, or group. Inexpensive tapes for purchase are available from jobbers, vendors selling book remainders, and producers.

Processing

Initial processing and labeling. Invest in an ownership stamp with small print so that you can neatly stamp each cassette tape label without stamping over important information. For items protected by copyright, consider a label regarding copyright restrictions.

Organization. Most often the preferred organization will be by subject, although this is a format that is easily arranged by accession or sequence if good indexing is provided. Many cassette tapes can be slipped into vertical-file envelopes or pockets.

Preservation and protection. Protect tapes from dust, heat, humidity, and excessive light by storing them on their edges in protective cases. Tapes should be played at least twice a year to remove tension. Do not place tapes near magnetic fields, which can cause tapes to be erased (including library security systems using magnetic sensors). Wood shelves are preferable to metal if you are establishing a special collection.

You may be able to make a circulating copy from your backup copy. Check with the producer or follow copyright regulations if you expect heavy use of the tapes. Some libraries shelve the case or a dummy book with a note to ask at the desk for the circulation copy. Cassette tapes can be sensitized with a special detection strip for security, but they must be passed around the security station to avoid desensitizing, which will erase the tape.

Housing. Cassette tapes can be classified and interfiled with books on the shelf, housed in a nonpublic area, or put into the vertical file.

Management

Promotion. Promote with various kinds of subject materials or biographical materials. Use recorded books with a copy of the book for reluctant readers, new readers, or nonreaders.

Circulation. Circulate tapes as needed.

Weeding. Weed when information is outdated. Replace when copy is worn.

COMPUTER PROGRAMS

Free and inexpensive computer programs are available. You will likely have requests for computer programs in your library. There are a number of issues that need to be addressed before offering this service, such as those regarding copyright and security. Copyright-free programs are available and will be less complicated for you to provide. Shareware is another category of computer software that can be made available. Shareware is a computer program that can be copied or shared with anyone. If the recipient buys the program and decides to use it on a regular basis, then a fee specified on the opening screen should be sent to the creator of the program.

Sources. Sources of free and inexpensive software include Educators Progress Service's *Guide to Free Computer Materials*.[1] Your area probably has a computer-users group that shares programs. There are also a number of bibliographies of shareware for Apple, Mac, and MS-DOS machines. Talking with a local computer buff will be useful in locating lists and software.

Selection. Decide what kinds of software you will collect (Apple, IBM, or other). Choose high-quality samples of software and provide reference sources for patrons to pursue others on their own. Advice from a local computer club or computer enthusiast will be invaluable.

Ordering. Try to locate a computer examination center near you. Most commercial computer software cannot be previewed, but you may have a computer consortium or examination center in your city or state. Large school districts may house a computer center with software available for preview. Free software is often available for only the cost of a disk, so you have little to lose if you do not want to keep the program. Check also with local computer clubs concerning what libraries they have for member access.

Processing

Initial processing and labeling. You may want to provide a computer with software installed for preview. Keep manuals handy for patron use. Be sure to clearly label programs regarding the copyright status and right to copy.

Organization. You will probably make this a special collection, although you may interfile computer programs with other audiovisuals if you have a special collection for them.

Preservation and protection. Make backup disks, clearly label them, and store them in a fireproof, safe place. Copies of copyright-free software may be circulated and the originals maintained as the master copy.

Housing. Store computer programs in dust-proof, protective containers. Control temperature and humidity. Do not touch, but handle by the permanent envelope. Do not label with a ballpoint pen (use a felt-tipped pen) and do not bend. Provide a secure place for computer programs, which are still temptations for theft in most libraries.

Management

Promotion. Prepare annotated bibliographies of programs available for each type of computer. Separate lists are important because people will only be interested in programs they can use on their personal computers.

Circulation. Many copyrighted programs cannot be circulated. Check with the licensing agreement on individual programs before you make your decisions. Programs that are available for copying can be circulated with instructions for patrons to copy onto their own disks if they want a copy. You may want a second copy of the manual to circulate.

Weeding. Remove when you have an updated version, a better program that does the same thing, or when the program is no longer useful.

FILMS, FILMSTRIPS, AND VIDEOTAPES

Free and inexpensive films, filmstrips, filmslips (short filmstrips), and videotapes are available from a number of sources. Although many librarians are now favoring video formats, there are still a great many films and filmstrips available.[2] Frequently videos are loaned with copying permissible.

Acquisition

Sources. Educators Progress Service will be one of your first choices for a source of free and inexpensive films. Many agencies, corporations, and institutions are listed here with specific instructions for ordering. Modern Talking Pictures circulates a number of free-loan association films. Embassies often provide films. Addresses of embassies are in most almanacs. You can write for general information about once a year. Agencies and corporations can be contacted directly, but expect that you will be referred to another company for distribution.

Selection. University and school libraries will choose items that support their curriculum by working closely with curriculum committees and individual teachers. Public libraries will select items as it is possible to respond to requests. These materials take a lot of space, so items should be selected carefully.

Ordering. Choose carefully items other than those requested by faculty or patrons for specific use or those for which there is a need. These materials present additional problems for storage and circulation. Generally you should not order in a particular format unless you have equipment available for viewing.

Processing

Initial processing and labeling. For materials you are adding to your collection, you should stamp each item with the ownership stamp. If materials have been borrowed for a teacher, attach a circulation slip to the film can or box with the date due clearly marked. Printed materials such as pamphlets, guides, or scripts are often sent with the borrowed film and can be added to the vertical file with instructions for borrowing the related film.

Organization. Purchased audiovisual materials are probably a separate collection in your regular collection. Free and inexpensive audiovisuals may be given the vertical-file treatment if you do not want to spend the time to catalog them fully. Your decisions will be determined by the volume of materials of this kind that you handle. Some libraries classify and intershelve audiovisual items with the regular circulating collection.

Preservation and protection. Films are best stored at temperatures between 30° and 70° F and at a humidity between 30 and 50 percent, with 40 percent being most desirable.[3] One of the best preservation ideas for films is to be sure that your users know how to use projection equipment properly. When you provide viewing equipment, attach clear, concise instructions to the equipment.

Housing. Store in boxes or cans on shelves. Do not touch the film surface with your fingers. Protect from dust and changes in temperature.

Management

Promotion. List with services and resources.

Circulation. Circulate films, filmstrips, and videos as needed but generally not longer than two days. A viewing room should be provided in the library.

Weeding. Weed when outdated or worn.

FLAGS

Flags of the United States, individual states, cities, other countries, and governments can add color and interest to your collection of materials. In addition, there are flags of the sea, flags for communication, and flags for sports teams and specific games. School, public, and university libraries as well as history and foreign language teachers may be interested in flags.

Acquisition

Sources. Information about the history of flags, flag terms, flag codes for display, and flag manufacture can be found in encyclopedia articles and books. Pamphlets and posters on state flags and U.S. historical flags are available for your vertical file. Cloth reproductions are available in several sizes, from small table displays to standard flags for wall or staff presentation. Companies supplying flags include school supply companies, foreign language supply companies, social studies companies, and small flag manufacturers. The United Nations is a good source of information about flags of member nations. Miniature flags are available individually or in sets. Flags Unlimited supplies larger sizes for U.S. current and historical, state and territory and international and fun flags. Embassies may furnish flag information about their countries.

Selection. Select flags that have meaning to your patrons, such as state flags, historical flags of the United States, or foreign flags. If you are in an area with sailboats or other sea vessels, you may also want flags of the sea.

Ordering. Order direct from the supplier or collect flags at conferences where the United Nations or U.S. Government Printing Office has a booth.

Processing

Initial processing and labeling. Label containers or use clasps or safety pins to attach identification tags that can be removed or tucked out of sight for displays.

Organization. Organize as a group under Flags or file with the country or subject in the vertical file or in the audiovisual collection.

Preservation and protection. Flags should be folded carefully for storage. The U.S. flag may be folded in the military style (twice lengthwise; then, starting at the stripe end, fold in a series of triangular folds). A flag permanently attached to a staff should be rolled around the staff and then wrapped with a cover. Flags may be mended, dry-cleaned, or washed as appropriate depending on the fabric.

Housing. House flags in boxes, bags, or pocket envelopes.

Management

Promotion. You can use flags in displays of travel, history, current events, food, language study, literature, art, music, or any other focus on countries, states, or regions. Rotate them in your library if your collection is large enough so that patrons will realize they are available. Post a sign near the displayed flags to indicate that others are in your collection.

Circulation. Establish a policy regarding circulation before you have a situation requiring a decision. Many teachers will want to keep them in their classrooms indefinitely.

Weeding. When worn out, flags should be destroyed in a dignified way, preferably by private burning.

FLASH CARDS

Flash cards present an alternate way to study material and to drill and practice and can be used by one person or a group. Flash cards are available for many types of information including such areas as geography, math, art, vocabulary for English and foreign language study, history facts and dates, and literature. Flash cards can be large enough for classroom use or 1"x2" for individual study. Flash cards will be of interest to teachers including teachers of new adult readers.

Acquisition

Sources. School supply companies and educational-materials companies offer a number of sets of flash cards; educational-toy stores or department stores may have some available; organizations and corporations may offer sets of flash cards with other vertical-file materials; and individuals may make their own flash cards to contribute to the library collection. School supply stores and college bookstores often have both blank and commercial flash cards for sale.

Selection. Order topics when teachers request alternate formats.

ABC School Supply, Inc., has a good selection of flash cards for presidents of the United States, the 50 states, countries of the world, traffic signs and symbols, transportation, and famous places. Many sets are less than $5 each.

Ordering. Consider purchasing flash cards when you find appropriate topics in catalogs, department stores, or bookstores.

Processing

Initial processing and labeling. Mark and label the container for a set of flash cards.

Organization. Flash cards most often come in sets. Keep the sets together and arrange by subjects. Flash cards can be put into a picture file, an information file, a game collection or in the general audiovisual section.

Preservation and protection. Large homemade cards can be laminated. Rubber bands (two-way or four-way) can be used to help hold boxes closed or keep cards together.

Housing. Flash cards can be slipped into files or pockets in your vertical file or housed in boxes in the audiovisual collection.

Management

Promotion. Consider a special collection or special list of fun educational items including educational games, flash cards, puzzles, and mind teasers. Provide an attractive listing, laminated for teachers to keep on their desks.

Circulation. Circulate as needed.

Weeding. Weed when worn.

GAMES

There are many educational games available commercially or from special groups. You may have commercially produced games in your library or game pieces for students to design their own. There are many educational games for adults, students, and younger children. There are a number of card games with pictures and information for subjects such as art masterpieces and presidents. Many games can be slipped into vertical-file folders, envelopes, or pockets; others will be a part of an audiovisual or special collection.

Acquisition

Sources. School supply or educational companies sell games of all kinds that have an application for education. Many teachers' books and magazines describe games that require few or no game pieces. Social Studies School Service offers a variety of supplementary materials including educational games and flash cards. Aristoplay offers various educational board games as well as card games. Topics include Greek myths and legends, children's authors, fairy tales, geometry, dinosaurs, and painters. Board games are available for great composers, human anatomy, elections, and pollution as well as a number of others.

Selection. School libraries should select games that have an educational base and will enhance the curriculum. Enlist the advice of teachers. Public libraries should establish a policy regarding games in the library.

Ordering. Order direct from the supplier. Friends of the library groups will probably donate new or used games if you make needs known to them.

Processing

Initial processing and labeling. Stamp and mark the envelope or box with an ownership stamp. Put a label on the outside listing a summary of pieces so that contents can easily be checked when returning. A four-way rubber band will help with the storage of boxes.

Organization. Games will be most useful if they are classified by subject, but they can be arranged in a number of ways. Cross-reference cards for subjects and names will be helpful.

Preservation and protection. You are bound to lose some pieces. You might get an extra set so that you can fill in missing items.

Housing. Store games with pieces in a closed container—either an envelope, a bag, or a box.

Management

Promotion. Let your teachers in your school or community know the games you have to support their classes. Let students know of games that you have to check out for home use.

Circulation. Check out games to students for home play. Even if pieces are occasionally lost, you have helped them learn something in an enjoyable way.

Weeding. Withdraw games when you have lost pieces that cannot be replaced.

MICROFORMS

Microforms, especially microfiche, are an inexpensive way to duplicate information. It is likely that you will have items in microform format. Microforms provide an alternative format to many kinds of library materials including books, periodicals, newspapers, catalogs, government documents, dissertations, as well as vertical-file materials. The microforms you have in your vertical-file or supplementary collections may be limited to the miscellaneous fiche you receive for ERIC documents or special reports.[4] The vertical-file treatment will be sufficient for many of these items.

Acquisition

Sources. Many government documents and reports are available on microfiche. Educational documents indexed in Resources in Education (RIE) are available from the ERIC Document Reproduction Service (1-800-443-ERIC) for a nominal charge. Frequently bibliographies, articles, and books will refer to ERIC documents and can be identified by ED followed by a six-digit number. Maps are sometimes reproduced on microfiche.

Selection. The use of microforms addresses a concern for space but presents an inconvenience to patrons by requiring them to use a machine for reading the material. The library that provides microform material must also provide equipment for reading and reproducing the material. You may not have a choice of format, but if you have a choice you should consider cost, space, and convenience before making your decision. Select microfiche collections if you have a space problem and there is a need to have the information available. Microfiche is usually less expensive than hard-copy formats.

Ordering. You may actively or inactively collect microfiche for your library. If you have a very large collection of microfiche, you will probably consider a fiche cabinet or special fiche holders for three-ring notebooks. Single fiche items can be placed in the vertical file if full cataloging is not needed.

Processing

Initial processing and labeling. Fiche or microfilm periodicals can be checked in like other serials. Individual titles may be cataloged individually or filed with the subject in the vertical-file cabinets if interest is limited. Provide author, title, and subject access for important items.

Organization. Use the same organization as used for other materials unless you are working with a special collection. Organize special collections for best use of materials.

Preservation and protection. Use separate acid-free envelopes and store vertically to protect fiche. Control temperature, humidity, and dust for all film formats.

Housing. File in metal cabinets or in fiche holders bound in three-ring notebooks.

Management

Promotion. People need to know what you have. Books on microfiche should have entries in your catalog; periodicals and newspapers should be listed with hard-copy issues; special collections can be listed in your library handouts.

Circulation. Do not circulate microfiche but do provide a good reader/printer for your patrons. You may want to consider providing a fiche-to-fiche copier for those like teachers with access to readers of their own. Inform your users of copyright laws regarding microfiche documents.

Weeding. Weeding microfiche is easier to postpone than other types of materials because of their small size. Microfiche should be weeded when the information is no longer current or relevant.

PUZZLES

There are several kinds of puzzles you might consider keeping in your library including children's wooden puzzles, puzzles on paper, and manipulative puzzles such as rings. A few nice puzzles add to a homey, friendly atmosphere in your children's department or school library.

Acquisition

Sources. Puzzles are available for purchase from school-supply companies and stores as well as toy and department stores. Sometimes puzzles are found in periodicals.

Selection. Select good-quality, preferably wooden puzzles appropriate to your patrons' interests. Give preference to educational puzzles that feature the United States or world cut-outs.

Puzzles for paper manipulation can be made available on occasion. Teachers and librarians may want to keep a few extra copies in their files for certain occasions if the sheet requires the user to write on it. Most issues of *The School Librarian's Workshop*[5] include a reference puzzle or pencil game. These can be tied in with displays or lesson plans for special interest or rotated each month to encourage library use. Brain-teaser puzzles frequently are found in *Reader's Digest* and other popular periodicals as well as in teacher materials.

Puzzles that involve the use of logic in the manipulation of actual pieces such as rings, balls, or cubes may be appropriate to have in limited numbers. Math supply companies have puzzles testing skill in logic and reasoning. You can keep these in your personal file cabinet if they are small enough to fit easily. Most likely you will house them with your collection of games.

Ordering. Let the word out to the friends of the library group or parents association and you will probably have more puzzles donated than you can handle.

Processing

Initial processing and labeling. If you have a number of the large-piece wooden puzzles that are likely to get mixed, you might want to put a letter or a distinguishing mark on the back of each piece of the same puzzle.

Organization. Unless you have lots of puzzles, you do not need to worry about organizing them. Wooden puzzles can be stacked.

Preservation and protection. Do not worry about preservation—use them then lose them!

Housing. Stack large puzzles on tables or shelves or in a puzzle holder. Smaller paper and pencil puzzles can be filed in personal files or information file cabinets. Larger manipulative kinds of puzzles can be housed with games.

Management

Promotion. Put puzzles out on the tables in the children's or youth services department. Children will find them.
Circulation. Do not circulate.
Weeding. Discard when you lose pieces or puzzles are worn.

SLIDES

Slides are another form of projected medium that is relatively inexpensive for libraries to acquire. Slides provide an alternative way to present information; you will consider them for your collection along with films, filmstrips, and transparencies. Good slides can be produced by most people with a little practice.

Acquisition

Sources. Inexpensive slides are available from a number of sources. Slides are available from many of the sources listed in the art reproductions section. Travel slides are available from individual attractions. Slide sets are available from school supply companies. Patrons will often donate slides from their travels if you let them know of your interest. You can make your own slide sets using a 35mm camera and a copy stand.

Take slides of special events in your library or school. Slides of library users and library events will be useful to have on hand for presentations to boards, administrators, and special groups. People love to see themselves, so take lots of pictures of individuals.

Selection. Purchase slides that will be used by your patrons. Ask faculty members for recommendations. Travel slides and art slides may make up a large part of your slide collection, though there are many slides available for other subject areas as well. Remember to collect a few good slides of each special event you sponsor. It is an excellent and easy way to summarize the activities of the year for groups.

Ordering. Order from jobbers or from galleries, museums, or educational companies. Buy travel slides on location. Plan the slides that you want to produce for the collection yourself.

Processing

Initial processing and labeling. Stamp the ownership on each slide. You can trace a magic marker diagonally across the top of a slide tray to indicate the position of each slide. Identify slides if they have no guide with them.

Organization. Small groups of specialized slides can be stored in transparent sleeves and filed by subject in your information files. Other groups may be organized as you do other audiovisual materials. Most sets will be easier to manage if left in sets.

Preservation and protection. Personal slides can be transferred to videotape for circulation and ease of handling.

Housing. Slides can be stored in plastic sleeves in binders, trays, or file drawers. Small groups of specialized slides are easily handled by housing in transparent sleeves and filing by subject in your information files. Large sets of slides may be better managed in trays or boxes.

Management

Promotion. Promote the concept of personal slides of teachers and librarians used to illustrate concepts.
Circulation. Circulate slides as needed.
Weeding. Weed when worn or uninteresting.

TRANSPARENCIES

The best transparencies are designed to communicate a single message in a very simple and clear way. Good transparencies can simplify an issue or a concept for your readers, and they can provide important information resources. Transparencies are used regularly by teachers and speakers with an overhead projector because they are an easy and effective way to communicate. You may house transparencies or transparency masters in your vertical files for convenience. You may have transparency masters or the transparencies themselves, either mounted or unmounted. Transparencies may be single items or they may be in sets.[6]

Acquisition

Sources. Educational transparency sets are available for purchase from many school materials supply companies, but unless you are in a school library you are more likely to add some of the free and inexpensive transparencies from companies and associations. Transparencies are easily made from masters or from any good copy.[7] Many teacher magazines or teacher guides to children's magazines have transparency masters in each issue. Examples include *Learning* and *Current Health.*

You can make transparencies in your own library or school if you have a copy machine that will use transparency film or if you have a thermal machine. Transparency film for both kinds of machines is available from most office supply companies or library supply companies. Many commercial copy centers make transparencies for a nominal charge.

Selection. Include transparency masters for topics your patrons will use. Prefer masters for your file and let individuals make their own transparencies if equipment is available and copyright is not a problem. Lettering should be large enough (at least ¼") to be easily read. A good rule of thumb for uncluttered transparencies is a maximum of six lines of six words each.

Ordering. Unless you are ordering sets of transparencies, you will not likely go out of your way to search for transparencies or transparency masters. They will be included in vertical-file materials from various sources, especially in educational materials. Free and inexpensive materials designed for schools frequently include transparency masters.

150 / 13—Other Free and Inexpensive Supplementary Materials

Processing

Initial processing and labeling. Label your accompanying material but try to keep the transparency master clear of extra marks including corrections. Every mark will be picked up by the film. Labels placed on the transparency itself may be projected as black spots. If it is necessary to mark the master, put marks on the back and make a clean copy for use in the machine. Transparency masters are designed to be copied, so it is unlikely that there are copyright restrictions, but read the accompanying material and make any restrictions clear to patrons.

Organization. File by the subject with related materials. Some libraries have a special collection of transparencies but most will file by subject in the vertical file or audiovisual collection.

Preservation and protection. Unmounted transparencies can be stored with tissue or typing paper between sheets of film. Protect from dust, heat, and excessive light. Avoid getting fingerprints on the film. Mounting frames give added protection but increase the size to 10¼"x11¾".

Housing. File transparencies in folders or envelopes in the vertical-file cabinets. Unmounted transparencies can be punched for a loose-leaf notebook or put in plastic mounts for notebooks. Oversize file cabinets are helpful for mounted transparencies. Sets can be stored in boxes or binders.

Management

Promotion. Promote with other vertical-file information. Add a note or label to appropriate files containing masters regarding the availability of transparency-making equipment. Masters can also be used to make paper handouts for group use.

Circulation. Circulate as needed. You can restrict circulation if you have copy equipment available.

Weeding. Weed when no longer useful.

NOTES

[1] Facts on File's *Public Domain Software on File* costs $200 and lists more than 200 programs for Apple or IBM. Minnesota Educational Computer Consortium (MECC) is another source of relatively inexpensive software.

[2] There are a number of sources for borrowing 16mm films and some 8mm films and film loops. Generally 16mm films are borrowed and 32mm filmstrips or filmslips are giveaways.

[3] See *Nonbook Media: Collection Management and User Services* (Chicago: American Library Association, 1987) for additional information regarding the care and maintenance of all kinds of nonbook materials.

[4]There are a number of commercial sources for microfiche and microfilm. Many kinds of materials are available including telephone directories, college catalogs, out-of-print books and plays, and educational documents (Educational Resources Information Center ERIC documents). Many of these are or will be available on CD-ROM. Watch the professional literature to keep up with new offerings.

[5]*The School Librarian's Workshop.* $40 per year for 10 issues. See also note 2 in chapter 14 (page 166).

[6]For additional information on the production of overhead transparencies and their use see Mildred Knight Laughlin and Patricia Ann Coty's "Overhead Transparencies," in *Nonbook Media: Collection Management and User Services* (Chicago: American Library Association, 1987), 214-16.

[7]The Facts on File series of ...*on File* books is designed to be copied and provides excellent transparency masters. The printing is done on card stock and housed in ring notebooks. Card stock will not work well with some transparency-making equipment, so you may need to make a good paper copy before you make a transparency. Examples of some of the titles are *Maps on File, Historical Maps on File*, and *The Human Body on File*. Most titles include about 300 pages for $145.

14
Supplementary Materials for Personal Files of Librarians and Teachers

Personal files are personal. It is impossible to say what teachers and librarians will want to put in their own files. The items listed are those more likely to be in personal or nonpublic files when they are collected. Undoubtedly teachers and librarians will collect some items from the materials already discussed. The groupings are not intended to be limiting in any way but simply to aid in reading. Items are included in the groups where it was felt that they fit best.[1]

Most items included in the list of materials for librarians and teachers fall into several natural groups of materials for programs, displays, and giveaways. Except for publisher catalogs the other items relate to public relations.

Programs:	book-talks, flannel-board materials, masks, puppets
Displays:	book jackets, bulletin-board materials, lettering guides, miniature books
Giveaways:	bookmarks, buttons, bumper stickers, handouts
General PR:	clip art

BOOK JACKETS

Book jackets can go into your vertical file if you do not keep them with the books. Your book-processing policy will dictate whether you keep jackets on the books or remove them. Most book jackets help promote the book by providing an illustration and interesting information about the book and the author. Public and school libraries usually keep them for that reason; many academic libraries remove them. There are many advantages to keeping them: They provide interesting information, they give protection to the binding, and they make your collection more appealing to patrons. Book jackets can be protected by putting a protective clear plastic jacket over the paper or by laminating. By keeping them you add an extra step in processing as well as the expense of the protective covering. Book jackets are excellent ways to promote materials through bulletin boards and exhibits.

Acquisition

Sources. Take jackets from the books. Occasionally you can get extra jackets from the publisher.

Selection. Keep jackets that provide important information about the author or provide an attractive illustration for a bulletin-board display.

Ordering. Extra jackets are sometimes available at library or education conferences in the vendors' exhibits area. Often children's book covers are reprinted as miniposters or postcards.

Processing

Initial processing and labeling. Put the call number of the processed book on the back of the jacket. Consider trimming so that you keep only the information you will use.

Organization. If you keep all jackets together for displays, file by classification number or put in folders by subject. Keep fiction together. If you clip from the jackets, just clip and file into your subject files. Author blurbs can be put in the author's file.

Preservation and protection. Do not bother with any preservation methods unless you are keeping jackets on the books or unless you want to mount flyleaf information. Clear plastic covers or lamination will help protect jackets you keep for use on the books.

Housing. If you keep all jackets together for displays you can put them in boxes in the back room to use for bulletin boards of new materials. The easiest solution is to keep the book jackets on the books.

Management

Promotion. Book jackets are great for bulletin boards. You can cover dummy books (blocks of wood, Styrofoam, or plastic) with jackets for displays so that the book is available for circulation.

Circulation. Do not circulate.

Weeding. If you do not put them on the book, keep only the ones you plan to use for exhibits or bulletin boards and discard them after use. Some librarians clip the author information and attach it to the inside of the book.

BOOKMARKS

Bookmarks provide an effective way to communicate a little bit of information. Some are appropriate for your vertical file, although most will be kept in the librarian's or teacher's personal files. Minibibliographies, the classification outline, the sign language alphabet, and the Gettysburg Address are examples of other useful bits of information that are available on bookmarks. Many special groups produce bookmarks with information related to their interest. For example, church libraries might include bookmarks with books of the Bible listed or the Ten Commandments.

Most bookmarks are effective tools for public relations. Many of them have quotes about reading and books which you can use for ideas for displays or decorations in your library or classroom. Some libraries print their own bookmarks using clip art or ready-to-use designs from various sources and photocopied on card stock. Bookmarks can be purchased, produced, or collected to give to patrons as part of the public relations of the library.

Acquisition

Sources. Look for bookmarks from associations and companies that use them to promote their ideas or products. Commercial bookmarks are available in bookstores. Bookmarks for library distribution are available from commercial vendors such as Upstart and Demco. The Perfection Form Company has a set of author bookmarks with caricatures of and famous quotes from famous authors including Twain, Dickinson, Shakespeare, Poe, Dickens, Hawthorne, Cather, Faulkner, Steinbeck, and Hemingway. Another set highlights twelve Olympian heroes from mythology.

You will save money if you can have your own printed. Camera-ready bookmarks are available from several sources including *Library Imagination Paper* from Carol Bryan Imagines and ALA Graphics. You can make your own bookmark shapes with an Ellison Lettering Machine, a minicutter that can be used with many different shapes. It can be used for bookmarks, letters, numbers, outlines of states, musical notes, math signs and many holiday, animal, and picture shapes. It can be used with paper, fabric, and other materials.

Selection. Choose bookmarks with appropriate information or a relevant library message.

Ordering. Order bookmarks direct from the vendor. Try to design your own bookmarks or sponsor a bookmark design contest for your users.

Processing

Initial processing and labeling. No processing or labeling is necessary.

Organization. Keep a personal file of bookmark samples and masters. Bookmarks that provide important information such as unique alphabets, lists, or speeches can be filed in the library vertical file under the subject of the information.

Preservation and protection. Consider laminating the best ones containing popular information that is frequently used.

Housing. Store your extra bookmarks with supplies.

Management

Promotion. Use bookmarks as a part of your public relations materials. Give them away with each circulated book, use them at book-talks, award them as prizes. Calendar bookmarks can serve as a reminder for the date due. Teachers can use them for rewards.

Circulation. Give away as many as you can afford.

Weeding. Discard bookmarks with dated information.

BOOK-TALKS

Librarians and teachers who work with children and youth use book-talking more than any other professionals, but many who work in public services use book-talking in one form or another. Book-talk information you prepare yourself can be recorded on note cards, a notebook, an audio- or videotape or—better yet—in your computer. You may also want to include notes of other presentations in your book-talk file, such as an annual talk to give to classes or parents on literature for children.

Acquisition

Sources. You can purchase wonderful books with ideas for book-talking and storytelling. Caroline Feller Bauer and Joni Bodart have written books containing many ideas for creative presentations for children and young people. You can get book-talk ideas from periodicals such as *Booktalker*, an insert in the *Wilson Library Bulletin* that appears five times each year.

Selection. If you do a lot of book-talking, it is a good habit to fill out an index card with enough information about each book to job your memory sufficiently to do at least a minitalk. You can code the ones you like the best. You should record your negative reactions to books as well as your positive ones.

Ordering. Books and tapes can be ordered through a jobber or direct. Your own collection of booktalks will be the result of a lot of self-discipline and a commitment to develop your collection. Many reading teachers, school librarians, and librarians who manage collections for children and young adults fill out an index card for every juvenile book they read.

Processing

Initial processing and labeling. Use a data management program to index by author, title, and subject.

Organization. If you have cards, you will probably want them filed alphabetically by author. Computer files can be indexed with multiple headings or you can use your collection category as an index.

Preservation and protection. You can use plastic card sleeves or laminate the cards you use frequently.

Housing. Use a card file for index cards or computer disk for book-talks.

Management

Promotion. If you work with youth, you will likely give frequent book-talks. You can easily put together a book-talk program from your book-talk notes on index cards.

Circulation. Book-talk notes are personal, so these will be your own files. You may want a review file available for students to access that might consist of other students' reviews.

Weeding. Put little-used titles in an inactive file. You might discard your cards for titles you no longer need for a book-talk or you can keep the information on your computer so it can be printed out anytime.

BULLETIN-BOARD MATERIALS

Materials for display boards are available in many types including hook and loop, magnetic, felt, paper, or miscellaneous items. Elementary teachers and librarians will develop an extensive collection.

Acquisition

Sources. Teacher-supply stores are available in large cities, but most items can be ordered from school supply catalogs. Card shops sell commercial holiday decorations that can be used for bulletin boards and displays. You may also make some of your own. An Ellison Lettering Machine will be helpful in making your own borders and cut-outs. Clip good ideas for bulletin boards from periodicals and newspapers. Some publications such as *The School Librarian's Workshop*,[2] include sketches and instructions for doing bulletin boards. Take notes or file the ideas you expect to use.

Selection. Choose items for purchase that can be used in different ways when possible. You will want to recycle all of these things. School and academic libraries will have the same students for several years, so you will want to vary each year's holiday decorations. Public and special libraries that have the same patrons each year will need to be even more creative in their use of bulletin-board materials. Consider exchanging decorations with librarians in other libraries and schools.

Ordering. Order what you can afford. Commercial decorations in your local stores will be on sale after the holiday, so that is a good time to stock up on additional items. Many librarians and teachers will buy these items themselves, as budgets do not always allow for decorative items.

Processing

Initial processing and labeling. Do not stamp or label.

Organization. You will probably have separate holiday boxes in your storage area for seasonal items. Materials can be arranged by holiday, subject, month of the year, or season. Label each box clearly.

Take a picture of the bulletin boards and displays that you may want to use again. Keep a file of pictures so that you can easily duplicate materials with little effort. Include a notation of the dates used.

Subject-specific ideas may be best filed with the subject. You may want to add index access by format to facilitate use.

Preservation and protection. You may want to laminate some materials. Use plastic sleeves to protect pictures.

Housing. Large cardboard file drawers hold a great deal of miscellaneous materials. You can use one for each holiday, each month, or each season. Lightweight boxes can be stored on high shelves in your back room.

Management

Promotion. This collection will probably be for your own use unless you are in a school library; then you can advertise it in your library handbook for teachers or in a newsletter for faculty members.

Circulation. Bulletin-board materials are for library or classroom use only.

Weeding. Get rid of materials when they look bad or when you are tired of them.

BUTTONS AND BUMPER STICKERS

Buttons are a special kind of supplementary item that comes under the category of public relations. They can add much to the interest and atmosphere of your library or classroom. They provide you with a means to communicate a brief message to the people you come in contact with. Many national campaign buttons are collectors' items, as are buttons of particular themes such as environment, reading, and history.

Bumper stickers often come with free and inexpensive promotional material. You can keep them in the file under the subject and use them for displays or bulletin boards when it is appropriate. Like buttons, bumper stickers provide a way to communicate with a few words. Bumper stickers kept in your files will be used like a minisign or banner.

Acquisition

Sources. Buttons and bumper stickers are available from many school supply companies, associations, local groups, and commercial vendors including the following: Upstart, Demco, Creative Publications, and the ALA. You can make your own buttons with a button-maker.[3]

Selection. Choose buttons and bumper stickers that promote reading, libraries, education, or subject areas you want to highlight. Teachers will appreciate your wearing buttons promoting their subjects.

Ordering. Order or buy as you find them available. Vendors in the exhibits area of conferences often offer buttons and other related promotional materials. Other kinds of supplementary promotional materials include bookmarks and pins.

Processing

Initial processing and labeling. No processing is necessary, but you may use a permanent felt-tipped pen to indicate ownership on the back of the button.

Organization. No formal organization is necessary, though you may choose to file campaign buttons and bumper stickers with the biographical information and specific subject-related buttons or bumper stickers with the subject.

Preservation and protection. No preservation is necessary.

Housing. You can display buttons on a bulletin board or pin them on hanging ribbons. File bumper stickers in the appropriate file folder or envelope.

Management

Promotion. Wear buttons frequently and give extras to faculty, students, and friends of the library. Some librarians have button vests or button sashes that display the full collection.

Circulation. Do not circulate. Give away what you can. Preserve those you feel have historical or local interest.

Weeding. Rarely or never weed.

CLIP ART

You can never have too much clip art. Copyright-free illustrations are available in books, periodicals, computer programs, and just by careful observation. When you are designing a flyer or newsletter it is hard to find the right illustration unless you have a large selection. You will use clip art for your own public relations, but your patrons will also appreciate the availability of clip art in your library.[4]

Acquisition

Sources. The easiest way to begin collecting clip art is to buy a few books or booklets of designs. Dover Press offers a large selection of inexpensive books with copyright-free designs including *Big Book of Graphic Designs and Devices*, $6.95; *Ready-to-Use Humorous Illustrations of Children*, $4.50; *Ready-to-Use Humorous Sports Illustrations*, $3.95; *Ready-to-Use School and Education Illustrations*, $3.95; *Ready-to-Use Whimsical Illustrations of Animals*, $4.50. Carol Bryan Imagines publishes *Library Imagination Paper*, a four-page quarterly with ready-to-use clip art for bookmarks, headings, miscellaneous illustrations, and ideas for public relations. It is excellent! *Library PR News* published by LEI, Inc., is a bimonthly publication with information on library publicity and promotion. Each issue includes a 11"x17" centerfold poster or two pages of clip art. Subscriptions are $26.95 per year.

Other clip art for libraries is available from ALA Graphics and Libraries Unlimited. There are many books of copyright-free illustrations on the market. There are also many computer files of clip art. An annotated bibliography of clip-art sources was compiled by Liz Austrom and Ken Haycock in the March-April 1989 issue of *Emergency Librarian*.

Selection. Choose subjects related to your needs and your patrons' interests, such as education and sports.

Ordering. Clip art is available from publishers or jobbers.

Processing

Initial processing and labeling. Be careful where you stamp and label clip-art materials since they will be copied.

Organization. Keep clip-art materials together.

Preservation and protection. To preserve your collection, you can make it "copy only" with no clipping. Provide a good photocopy machine near the collection.
Housing. Use files, notebooks, envelopes, pocket envelopes, or boxes.

Management

Promotion. List with your special services for faculty. Add footnotes on flyers indicating that the illustration is from the library clip-art file.
Circulation. Do not circulate. Provide a photocopy machine.
Weeding. This is one file you will probably never weed unless items are falling apart.

FLANNEL-BOARD MATERIALS

Teachers and librarians who work with young children will probably have a collection of materials for flannel or felt boards. These boards are valuable tools for the education and entertainment of children. They are useful in storytelling and in presenting concepts. They are flexible because the pieces can be added, removed, and manipulated easily for presentations.

Acquisition

Sources. Felt is the most popular material used for flannel and felt boards. School specialty companies and school supply stores in large cities often have cut-outs available. Fabric stores may have cut-outs for appliqué. Another option is to make your own designs from simple outline pictures you find in coloring books or stencil guides.[5]
Selection. Buy or make figures to illustrate concepts or stories you use with children. Choose shapes that can be used in more than one story.
Ordering. Buy at local school supply stores or order from school specialty companies. Some cut-outs may be available in sets or individual items.

Processing

Initial processing and labeling. If you have groups of felt figures that illustrate a specific story or teach a specific concept, they can be grouped in one transparent plastic bag and filed accordingly.
Organization. Keep felt cut-outs together as a collection in a box or hand them in plastic bags on racks. Some librarians may prefer to file by subject or title (for storytelling) in the vertical file.
Preservation and protection. Store flannel-board materials in transparent plastic bags.
Housing. House cut-outs in boxes, envelopes, or files.

Management

Promotion. List with services to teachers. Promote by subject area, for example, math items to math teachers, music items to music teachers, and language arts items to reading teachers. Children's librarians in school and public libraries may keep these in a private file.

Circulation. Public library children's librarians as well as school librarians may want to develop a collection of felt figures that teachers and adults working with children could check out.

Weeding. Discard or replace when items are worn or soiled.

HANDOUTS

You may want to provide a literature rack of free handout materials for your patrons. Some handouts you will prepare yourself but others will be available to you from many sources. These may include local bus schedules, college and university class schedules, opportunities to volunteer, voter information, health information, bibliographies, information about municipal government, membership information for appropriate organizations (friends of the library groups, Literacy Project) or any other public service information you think is appropriate to make available to your patrons.

Acquisition

Sources. Many organizations, special groups, clubs, and other community groups will gladly provide handout materials for your patrons.

Selection. Carefully select material to put on your free literature rack. Beware of propaganda in free literature.

Ordering. Pamphlets, brochures, information cards, and other related materials are available by writing to the organization or company. Bus schedules, class schedules, and other local information may be delivered if you call to tell the institution or group that you will make information available. You may need to pick up some materials yourself.

Processing

Initial processing and labeling. No processing is necessary for materials you are putting out for patrons to take, but you may want to keep track of the number you are distributing if you expect to offer the items again.

Organization. It is important to keep your literature rack neat and tidy. If you have a great deal of information, you may want to group it and use labels such as Educational Opportunities, Municipal Meetings, and Library Aids.

Preservation and protection. Keep a master copy so that you can copy or order more.

Housing. Put all free materials together in a literature rack or stacked on counters and tables clearly away from library materials for loan. You may want copies of some of the handouts in your information file.

Management

Promotion. Put up a good sign. To avoid confusing patrons, separate free materials from materials they are expected to borrow.
Circulation. Clearly indicate when materials are available to keep.
Weeding. Remove extra copies of handouts promptly when they are no longer relevant or needed.

LETTERING GUIDES

Lettering guides for calligraphy, outline letters, and stencils and symbols for alphabets of other languages and means of communication may be popular items in your school or library. Similar information is available in books on lettering, but users often want something they can trace or copy. These materials can be in personal files for librarians and teachers, in the public information files, or in the audiovisual collection.

Acquisition

Sources. School specialty suppliers and library supply companies sell stencils and commercially prepared letters. Dover Publications has a large selection of inexpensive guides. Large cities often have school supply stores with samples of cut-outs.
Calligraphy guides are available from publishers. An American sign-language alphabet is available on a poster from Giant Photos and from a number of other sources. Samples of braille alphabets, international signals, and other alphabets may be helpful.[6]
Selection. Choose styles that you or your patrons will use. Include a variety of sizes and styles.
Ordering. Order direct from the supplier.

Processing

Initial processing and labeling. Mark lettering guides with an ownership stamp.
Organization. Keep like alphabets together.
Preservation and protection. Laminate calligraphy guide sheets. Mount or laminate posters if you expect heavy use.
Housing. Use large 8½"x11" envelopes for each letter or set of alphabet. File the set in a box or vertical file.

Management

Promotion. Use the letters in your displays and indicate their availability.
Circulation. Be flexible if you are loaning your letter sets.
Weeding. Discard punch-out or stencil letters when they are worn. These materials will not go out-of-date.

MASKS

Masks are another of those additional items you can have in your collection to add interest to displays, storytelling, role-playing, or drama activities. The easiest to manage in your vertical file are the stick masks or small cloth or paper masks that attach with an elastic band. Paper-sack masks that will fold will also slip into your file with no problem.

Acquisition

Sources. There are a number of sources of masks from school specialty companies and library suppliers including Demco, Dover, Rivershore Library Store, and Simon & Schuster. Masks can also be made in the classroom or library.
Selection. Choose set of masks that can be used for storytelling, role-playing, or other activities by teachers, youth leaders, or children's librarians.
Ordering. Order direct from the source along with other materials.

Processing

Initial processing and labeling. Stamp and label the back of face masks.
Organization. Organize masks by subject or keep all masks together in a mask section. If you have all masks together, you will want to group by category such as dinosaurs, farm animals, people, etc. Be sure to cross-reference with the subject area.
Preservation and protection. Laminate flat masks to help preserve your collection. Transparent bags will give additional protection.
Housing. Flat masks can be placed in envelopes or plastic bags and housed in files or folders. Larger masks will need additional space and can be housed in large transparent bags in boxes.

Management

Promotion. Promote with teachers, youth workers, and librarians to use with theater classes, role-playing, and the study of subjects and foreign languages. Masks may be used in many ways similar to puppet use.
Circulation. Be flexible in your circulation, but in most cases masks will not be circulated for long periods of time.
Weeding. Weed masks only when they are worn out.

MINIATURE BOOKS

Miniature books are more of a curiosity than a source of information. You may not want to bother with something of this type, but it can be a great attention-getter. You may find miniature books in all subjects for adults and children. Public libraries would probably have the most interest in a collection of miniature books.

Acquisition

Sources. Publishers of children's books occasionally offer miniature books. Running Press has a series of miniature books (2½"x3") of classics such as *Love Sonnets of Shakespeare, Rubaiyat of Omar Khayyam, Sonnets from the Portuguese, A Child's Garden of Verses*, and *Aesop's Fables*. Dover Publications has a number of facsimile children's books. The Library of Congress sells *A Visit from St. Nicholas* in a facsimile of an 1864 edition that is about the same size. Facsimile shape-books of nineteenth-century rare books are also available from the Library of Congress for $4.95 each for the 20-page books, which measure less than 7" high and are shaped like the people they represent.

Selection. Choose titles that will add to your permanent or temporary displays in subject areas.

Ordering. Order direct from the vendor.

Processing

Initial processing and labeling. Use a small stamp or write in the ownership and other information. Avoid using a standard-size stamp.

Organization. Miniature books should be kept together so that they are not lost.

Preservation and protection. Losing miniature books will be more of a problem than preservation. They will be subject to theft because of their curious format and they will be easily lost because of their size.

Housing. Put them in something larger, such as an envelope or box.

Management

Promotion. Use as enhancements to your displays and storytelling sessions. Children love miniature books and will be fascinated by them.

Circulation. Consider a noncirculating status for these items.

Weeding. Weed miniature books only when they are worn.

PUBLISHERS' CATALOGS

Publishers' catalogs are the trade tool of salespeople. You will want to keep some of the catalogs for your own or public use. This collection may be housed in the technical services department or a workroom in the library.

Acquisition

Sources. Once sales representatives know you and your library, you will begin getting catalogs of furniture, supplies, and equipment in addition to catalogs for library resources for both print and nonprint formats. You may need to find a source for items you do not find listed in your supply of catalogs. A couple of resources will be helpful in identifying sources. The *Books in Print* volume of publishers lists addresses and telephone numbers and is one of your best sources for books. *Bowker Annual* lists sources of other kinds of library materials, supplies, and equipment.

Selection. Request catalogs you really want from the sources. Ask to be taken off the mailing lists of companies you will not buy from.

Ordering. Many companies have an 800 number so that you can talk to a representative or request a catalog without charge. Do not be surprised when your call initiates a visit from the local salesperson.

Processing

Initial processing and labeling. You should put the date of receipt on the catalogs. You may want to add a label with the beginning letter of the name of the company so you can do a general alphabetical sorting. This is convenient if you are using pamphlet boxes to store your catalogs. You might consider using large colored dots with the letter indicated. If you change colors every year, you can easily spot the old catalogs for discard.

Organization. An alphabetical arrangement by the name of the company serves most libraries very well. If you have a large collection, you may want to group catalogs by product (such as computer equipment, furniture, microfiche). Since many companies supply more than one kind of product, it may work best to file them alphabetically and color-code labels or use colored dots to indicate the product or products they sell. Choose the easiest system that works for you.

Preservation and protection. Put your name on personal catalogs you want to keep if you open the collection to faculty members or the public.

Housing. You can file catalogs in folders in a vertical filing cabinet. Many libraries use Princeton files or magazine boxes with a box or so for each letter, then simply sort by letter.

Management

Promotion. You probably do not need to promote this collection. People who need catalogs will ask, or you can make your collection known to them individually. You may want to promote catalogs for textbooks and educational resources with groups of teachers.

Circulation. Circulate on your standard vertical-file forms.

Weeding. Keep only the latest catalog. Instruct those filing catalogs to try to discard an old catalog for every one filed. This practice will keep your files current.

PUPPETS

There are a number of kinds of puppets available for library and classroom use. Most of the ones you will use in your library will be either hand, finger, or glove puppets. Some are "turn-around." They can be used with children and youth for storytelling, role-playing, creative dramatics, music, foreign language, speech, and health study. They can add interest to both presentations and teaching situations. Puppets are often used in counseling or therapy sessions and can be very useful with special students.

Acquisition

Sources. There are many sources of puppets, including school supply distributors, toy stores, and library companies.[7] You can make your own puppets. A few examples of commercial suppliers are

WatchMe Blossom Theater Works. For animal hand puppets 8" to 16" in size.

Playful Puppets. For animal hand puppets from a 14" spider to a 55" bear. Most puppets are 10" to 12" for $18.

Nancy Renfro Studios. Hand and finger puppets are available as well as kits for making puppets. Some kits include a puppet, story, props, and activity manuals. Sets of puppets are available as well as puppet books, story aprons.

Demco has a good selection of puppets available, particularly the hand puppets.

Selection. Choose characters that can be used in a variety of stories and situations. Select puppets that appeal to children. Choose washable fabrics if possible so that children can play with them.

Ordering. You may be able to purchase some puppets in your local toy stores, but before purchasing you will probably want to look at a number of catalogs for the best selection and so that you get puppets you can mix and match.

Processing

Initial processing and labeling. You may want to use iron-on labels to mark your ownership.

Organization. Group puppets in sets or keep all of them together.

Preservation and protection. Handle with care.

Housing. Store in boxes. Each puppet can be stored in a separate plastic or mesh bag.

Management

Promotion. Encourage teachers to use puppets by providing books and ideas for using them in the classroom. Invite classes to storytelling sessions where you use puppets to illustrate a story. Use a puppet as a library mascot.

Circulation. Circulate to teachers and adults working with children for the period needed. Consider circulations to children.

Weeding. Weed puppets only when they are worn out.

NOTES

[1] School librarians will consider purchasing a ready-made vertical file of ideas for library management in *School Library Media Folders of Ideas for Library Excellence*, which is available from Libraries Unlimited. Information sheets are issued in loose-leaf format with subject headings printed on the side of the pages for easy filing and come complete with file-folder labels. There are more than 100 ideas in each set. No. 1, 1989, and No. 2, 1991. $27.50 each.

[2] *The School Librarian's Workshop* is published monthly except July and August by Library Learning Resources, Inc., 61 Greenbriar Drive, Berkeley Heights, New Jersey 07922 ($40 per year). This aid for librarians contains a number of regular items in addition to bulletin-board ideas such as bibliographies, library skills units, library related pencil games, and reference question exercises. It is designed for use with upper-elementary to middle-school students but many ideas are adaptable for high school and general use.

[3] Badge-a-Minit has a starter kit beginning at about $30 and offers ideas for making your own buttons.

[4] Creative Media Services offers a variety of 50-page theme art in collections for $27.95 each, punched for three-ring notebooks. They offer a business collection for desktop publishers for both IBM and Macintosh computers.

[5] Use an Ellison Lettering Machine to cut felt in a variety of shapes using special dies. Many elementary schools and libraries have the machine and dozens of dies available to use. The Ellison Lettering Machine ($300) has nine alphabet styles and more than 300 shapes available for purchase, with most prices for dies ranging from $25 to $50 each. Felt and other materials such as vinyl, Contact paper, poster board, and all kinds of paper can be cut using the equipment.

[6] The Ellison Lettering Machine has nine different lettering styles including roman letters, as well as the Greek alphabet. Dies are expensive, but a school district or network library can share equipment. Extra letters can be cut ahead and filed for later use. You can use patterned wrapping paper, wallpaper, fabric, plastic, or other materials for variation.

[7] Information on the use of puppets is available from Puppeteers of America (#5 Cricklewood Path, Pasadena, California 91107).

15
Special Collections of Supplementary Materials

Special collections are formed for a variety of reasons, but probably the most compelling factor is the flexibility that they provide for alternatives in such areas as physical location, organization, housing, and circulation. These options can provide ways of addressing the needs of users and simplifying the organization and management of materials. There is no magic formula to suggest when special collections should be established, but they are most often created to group materials of the same format (type) or subject or because the size of an accumulated collection has made special-collections status desirable.

Grouping general library materials by format is a common practice. Examples of format-based collections in libraries include periodicals, newspapers, microfiche, and videotapes. Materials that are frequently made into special collections include the clippings, maps, and pictures, plus others from our general list of supplementary items, such as annual reports, college catalogs, reports, scripts, and sheet music. Many of these special-collections materials lend themselves to special arrangements, such as government documents arranged by SuDoc's number, report series arranged by report number, college catalogs arranged by state, or career materials arranged by *Dictionary of Occupational Titles* number. Check the literature for books on the organization of special collections of materials such as government documents, maps, and picture collections. Materials may be grouped because their format requires special housing or handling for preservation (such as control of temperature, humidity, dust) or for shelving convenience, as in the case of oversized or odd-sized materials.

Grouping materials by the size of the item is a question of format and is not a new issue for librarians. Most libraries have a section for oversized books. Supplementary materials come in a variety of sizes that may present a challenge to convenient and logical organization of like materials. Collections of large maps, posters, audiovisual materials, and other items that do not conform to your standard-sized file cabinets or shelves can be grouped by size. File cabinets, hanging folders, adjustable shelves, and special boxes will aid in your organization of oversized or undersized materials. Arrangement in this case may simply be an adaptation of your basic system for the organization of general supplementary materials.

Decisions to form a special collection may also be based on the size of the collection. For example, if you have a sufficient number of pieces of a collection and it is more convenient to pull them together for a special collection, then you should do it. For example, say you have 100 annual reports in your vertical file. They could be (1) filed alphabetically throughout the files under the name of the company, (2) grouped in your file under a general heading "Annual Corporation Reports" and then arranged alphabetically by name of the company, or (3) put into a special collection, either in a file cabinet or on the shelves, and arranged by name or by SIC number.

Special collections may also be "special" because of the subjects included. There is, of course, a wide range of subjects that can be collected. Teachers will have special collections of materials based on the subjects they teach. Associations or clubs may have special collections based on the interests of the members. Libraries may have special collections based on curriculum emphasis such as art, business, drama, education, health, language, literature, music, science, social studies, and travel. Forming a special collection based on subject may mean that materials can be physically located near related information, or they may be placed in a part of the library where a subject specialist can more easily assist users, or perhaps it is just easier for patrons to use a collection when the materials are grouped by broad subject area. Two examples are addressed in detail: local history and career collections.

Once a special subject collection is identified as a separate unit, then its treatment determines whether it is officially a part of the regular collection or whether it remains as supplementary. For example, if full cataloging is not given to college catalogs or telephone directories, then they essentially are treated as supplementary. Groups of items that need to be cycled in and out of your collection with a minimum of processing are the candidates for vertical-file treatment, whether in a special collection or as part of your information files. The organization of materials for special subject areas will give you an opportunity to be creative with your approach to supplementary materials. You can find special guides to establishing special collections of library materials such as music libraries, art libraries, local history and career centers.

In some libraries these supplementary materials would be incorporated into the general information file, while in other situations there may be special collections for these as well as additional materials. Organization within the grouping may follow one of the standard forms of organization discussed for general vertical files or may follow a unique system.

The organization of special collections will be based on an alphabetical arrangement, a numerical arrangement, or a special code or classification system. Alphabetical arrangement alternatives to a subject arrangement include examples such as author, title, geographic location, publisher or issuing body. Numerical subarrangement can be based on date, volume, age, grade level, or rank (such as the largest to the smallest).

Examples of specialized classification systems include the U.S. Government Documents classification system which arranges materials by the issuing body of the federal government, the *Dictionary of Occupational Titles* classification for career materials, and the SIC (Standard Industrial Code) code for business and industry. Alternatives for organization of materials are discussed under the various types of supplementary materials.

This chapter presents three examples of special collections of supplementary materials. One is based on format (maps) and two on subject (careers and local history). The three examples represent special collections found in many libraries. Some of the guidelines for collections of these materials may be generalized to other special collections. However, it is expected that readers will use this book as a starting point and will consult resources in their area of focus when working with special collections. Examples follow the same basic format as other supplementary materials with expanded discussions of unique features and problems for the topic. These examples are not intended to be limiting in any way, and it is hoped they will serve as springboards for ideas for creation of appropriate special collections for your library.

MAP COLLECTIONS

Maps play an important role in our lives, and it is likely that every library will have some in their collection of supplementary materials. You will use them to answer your travel questions and in the study of history, politics, economics, etc. Individual maps will complement the atlas collection by providing more details and giving specialized information that cannot be conveyed in general atlases. There are land, water, and sky maps of many types including aerial, agricultural, antique, bicycle route, census, political subdivision, energy, geologic, highway, historical, land ownership, land use, military, natural resources, oceanic, outline, park and forest, political, railroad, recreation, river and lake, state, topographic, trail, treasure, universe, weather, wildlife, and world.[1] Maps also have the advantage of being very portable for easy patron use. They can be displayed in exhibits, presentations, and bulletin boards.

Acquisition

Sources. There are local, state, federal, and foreign maps available. The federal government publishes hundreds of maps. Some are available through the U.S. Government Printing Office, and others are available only from the specific agency issuing the map. A number of these sources are listed in the appendix. State governments often provide highway maps; mileage charts; hunting, fishing, and camping maps; and maps showing points of interest (e.g., museums, parks). Local governments and organizations provide city street maps, transit system route maps, and school district boundary maps. Foreign maps are available from embassies and travel bureaus.

There are a number of excellent commercial vendors such as Rand McNally and Nystrom. Maps are also available from businesses and associations such as the chambers of commerce, the American Automobile Association (AAA), car rental companies, and the American Association of Petroleum Geologists.

Map supplements to the *National Geographic* magazine are readily available, and those and others are offered for sale by the National Geographic Society. A subscription to the *World Newsmap of the Week*, incorporating *Headline Focus Wall Maps*, is available from the Curriculum Innovations Group, with 30 maps each school year.[2] Additional sources are listed in the appendix.

Selection. Consider the following when choosing maps:

1. The reputation of the publisher. Learn the names of some good publishers.
2. The date of the map. Generally, the more recent, the better, except in the case of material that does not go out of date, e.g., historical maps.
3. The geographic area covered. Does the map properly emphasize the area in which you are interested?
4. The subject covered. Is the subject one that is needed by your patrons?
5. Detail included on the map. Does it show enough detail for your needs?
6. Scale. What is the relationship between a given measurement on the map and the actual distance on the ground?
7. The use of color. Are physical features, political units, or thematic characteristics distinctive?
8. The use of symbols. Are they easily located and clearly interpreted?
9. Textual information. Are place-names or other word designations on the map clearly printed and readily legible? Are adequate explanations and instructions provided? Are textual portions of the map in English or in a foreign language?
10. Indexing. Does the map carry its own place-name index? Is there a separate index? A good index is very important in helping to locate points on the map and also in serving as a minigazetteer when trying to identify an elusive town.
11. Special features. Some maps carry extra bonuses such as mileage charts or enlarged inserts of important areas.
12. Format. What size is the map? How permanent is it? Is it flat, folded, or rolled? Will it present a housing problem?

Ordering. Order maps that reflect the interests of your users. Provide local and state maps.

Processing

Initial processing and labeling. Stamp and label in the same corner on the back of the maps. Be sure to indicate the source and date received. The date of publication is an important item that should be on the map.

Organization. Maps can be arranged by country, by continent, by subject, or numerically in the order they were accessioned. Items that may be considered in processing are subject, type of map, and size.

Housing. Large maps should be housed in large flat map cases. Alternatives include folding or rolling for storage in tubes.

Preservation and protection. Maps can be laminated or cloth backed. Both processes require a dry-mount press or laminator. Many maps are now available on plastic, so they are much more permanent than paper maps.

Management

Promotion. You should promote maps through displays and with patrons who travel, teach, or are involved in history, hobbies, community planning, or many other areas where a map would be helpful.

Circulation. Circulate maps as you would other vertical-file materials.

Weeding. Weed regularly. Maps should have dates printed on them, so you can often weed by date when changes have taken place in the area covered by the map.

CAREER COLLECTIONS

Interest in career information comes from all ages: Young children are fascinated with careers of policemen and astronauts; high-school and college students look for career information as they begin to think about their future; many adults change careers at mid-life; and many senior citizens are looking for ways to supplement their retirement income. Public and school libraries can make a big contribution to users by maintaining up-to-date, well-organized files of career material.

Acquisition

Sources. Many tools that are useful in selecting general vertical-file materials also provide information for vocational files. *Vertical File Index* lists career materials. Specialized guides include *Educators Guide to Free Guidance Materials, Vocational Guidance Quarterly, Counselor's Information Service,* and *Occupational Outlook Quarterly. Professional Careers Sourcebook: An Information Guide for Career Planning* (Detroit: Gale Research, 1990) provides additional resources.

Serial indexes and expensive specialized bibliographies are tools that should be examined before purchase if possible. Career information can be found in many places. School librarians may be able to borrow some titles from the counselors or district offices.

The U.S. government is a rich source for career information. Many agencies prepare pamphlets and leaflets about the career opportunities they offer. *Guide to Federal Career Literature* is a directory aimed at the college graduate or experienced adult and describes the principal publications used by various federal departments and agencies in nationwide recruiting. *Occupational Outlook Handbook* is comprehensive and revised biennially with additional references given at the end of each article. Reprints of some of the individual articles are available. It is supplemented and updated between editions by *Occupational Outlook Quarterly*.

State vocational materials that reflect conditions in a particular state are also important. Contact the employment office in your state to discover what publications it can provide for your career files. Government agencies that license or certify members of occupations (e.g., cosmetology, nursing, teaching) may have materials on requirements for entering the profession, and some may provide sample tests for your files.

Public libraries, academic libraries, and high-school libraries should arrange to receive announcements of license and position examinations as well as other descriptive literature available on jobs in the state civil service system. The announcements will inform patrons of immediate job openings and also help them to plan ahead for future job possibilities.

Local government units in large cities may have recruiting leaflets and examination announcements for local government positions. Local chambers of commerce often prepare lists of local industries, processors, and retail firms that are appropriate for career study as well as provide a record of community activity.

Organizations, societies, institutes, and associations provide free pamphlets and brochures describing career possibilities in their areas of activity. To locate names and addresses of organizations, the following will be useful: *Encyclopedia of Associations, Occupational Outlook Handbook*, and *Encyclopedia of Careers and Vocational Guidance*. In addition, the career briefs and monographs for sale by commercial publishers and career-counseling organizations often contain lists of associations connected with a particular occupation.

Large businesses and industries sometimes publish occupational brochures. They are usually designed to recruit people for their own company, but often they will present a detailed study of a career field or survey occupational opportunities in the industry as a whole. Although they tend to be generalized and overly optimistic, these company publications can be useful.

Brochures on career areas relating to programs offered by colleges and universities are often available from individual institutions. They usually describe the program of the school but can provide good general information about the vocation itself. Some colleges and universities have produced studies of current and future employment opportunities in the local community.

Magazines often run feature articles on interesting careers. This information is generally very current, so you may want to consider clipping it for your file. There will often be references to additional sources of information.

There are quite a number of commercial vocational aids, including *Chronicle Occupational Briefs* (Chronicle Guidance Publications, Inc.), *Chronicle Occupational Reprints* (Chronicle Guidance Publications, Inc.), and *Career Briefs* (Careers, Inc.). Publishers of career material frequently offer discounts for large-volume purchases. This can fill your file quickly, but it may also burden the library with unwanted and unused items. Consider the package plans carefully.

Selection. General selection principles for career materials should be considered with particular attention to the following: current information, a realistic approach, an appropriate style, and specific occupations. It is advisable to examine several selections from a career series before making an investment. Calculate what proportion of your total vocational budget you want to commit to a single series. Each series has its strengths and weaknesses.

Related information that can be grouped with career materials includes

1. College and trade-school catalogs.
2. Annual reports of corporations.
3. Files of local residents willing to talk to youth about their jobs.
4. Materials on labor-related laws.
5. Booklets on rehabilitation and employment of the handicapped.
6. Special training and placement programs for the unemployed.
7. Information about scholarships, fellowships, and student loans.
8. Part-time or summer job announcements.
9. Materials on service organizations, e.g., the Peace Corps.
10. Information on the military: air force, army, marines, navy, coast guard.

Ordering. Consider standing orders for purchased career materials to ensure that you get the latest information as soon as it is available.

Processing

Initial processing and labeling. Be sure that every item has a date printed or written on it.

Organization. The first option, particularly for small collections, is to put the materials in the general vertical file under Careers or Vocations.

Libraries that have a special collection of career materials have a number of ways to indicate the separate collection. The use of color is one way in which this can be done, for example, colored files, colored ink for marking, colored labels, or colored stars or dots. A special stamp marking materials Career File is useful and will not peel off. Whatever the distinguishing mark, it should be clear so that files do not mistakenly get misfiled in the wrong information file.

Within the collection there are several options for arrangement of career materials. Each of the following systems is based on an alphabetical or numerical arrangement.

Classification of job families (*Dictionary of Occupational Titles*) *system.* This system is based on the elaborate classification of job families and has the advantage of keeping related occupations in close physical proximity allowing a quick overview of jobs that share certain common elements. This correlation of jobs is particularly attractive to vocational guidance counselors. A disadvantage is that the alphabetical index must be used to find specific jobs; however, if the classification system is adhered to strictly, the index in the back of the volume can be used.

Subject, classified (Dewey Decimal Classification *or* Library of Congress). Materials arranged by this system could be placed on the open shelf in pamphlet boxes, in a special collection in pamphlet boxes, or arranged in files. This system requires an index but parallels the book collection.

Subject, alphabetical. If most of your patrons want information of a specific job and are not concerned with the relationship between job families, this is an arrangement to consider. If this system is adopted you have two methods of approach: (a) terms that describe the job (optometry, law) and (b) terms that describe the person (optometrist, lawyer, actor). The second system is preferred. You should be consistent in the approach you choose. Avoid general subject headings, e.g., Air Transportation or Restaurant Work. Consider using an alphabetical job index in the back of one of the standard career references. You can easily change the terms from the job to worker.

Curriculum-based. Some school counselors have argued for vocational files that are oriented to courses taught in the school. Using this as an arrangement guide presents problems and is not advisable. You could instead provide a list or index to materials under school subjects.

Preservation and protection. There is probably no need to worry about preservation for career materials; you should weed them before they become worn.

Housing. House in filing cabinets, pamphlet boxes in the career collection, or on classified shelves.

Management

Promotion. Your school or university may have a career fair that would be a good place to exhibit materials from your collection. A date near graduation or possibly in August when students are about to begin classes is a logical time for a career focus. Many subject exhibits can have an added element showing career possibilities in the field.

You may want to keep one bulletin board or exhibit area reserved for career materials and change the exhibit frequently. Using a few pamphlets or prepared materials from the career field and pictures of well-known people in the field and a few books, you can have an easy career series with very little preparation.

Circulation. People will want to check out career materials. It is a heavily used collection in many libraries, so you may want to limit circulation and provide a copy machine near the files.

Weeding. Keeping materials current by weeding outdated materials is extremely important. Generally, you should have nothing older than five years unless it is needed for historical purposes, and then it should be labeled. If you cannot keep your collection up-to-date, consider providing the information through a few choice reference books.

LOCAL HISTORY COLLECTIONS

One area for which many libraries have some responsibility is the collection of local history materials. This is not only a responsibility but an opportunity to collect information unique to the region, community, or institution. Public, academic, and school libraries will have patrons interested in broad topics of local history; special libraries may limit their collections to the history of their own institution.

Generally, archival materials should be handled by state or local archivists who are familiar with techniques for preservation and handling of those unique items. Cooperation and coordination with other groups such as historical associations, genealogical societies, museums, and universities is important to avoid duplication of efforts in some areas and to ensure that important materials are collected.[3]

Acquisition

Sources. Books about your area will help you to identify names and events that you should include as subjects in your file. Any special events or disasters should also be represented by a file in your collection. Local history is one area for which you may clip the local newspaper. A number of items will come to you as gifts.

Selection. Some obvious types of items to collect for local history include books about the area, pamphlets, articles, school yearbooks, telephone books, and books by local authors. Local history vertical-file items may include information about native or ethnic groups, pictures, postcards, maps, songs or poems about the area, annual reports of local groups, and obituaries. Other items frequently requested include obituary indexes, information on street-name origins, files of early cemetery inscriptions, early records of marriages, births and deaths, and information on local clubs and organizations. The checklist in figure 15.1 includes items that should be considered for preservation in the community.

Ordering. Gifts should be recorded in some type of file or log that includes the name and identity of the donor and a description of the gift including the quantity and condition. A form for gifts will be helpful to avoid any legal complications. The attorney for your institution can advise you on the content. Generally, it is not a good idea to accept items on an indefinite loan.

Processing

Initial processing and labeling. Be sure to record and identify each item by subject and date. Note the source.

Organization. You will most likely prefer an alphabetical subject approach to organizing your local history materials. Subjects may be subdivided chronologically. *New York Times Index* entries under New York State and New York City may be helpful in establishing subject headings. Use generous cross-references in your index.

*Selective Checklist of
Ingredients for Local History Collections**

County, city, village, or township governments

    Agendas or minutes of meetings

    Annual reports

    Budgets

    Charters

    Directories of officials

    Economic reviews

    Ordinances

    Organizational charts and booklets describing the functions of local government

    Population statistics

    Sample ballots

    Special surveys or studies of housing, recreation, etc.

    Reports on zoning and planning

School systems

    Annual reports

    Brochures issued when new buildings are opened

    Census reports of the schools

    Commencement programs

    Curriculum guides and studies

    Directories of teachers

    Evening school announcements

    Minutes of boards of education

    Publicity and programs for student activities such as plays and concerts

    Report card samples

    School publications

    Studies of future needs for buildings and capital improvements

    Superintendents' bulletins

---

*Based on Shirley Miller's list in *The Vertical File and Its Satellites*, 2d ed. (Littleton, Colorado: Libraries Unlimited, 1979), 133-35. Some of these items may be a part of your supplementary collection, some may be fully cataloged and processed, and some may be directed to the local or state historical group. Efforts in local history should be coordinated with related interest groups.

Fig. 15.1. Example of a checklist for local history.

Businesses and industries
- Account books
- Advertisements
- Annual reports
- Charters
- Company histories
- Financial statements
- House organs
- Newspaper articles on local businesses (major articles only)
- Patents (copies) that are key in the firm's development
- Sales catalogs
- Speeches describing business activities

Political parties, candidates, and interested citizens' groups
- Ads and program notes for political rallies and picnics
- Campaign leaflets
- Campaign speeches of importance
- Newsletters from local legislators
- Posters depicting candidates
- Records of county meetings of political parties
- Studies of candidates or campaign issues

Service, social, and hobby groups
- Constitutions and bylaws
- Exhibition catalogs of art or photography groups
- Histories (compiled) of the club or organization
- Literature for fund-raising campaigns
- Minutes of meetings
- Newsletters
- Program notes of theatrical or musical groups
- Rosters of members and officers

(Figure 15.1 continues on page 178.)

Religious institutions
    Anniversary publications
    Birth, baptismal, marriage, death, and burial records
    Brochures of groundbreakings or dedications
    Funeral orations for prominent citizens
    Membership lists
    Minutes of meetings of church officials
    Newsletters
    Records of clergymen who served the institution
    Sermons centered around local events or people

Personal papers and memorabilia (These must either represent prominent citizens or be old enough to justify inclusion because they give the flavor of a past era.)
    Account books
    Correspondence
    Diaries
    Diplomas
    Land grants, deeds, bills of sale
    Photographs
    Records of marriages, births, or deaths
    Scrapbooks
    Wills

Preservation and protection. Some local history materials will not be weeded, so you will probably want to put some effort into the protection of these items such as the use of acid-free storage materials, encapsulation, mounting, or laminating. Photocopies (within copyright law) should be considered for patron use of fragile materials. Metal paperclips, metal staples, rubber bands, and rubber cement should be avoided. Consult your state or local archivists for recommendations or consult the Library of Congress leaflets on preservation.

Housing. Materials can be stored in files, envelopes, or pockets in boxes or file cabinets. Consider using archival acid-free materials for items you expect to keep indefinitely.

Management

Promotion. Display parts of your collection with appropriate exhibits. Indicate that materials are from the local history file.

Circulation. Provide a photocopy machine instead of circulating your local history materials.

Weeding. Weed local history collections infrequently.

Three different examples of possible materials for special collections have been highlighted. Undoubtedly you have others in mind for your library. The interesting thing about special collections of supplementary materials is that they can vary so much.

In addition to providing variety, special collections present unique challenges and opportunities to provide in-depth resources for your users. They also provide the added advantage of permitting the patron to browse through like or related materials.

Special collections allow you to be creative within a system that is by nature very structured. If you see the need, respond to it. Another advantage of special collections is that by pulling like items together you have a group of materials that can be featured for public relations.

Outstanding, well-planned, carefully developed special collections can become realities in any library no matter how small. They are not expensive to create, but they can be extremely valuable to your library users and perhaps also to your region, state, or beyond.

NOTES

[1] There are many map libraries and a number of books written on map collections. One you may want to consult is Mary Larsgaard's *Map Librarianship*, 2d ed. (Littleton, Colorado: Libraries Unlimited, 1987).

[2] *World Newsmap of the Week* is designed for secondary schools, but the attention to current events will have appeal for adults as well. Display boards are available for rotating maps each week.

[3] Many libraries will leave the major collection of rare and historical materials to major libraries and historical collections and concentrate their efforts on currently published state materials. Some possible resources include the state handbook (often called the blue book), organizational charts of state government, and state telephone directories. Check with your state library for recommendations.

Appendix
Vendors

This list of vendors of materials and supplies related to vertical files, supplementary materials, and alternatives is a representative list and does not claim to be complete. The list was compiled from sources used as examples in the text, from examples used in Miller's *The Vertical File and Its Satellites*, and from sources the author was familiar with or discovered in the preparation of this work. Telephone numbers (800 toll-free numbers where possible) and FAX numbers are included if they were available. An explanation of the type of goods or services and/or examples of specific titles is included. Current prices for specific titles are included. Every attempt was made to provide the most current information, but the reader is cautioned that there will be changes.

AAA Foundation for Traffic Safety 1730 M Street N.W., Suite 401, Washington, D.C. 20036 (202-775-1456).
Catalog of booklets, reports, videos, slides, television, and radio spots.
Research Reports series. $2 each.

ABC School Supply, Inc. 3312 N. Berkeley Lake Road, P.O. Box 100019, Duluth, Georgia 30136 (800-669-4ABC) FAX 800-93FAX-US.
Flash cards for U.S. presidents, countries of the world, traffic signs and symbols, transportation, and famous places. Most sets are less than $5.50.

Accents Publications Service, Inc. 911 Silver Spring Avenue, Suite 202, Silver Spring, Maryland 20910 (301-588-5496) FAX 301-588-5249.
Distributor of U.S. government and association publications.

Alcoholics Anonymous World Services P.O. Box 459, Grand Central Station, New York, New York 10163 (212-686-1100).
Publications.

Aluminum Association, Inc. 900 19th Street N.W., Washington, D.C. 20006 (202-862-5100) FAX 202-862-5164.
Aluminum Recycling: Your Next Assignment. n.d. Video
Aluminum Recycling: America's Environmental Success Story. 1990. Free booklet.

American Association for Counseling and Development 5999 Stevenson Avenue, Alexandria, Virginia 22304 (800-347-6647).
Brochures (free samples), other publications, videos.

American Association for State and Local History 172 Second Avenue N, Suite 102, Nashville, Tennessee 37201 (612-255-2071).
Directory.

American Association for the Advancement of Science Reprint Sales, 1333 H Street N.W., Washington, D.C. 20005 (202-326-6500).
Reprints from *Science* magazine. $1 each.

American Association of Petroleum Geologists P.O. Box 979, Tulsa, Oklahoma 74101-0979 (918-584-2555).
Maps including the AAPG geological highway map series. $5-$8 each.

American Bar Association 750 N. Lake Shore Drive, Chicago, Illinois 60611 (312-988-5555).
Bill of Rights Bicentennial Resource Book. 1990. $6.95. (Also from ALA)
Passport to Legal Understanding: The Newsletter on Public Education Programs and Materials. 2 each year. Free.
Update on Law-Related Education. 3 per year for $12.95. Includes references to free and inexpensive materials.

American Chemical Society 1155 Sixteenth Street N.W., Washington, D.C. 20036 (202-872-4446).
Transcripts of radio program "Dimensions in Science." Free on request.

American Classical League Miami University, Oxford, Ohio 45056 (513-529-4116).
Books, pamphlets, greeting cards, coins, computer software, games, posters, maps, charts, slides, tape recordings, and other teaching materials related to Latin, Greek, and classical humanities.

American Council on Life Insurance 1001 Pennsylvania Avenue N.W., Washington, D.C. 20004 (202-624-2000) FAX 202-624-2319.
Pamphlets.

American Fiber Manufacturers Association, Inc. (formerly Man-Made Fiber Producers Association) 1150 Seventeenth Street N.W., Suite 310, Washington, D.C. 20036 (202-296-6508).
Man-Made Fibers Guide, 1988. Free.
List of resources.

American Forest Council (formerly American Forest Institute) 1250 Connecticut Avenue N.W., Suite 320, Washington, D.C. 20036 (202-463-2455).

American Hospital Association 840 N. Lake Shore Drive, Chicago, Illinois 60611 (312-280-6000).
Hospital Literature Index. Quarterly. $200/year.

American Humane Association P.O. Box 1266, Denver, Colorado 80201-1266 (303-695-0811).
Eight-page catalog of pamphlets, bookmarks, posters, flyers, audiovisuals, educational materials, and miscellaneous items. Free or inexpensive.

American Library Association 50 East Huron Street, Chicago, Illinois 60611 (800-545-2433) FAX 1-312-440-9374.
ALA Graphics Catalog. Including bibliographies, posters, buttons, banners and other promotional items, clip art.
Best Books for Young Adults Series. Annual. (Camera-ready sheets available)
Caldecott Medal Books. Annual.
Gotsick, Priscilla, et al. *Information for Everyday Survival: What You Need and Where to Get It.* Out of Print.
Newbery Medal Books. Annual.
Nonbook Media: Collection Management and User Services. 1987. $35.
Notable Books. Annual.
Outstanding Books for the College Bound Series (theater, biographies, fine arts, nonfiction, fiction). New edition 1991.
Quick Clips. Clip art for libraries.
Segal, Joseph P. *Evaluating and Weeding Collections in Small and Medium-Sized Public Libraries.* 1980.

American Paper Institute 260 Madison Avenue, New York, New York 10016 (212-340-0600).
Careers in the Paper Industry. Free 5-page reprint.
How Paper Came to America. 1987. Free poster.
How You Can Make Paper. 1985. Free leaflet.
Paper and Paper Manufacture. 1987. Free booklet.

American Psychological Association 1200 17th Street N.W., Washington, D.C. 20036 (202-955-7600).
Thesaurus of Psychological Index Terms. 6th edition. 1991.

American Quarter Horse Association P.O. Box 200, Amarillo, Texas 79168 (806-376-4811).
American Quarter Horse. Free chart.
For You, an American Quarter Horse. 1990. Free booklet.
Prime Time. List of free-loan films and videos.

American Universities Field Staff, Inc.
Fieldstaff Reports Series. Discontinued.

Applause Learning Resources & Goldsmith's Music Shop 57B Summit Drive, Smithtown, New York 11788-1515 (516-979-6670) FAX 516-979-9347.
Supplementary teaching materials elementary-adult for 31 foreign languages (primarily French, German, Italian, Latin, Russian, and Spanish) including books, periodicals, audiovisuals, posters, maps, educational games, stamps and coins, flash cards, computer software, art reproductions, flags, music. Free catalog.

Applause Video 85 Longview Road, Port Washington, New York 11050 (516-979-6670).
Great Performances on Video: Opera, Ballet, Theater, Concerts. Free catalog.

Argus Communications P.O. Box 6000, Allen, Texas 75002-1305 (800-527-4747).
Posters. $2.50 each; discount for quantity orders.
Postcards.

Arizona Educational Information System (AEIS) Bureau of Educational Research and Services, College of Education, Arizona State University, Tempe, Arizona 85287-2611 (800-525-0527) FAX 602-965-9423.
The Gold File Catalog. Gold Files each contain 60 to 100 pages of selected current journal articles related to a topic in education; some files include additional information on microfiche.

Arrow Map Inc. Myles Standish Industrial Park, 25 Constitution Drive, Taunton, Massachusetts 02780 (800-343-7500).
Folding pocket street maps, wall maps. Most $2-$5.

Art Extension Press 21 (formerly Artext) Box 389, Westport, Connecticut 06881 (203-531-7400).
Art prints. 3"x4" to 8"x10", 15 cents to $1.75 each.

Asia Society 725 Park Avenue, New York, New York 10021-5088 (212-288-6400) FAX 212-517-8315.
Focus on Asian Studies. $5-$7 each.
Asian Agenda Reports. Paper copies $5-$6.50 each.
Asian Updates (formerly Media Briefing Series). $4 each.
Free list of publications and educational materials.

Aristroplay P.O. Box 7529, Ann Arbor, Michigan 48107 (800-634-7738).
Various board and card games for fun and learning.
Card sets including inventors, Greek myths and legends, great women, American history and Black history, American authors, children's authors, fairy tales, Old Testament stories, painters, dinosaurs, geometry. $10 and under.
Board games including pollution, community, American history, classical myths, musical instruments, great composers, geography, architecture, dinosaurs, human anatomy, elections. $22 and under.

Automobile Quarterly 245 W. Main St., P.O. Box 348, Kutztown, Pennsylvania 19530-0348 (800-523-0236) FAX 215-375-8426.
Quatrefoil. Free magazine and sourcebook.
Pictures $4 each; posters $5.95 each.

Avery Aigner Products Division, 850 Algonquin Road, Schaumburg, Illinois 60173.
Quick Speller's Guide. Available at office supply companies.

Badge-A-Minit Department IN491, 348 North 30th Road, Box 800, La Salle, Illinois 61301 (800-223-4103)
Button maker. Prices start at $29.95.

Bank of America Dept. 3631, P.O. Box 37000, San Francisco, California 94137.
Small Business Reporter Series. $5 each.

Bantam Doubleday Dell Publishing Group Inc. 666 Fifth Avenue, New York, New York 10103.
Caplan, Frank, ed. *Parents' Yellow Pages*. Out of print.
Greenfield, Stanley *National Directory of Addresses and Telephone Numbers*. Out of print.
Weisinger, Mort *1001 Valuable Things You Can Get Free*. Out of print.

Bowker, R. R. 245 West 17th Street, New York, New York 10011 (800-521-8110) FAX 212-337-7157.
Magazines for Libraries. 7th ed. 1992. $139.95.
Magazines for Young People. 2nd ed. 1991. $34.95.
Annual Reports (Annual reports and 10K filing for 2,000 companies). Microfiche, monthly. $954 per year.

Brigham Young University David M. Kennedy Center for International Studies Publication Services, 280 Herald R. Clark Building, Provo, Utah 84602 (801-378-6528).
Building Bridges. Free catalog of publications.
Culturgram Series. $1 each; $40 for set of 100+
Ethnigram Series. $1 each.
Infogram Series. $1-$1.50 each.

Britannica Encyclopaedia Britannica Educational Corporation, 310 S. Michigan Avenue, Chicago, Illinois 60604 (800-554-9862) FAX 312-347-7903.
Study prints and other audiovisual items.

Bryan, Carol. *See* **Carol Bryan Imagines**.

CINAHL Information Systems 1509 Wilson Terrace, P.O. Box 871, Glendale, California 91209-0871 (818-409-8005).
Cumulative Index to Nursing and Allied Health Literature. Quarterly index to journals including some serials and pamphlets. Annual subscription is $220, but the Subject Heading List can be purchased for $35.

California Medical Association 221 Main Street, P.O. Box 7690, San Francisco, California 94120-7690 (415-541-0900).
Health Tips. 24/year. 2-4 page handout on health issues; permission to reproduce with credit to Association. Free.
Health Tips Index: A Directory of Health Education Publications Prepared by Physician Members of the California Medical Association. 1988, plus supplement. Free catalog listing back issues of *Health Tips*. Back issues $.30 each; $30 for complete set of 400+ titles in print.

Canadian Embassy Public Affairs Division, 501 Pennsylvania Avenue N.W., Washington, D.C. 20001 (202-682-1740).
Canada Today/Canada d'Aujourd'hui. Ceased publication.

Canadian Government Office of Tourism, Industry, Science & Technology Ottawa, Canada K1A-OH5.
Canada Travel Information. Free booklet.

Canadian Library Association 200 Elgin Street, Ottawa, ON K2P 1L5, Canada (613-232-9625).
Nonbook Materials: The Organization of Integrated Collections. 3d edition. 1989.

Career Guidance Foundation. 8090 Engineer Road, San Diego, California 92111.
College catalogs on microfiche.

Careers, Inc. 1211 10th St. SW, P.O. Box 135, Largo, Florida 34649-0135 (813-584-7333).
Career Guidance Index. 8/year for $11.50. Lists free and inexpensive materials.
Career Briefs. $1.25 each; $129 for set of 167; subscription (40/yr) $31.25.
Career Job Guides. $1 each; $55 for set of 90; subscription (20/yr) $9.
Career Reprints. $1 each; $66 for set of 100; subscription (20/yr) $11.50.
Career Summaries. $1 each; $167 for set of 341; subscription (80/yr) $38.75.

Carol Bryan Imagines 1000 Byus Drive, Charleston, West Virginia 25311.
The Library Imagination Paper. Quarterly for $24 per year. Clip art.

Celestial Arts P.O. Box 7123, Berkeley, California 94707 (800-841-2665).
Posters various sizes $3.50 to $14.95; some glow in the dark.

Center for Research and Development in Law Related Education (CRADLE) Wake Forest University School of Law, P.O. Box 7206 Reynolda Station, Winston-Salem, North Carolina 27109 (919-761-5872).
Sharing Lessons in Citizenship Education (SLICE). Catalog of teaching materials.

Chadwyck-Healey Inc. 1101 King Street, Alexandria, Virginia 22314 (703-683-4890).
Microfiche collections for art, pamphlets, playbills.
Museum of Modern Art Artists Scrapbooks and *Artists Files.* Vertical files on microfilm. 600+ microfiche for $3,900.
New York Public Library Artists File. Microfiche copy of the complete clippings file of over 1.5 million items. More than 10,000 microfiche for $22,800.
New York Public Library Print File. Vertical files on approximately 5,800 microfiche for $14,850.

Chase Manhattan Bank, N.A. 1 Chase Manhattan Plaza, New York, New York 10081.
Business in Brief. Discontinued.

Childswork/Childsplay Center for Applied Psychology, 3rd Floor 441 North 5th Street, Philadelphia, Pennsylvania 19123 (800-962-1141)
Games, puppets, toys, books, and other products geared toward the mental health of children.

Chronicle Guidance Publications, Inc. Aurora Street, P.O. Box 1190, Moravia, New York 13118-1190 (800-622-7284).
Occupational Briefs. $2 each or $213.25 for set of 600.
Occupational Reprints. $2 each or $62 for set of 125.
Professional Articles. $2 each or $63.60 for set of 145.

Cliffs Notes P.O. Box 80728, Lincoln, Nebraska 68501 (800-228-4078).
Study guides for literary works. More than 200 titles in the series. Most titles under $4. Hardbound set available from Moonbeam Publications, Inc.
Test preparation guides; 17 titles in the series.

Commission on the Bicentennial of the U.S. Constitution 808 Seventeenth Street N.W., Washington D.C. 20006 (202-USA-1787).
The Commission is scheduled to terminate December 31, 1991.
Constitution of the United States. Pocket-size. Free.
Constitution of the United States. Parchment. $.25 each.
Many other pamphlets, bibliographies, calendar, guides, posters, clip art, activities, newsletter, videos. *See also* **Center for Research and Development in Law Related Education (CRADLE)**

Congressional Quarterly, Inc. 1414 22nd Street N.W., Washington, D.C. 20037 (800-432-2250).
Editorial Research Reports. Weekly. Individual reports $7 each.
Catalog of publications.

Council of State Governments P.O. Box 11910, Iron Works Pike, Lexington, Kentucky 40578-9989 (606-231-1939).
State Administrative Officials Classified by Function. Published biennially. $30.

Cram, George F., Co., Inc. 301 South LaSalle Street, P.O. Box 426, Indianapolis, Indiana 46206 (317-635-5564).
Student Quick Reference for Social Studies. Paper atlas. $3.50.
Free catalog.

Creative Media Services P.O. Box 5955, Berkeley, California 94705.
Clip art.

Creative Publications 5040 West 111th Street, Oak Lawn, Illinois 60453 (800-624-0822).
Teaching aids including activity books, puppets, game components, posters, buttons, charts, etc. for mathematics, science, and some language arts. Free catalog.

Croner Publications, Inc. 211-05 Jamaica Avenue, Queens Village, New York 11428.
American Trade Schools Directory.

Curriculum Innovations Group P.O. Box 16504, Columbus, Ohio 43216-6504.
Career World. 9/year. $15.95.
Current Consumer & Lifestudies. 9/year. $15.95.
Current Health I. 9/year. $15.95.
Current Health II. 9/year. $15.95.
Current Health II Sexuality Supplement. 9/year. $1.95.
World Newsmap of the Week, incorporating *Headline Focus*. 30/year. $59.90.
Writing. 9/year. $15.95.

Data-Guide Inc. 154-01 Barclay Avenue, Flushing, New York 11355.
Single 8½"x11" plastic notebook insert charts of core facts about the particular subject. The Quick Chart series has more than 60 titles available at $2.50 each.

Defense Mapping Agency Customer Assistance Office, Director DMACSC, Attention PMA, Washington, D.C. 20315-0010 (800-826-0342).
Public Sale Catalog: Topographic Maps and Publications.
Public Sale Catalog: Aeronautical Charts and Publications.

Demco Box 7488, Madison, Wisconsin 53707 (800-356-1200) FAX 608-241-1799.
General library supplies and promotional items including posters, buttons, bulletin-board materials, puppets, bookmarks, games, face masks, activity books.
Book Preservation and Repair Guide. 1989. 36-page booklet. $2.49.
Book Preservation Workshop. Videotape. $59.95.

Denison, T. S., & Company, Inc. 9601 Newton Avenue South, Minneapolis, Minnesota 55431 (800-328-3831) FAX 612-888-9641.
Educational resource materials including charts, posters, activity books, bookmarks, storytelling apron, bulletin-board packages.

Detroit Institute of Arts Mail Order Sales, 5200 Woodward Avenue, Detroit, Michigan 48202 (313-833-7948).
Poster Collection. Flyer showing individual posters at $10 to $20 each.

Disclosure, Inc. 5161 River Road, Building 4, Bethesda, Maryland 20816 (301-951-1300) FAX 301-657-1962.
Company annual reports.

Dover Publications, Inc. 31 East 2nd Street, Mineola, New York 11501.
Complete Catalog of Books in All Fields. Also specialized catalogs.
Clip art, postcards, posters, books of masks, books of paper models, coloring books, books of stencils, calligraphy, prints, song books, musical scores.

Dow Jones & Company, Inc. Educational Service Bureau, P.O. Box 2000, Riverside, California 92516.
List of educational resources related to the *Wall Street Journal*.

Dramatists Play Service 440 Park Avenue South, New York, New York 10016 (212-683-8960).
Scripts for plays.

Eastman Kodak Company Department 412-L, Rochester, New York 14650-0608.
Finishing Prints on Kodak Water-Resistant Papers (No. E-67). 1990. $1.
Kodak Index to Photographic Information (L-1). $1.

Educational Resource & Research Service P.O. Box 66, Barnesville, Minnesota 56514 (800-752-4243).
Vertical-file materials on diskette for Apple computers.

Educational Resources 1550 Executive Drive, Elgin, Illinois 60123 (800-624-2926) FAX 708-888-8499.
Commercial computer programs and products.
Timeliner.

Educators Progress Service, Inc. 214 Center Street, Randolph, Wisconsin 53956.
Educators Grade Guide to Free Teaching Aids. Annual. $43.95.
Educators Guide to Free Audio and Video Materials. Annual. $23.95.
Educators Guide to Free Films. Annual. $27.95.
Educators Guide to Free Filmstrips and Slides. Annual. $20.50.
Educators Guide to Free Guidance Materials. Annual. $25.95.
Educators Guide to Free Health, PE and Recreational Materials. Annual. $26.50.
Educators Guide to Free Home Economics and Consumer Education Materials. Annual. $23.
Educators Guide to Free Science Materials. Annual. $26.25.
Educators Guide to Free Social Studies Materials. Annual. $27.95.
Educators Index of Free Materials. Annual. $45.75.
Elementary Teachers Guide to Free Curriculum Materials. Annual. $23.75.
Guide to Free Computer Materials. Annual. $36.95.

Ellison Lettering Machine P.O. Box 8209, Newport Beach, California 92658-8209 (714-724-0555) FAX 714-724-8548.
Ellison Lettering Machine. $300.
Cut-outs, borders, shapes.
Genovese, Sandi, and Lori McCaughey. *Cut It Out.* $6.50.
Jenkins, Lee. *Manipulatives.* $8.

Exxon Corporation P.O. Box 101, Florham Park, New Jersey 07932.
The Lamp. Quarterly magazine. Free.

Facts on File, Inc. 460 Park Avenue South, New York, New York 10016 (800-322-8755) FAX 800-678-FOF3.
There are many titles in the "on file" series; all have copyright-free illustrations; available in looseleaf notebooks designed to be copied.
American Historical Images on File series. Including prints, drawings, portraits, photographs, maps, charts, documents, paintings. $145 each. The series also includes *Faces of America*, I-IV. 300 portraits. $145 each set.

Charts on File. 300+ charts in the sciences, humanities, health for $145.
Design on File. 750 patterns and designs for $95.
Forms on File (Business and Personal) 2 volume set for $155; also individual.
Geography on File. 300+ maps, charts, and graphs for $145.
Historical Maps on File. 300+ maps for $145.
Human Body on File. $145.
Maps on File. 400+ maps for $165; updates for $35. Also *State Maps.*
Public Domain Software on File. 200 programs; Apple or IBM.
Science Experiments on File and *More Science Experiments on File.* $145.
Surgery on File Series. $85 each volume.
Time Lines on File. 300+ for $145.

Faxon, F. W. Company Inc.
Ireland, Norma O. *Pamphlet File in School, College, and Public Libraries.* Revised edition. 1954. Out of print.

Fearon/Janus 500 Harbor Boulevard, Belmont, California 94002 (800-877-4283).
High-interest, low-reading-level booklets for biography, health, lifeskills, vocational, etc.

Fearon Teacher Aids 1204 Buchanan St., Box 280, Carthage, Illinois 62321 (800-242-7272).
Books of forms, activities, maps, calendars, games, charts, projects, bulletin-board ideas, puzzles, puppets. Many items under $10.
Teacher Aids. Free catalog.

Field Museum of Natural History Roosevelt Road at Lake Shore Drive, Chicago, Illinois 60605 (312-922-9410).
In the Field: The Bulletin of the Field Museum of Natural History. Bimonthly. $6/year ($3 to schools).

Flags Unlimited 1490 Lake Drive S.E., Grand Rapids, Michigan 49506 (800-648-3993) FAX 616-458-0915.
U.S., International, and fun flags.

Ford Motor Company The American Road, P.O. Box 1899, Dearborn, Michigan 48121-1899.
A History of Measurement. Chart. Free.

Foster Manufacturing Company 414 N. 13th Street, Philadelphia, Pennsylvania 19108 (800-523-4855) FAX 215-625-0196.
Vertical file cabinets and storage envelopes in a variety of sizes.

Freeman, W. H. and Co., Inc. 41 Madison Avenue, 37th Floor, New York, New York 10010 (212-576-9400).
Scientific American. Reprints.

French, Samuel Inc. 45 West 25th Street, New York, New York 10016 (212-683-8960).
Scripts for plays.

Gale Research Inc. 835 Penobscot Bldg., Detroit, Michigan 48226-9948 (800-877-GALE).
Encyclopedia of Associations. 3 volumes. Annual.
Encyclopedia of Associations: Regional, State & Local Organizations. 5 volumes for $450, or $95 each region.
The International Portrait Gallery. 3,600 black-and-white portraits 8½"x11" published in 12 units between 1968-1983. No longer published.
Hobbyist Sourcebook. 1st edition. 1990. $49.95.
Newsletters in Print. 4th edition. 1991. $175. (Formerly *Newsletters Directory.*)
Professional Careers Sourcebook. 1st edition. 1990. $69.95.
Vocational Careers Sourcebook. 1st edition due 1992.

Gaylord Bros. Box 4901, Syracuse, New York 13221-4901 (800-634-6307) FAX 315-457-8387.
Library supplies.
Bookcraft: Protection, Maintenance and Repair of Library Materials. 1987. 32-page booklet. $2.95.

George F. Cram Co., Inc. *See* **Cram, George F., Co., Inc.**

Giant Photos, Inc. P.O. Box 406, Rockford, Illinois 61105 (800-826-2139).
Posters: "American Sign Language Alphabet" and "U.S. Currency & Coins."
"Geographer Wheel." $3.99.
"President Profile Wheel." $3.99.
Personalities in History. 3 sets of 64 portraits each set for $4.99 each.
Posters, portraits, maps, stickers. Free catalog.

Greenhaven Press, Inc. P.O. Box 289009, San Diego, California 92128-9009 (800-231-5163) FAX 619-485-9549.
Opposing Viewpoints Pamphlet Series. Each pamphlet is a chapter from an Opposing Viewpoints book. $2.95 each.
Opposing Viewpoints Sources Series. 100 viewpoints/sourcebook. Discontinued in 1991. Continued by Current Controversies Series.
Opposing Juniors Viewpoints Series. (Elementary/Junior High) 32-page booklets. $4.95 each. 12 different topics.
World History Program. 64 booklets. $2.45 each.

Haddad's Fine Arts, Inc. P.O. Box 3016-C Anaheim, California 92803 (800-9HADDAD).
Haddad's Reproductions Catalog. 5th ed. 400 pages, hardbound. $25.
Art posters and reproductions. $1.50 and up.

Hammond Incorporated 515 Valley Street, Maplewood, New Jersey 07040 (800-526-4953) FAX 201-763-7658.
Captain Atlas and the Globe Riders Series. 48-page booklet, chart in comic format. $6.95 each.
Smart Chart Series. Booklet, chart. $4.95 to $5.95 each.
Wall maps folded or rolled. $2.95 to $4.95.
Bartholomew world travel maps. Most under $10.
Hammond Education Catalog. Skills books, desk atlases, outline maps. Free.

Hannecke Display Systems, Inc. 370 Franklin Turnpike, Mahwah, New Jersey 07430 (800-345-8631).
Revolving displays for materials.

Hennepin County Library 12601 Ridgedale Drive, Minnetonka, Minnesota 55343 (612-541-8530).
HCL Cataloging Bulletin. 6 issues per year. $12.
HCL Authority File. Quarterly. $7.50 per cumulation. Microfiche.

Hershey Chocolate U.S.A. (125) Consumer Relations Department, P.O. Box 815, Hershey, Pennsylvania 17033-0815 (800-468-1714).
Miscellaneous items about the company and chocolate.

Highsmith Co., Inc. W5527 Highway 106, P.O. Box 800, Fort Atkinson, Wisconsin 53538-0800 (800-558-2110) FAX 414-563-7395.
General library supplies.
Highsmith Book Repairs. 4-page leaflet. Free.
Care & Repair: Book-Saving Techniques. 1990. 22-page booklet. $2.75.

Hogg Foundation for Mental Health The University of Texas, P.O. Box 7998, Austin, Texas 78713-7998.
Pamphlets, leaflets, cassette recordings.

Images of Excellence Foundation P.O. Box 1131, Boiling Springs, North Carolina 28017.
Images of Excellence. 6/year for $5.

Incentive Publications The Kids' Stuff People, 3835 Cleghorn Avenue, Nashville, Tennessee 37215 (800-421-2830).
Materials for early learning through middle grades. Free catalog. Many items under $10.
George Peabody College for Teachers. *Free and Inexpensive Learning Materials.* Last published in 1987. Out of print.

Information Plus (formerly Instructional Aides) 2812 Exchange Street, Wylie, Texas 75098-9990 (214-442-0167).
Paperback series containing statistics, polls, laws, court decisions, charts, tables. 8½"x11" format. 22 titles revised biennially. $18.95 to $23.95 each; discounts available.

International Reading Association 800 Barksdale Road, P.O. Box 8139, Newark, Delaware 19714-8139.
Catalog of Publications of books, booklets, bibliographies, and posters; some Spanish; free and inexpensive. Many brochures for parents.
100 Favorite Paperbacks 1989. Bibliography. Single copies free with SASE.
Children's Choices. Bibliography. Single copies free with SASE.
Magazines for Children. 1989. $5.25.
Teachers' Choices. Bibliography. Single copies free with SASE.
Young Adult's Choices. Bibliography. Single copies free with SASE.

Jackson-Hirsh, Inc. 700 Anthony Trail, Northbrook, Illinois 60062 (708-272-1844) FAX 708-272-3588.
Laminating pouches.

Journal Graphics 267 Broadway, New York, New York 10007 (212-227-7323).
Transcripts of over 70 different news documentary and public policy programs including "60 Minutes" and "20-20." $3-$5 each.

Kapco Library Products 930 Overhold Road, P.O. Box 626, Kent, Ohio 44240 (800-843-5368) FAX 800-843-5368.
Easy Cover, self-adhesive book covers. Free sample.
Easy Hold, magazine and pamphlet reinforcement. Free sample.
Easy Lam, no hassle laminating film. Free sample.

Knowledge Unlimited Box 52, Madison, Wisconsin 53701-0052 (800-356-2303).
Posters, art reproductions, charts, other educational audiovisuals.
Cartoons by Kids (editorial cartoons). $7.95.
Understanding and Creating Editorial Cartoons: A Resource Handbook. $29.95.

Kraus International Publications One Water Street, White Plains, New York 10601 (800-247-8519).
Annual collection of approximately 300 curriculum guides in microfiche.
Worldwide Bibliography of Art Exhibition Catalogs, 1963-1987. 3 volumes. Due 1992.

LEI, Inc. RD 1, Box 219, New Albany, Pennsylvania 18833 (717-746-1842).
Chase's Annual Events: Special Days, Weeks, and Months. $27.95.
Library PR News. Bimonthly for $26.95 per year. Ideas for promotion, clip art.
"Low Cost/No Cost Resources for Librarians and Teachers."

League of Women Voters of the United States 1730 M Street N.W., Washington, D.C. 20036 (202-429-1965).
Publications catalog.

Libraries Unlimited P.O. Box 6633, Englewood, Colorado 80155-6633 (800-237-6124) FAX 303-220-8843.
Bailey, William G. *Guide to Popular U.S. Government Publications*. 2d ed. 1990. $35.
Bradbury, Phil. *Border Clip Art for Libraries*. 1989. $26.
_____. *Holiday and Seasonal Border Clip Art*. 1990. $16.
_____. *Button Art: Reading and Libraries*. Coming in winter 1992. $27.50.
C. A. Cutter's Three-Figure Author Table. 1969.
C. A. Cutter's Two-Figure Author Table. 1969.
Cutter-Sanborn Three-Figure Author Table. 1969.
Ekhaml, Leticia T., and Alice J. Wittig. *U.S. Government Publications for the School Library Media Center*. 2d ed. 1991. $22.50.
Larsgaard, Mary Lynette. *Map Librarianship: An Introduction*. 2d ed. 1987. $43.50.

194 / Appendix—Vendors

Matthews, Judy Gay, Michael Mancarella, and Shirley Lambert. *ClipArt & Dynamic Designs for Libraries & Media Centers: Volume 1: Books & Basics.* 1987. $28.

_____. *ClipArt & Dynamic Designs for Libraries & Media Centers: Volume 2: Computers and Audiovisual.* 1989. $26.50.

Pokorny, Elizabeth J., and Suzanne M. Miller. *U.S. Government Documents: A Practical Guide for Non-Professionals in Academic and Public Libraries.* 1989.

Print Shop Graphics for Libraries. 9 volumes. For IBM, Apple, and Macintosh computers. 1987-1990. Including clip art, calendars, books and fonts, states and politics, American heritage, world nations, and history.

School Library Media Folders of Ideas for Library Excellence. A ready-made vertical file for library management with information sheets that are issued in loose-leaf format with subject headings printed on the side of the pages for easy filing and complete with file-folder labels. More than 100 ideas in each set. No. 1, 1989 and No. 2, 1991.

Slide Buyers' Guide: An International Directory of Slide Sources for Art and Architecture. 1985. $30.

Slote, Stanley J. *Weeding Library Collections.* 3d ed. 1990. $29.50.

Smallwood, Carol. *Exceptional Free Library Resource Materials.* 1986.

Smallwood, Carol. *Guide to Selected Federal Agency Programs and Publications for Librarians and Teachers.* 1986.

Spencer, Michael. *Free Publications for U.S. Government Agencies: A Guide.* 1989. $18.

Library Learning Resources, Inc. 61 Greenbriar Drive, Berkeley Heights, New Jersey 07922.

School Librarian's Workshop. Monthly except July and August. $40 per year.

Library of Congress Washington, D.C. 20540

_____. **Center for the Book** (202-707-5221).

Publications list, camera ready clip art, ideas for promotion.

_____. **Children's Literature Center** (202-707-5535).

Books for Children. Annual list.

_____. **Copyright Office** Washington, D.C. 10559 (202-707-9100).

Information kit of application forms, circulars, and regulations. Revised, 1990.

_____. **Geography and Map Division**

List of Publications.

Selected List of United States Dealers in Out of Print Maps and Atlases. Free.

_____. **Office for Subject Cataloging Policy**

Library of Congress Subject Headings.

_____. **Preservation Office.** (202-287-1840).

Marking Paper Manuscripts. (Preservation Leaflet No. 4) 1983. Free.

Newsprint and Its Preservation. (Preservation Leaflet No. 5) 1981. Free.

_____. **Publications** (202-707-5112).

Library of Congress Selected Publications, 1989-1990. Free catalog.

_____. **Science and Technology Div.** 10 First Street S.E., Washington, D.C. 20540.

LC Science Tracer Bullets. Literature guides; about 100 in print. Free.

Library Reference Service, Inc. 8225 44th Avenue West, Suite G, Mukilteo, Washington 98275 (800-622-9444).
LRS Vertical File Update. Information on products.
More than 80 topics available; each topic includes 25 reprints for $24.50. Available in print or on computer diskette (3.5 and 5.25 for IBM and Apple).

Library Research Associates, Inc. Dunderberg Road, RD#5, Box 41, Monroe, New York 10950 (914-783-1144).
Gilbert, K. *Picture Indexing for Local History Materials.* 1974. $4.
Perica, E. *Newspaper Indexing for Historical Societies, Colleges and High Schools.* 1975. $4.

Library Store, Inc. Box 964, 112 E. South Street, Tremont, Illinois 61568 (800-548-7204).
Catalog for general library supplies.

Life Skills Education Inc. 226 Libbey Parkway, Weymouth, Massachusetts 02189 (800-783-6743).
More than 100 different pamphlets on health, drug and alcohol education, family life, social awareness, job and vocational guidance. $1.50 each; $65 for 100 titles.

Magafile Company P.O. Box 66, 606 South Maple, Vandalia, Missouri 63382 (314-594-3713).
Heavy kraft-board protection for magazines, letters, books, pamphlets, sheet music available in a variety of sizes.

Malaysian Rubber Bureau United States of America, Malaysian Rubber Research & Development Board, 1925 K Street N.W., Washington, D.C. 20006-1163.
Leaflet with available videos and literature.

Marketing Information Guide 224 Seventh Street, Garden City, New York 11530.
Marketing Information Guide. Ceased publication.

Massachusetts Department of Public Health Office of Health Resources, 150 Tremont Street, Boston, Massachusetts 02111.
AIDS education and information resources directory.

McDonald Publishing Co., Inc. 10667 Midwest Industrial Boulevard, St. Louis, Missouri 63132 (800-772-8080).
Poster sets, exercises for all subject areas.

McFarland Box 611, Jefferson, North Carolina 28640.
Interesting People (Black history). Black-and-white prints with 100- to 150-word biography. Sets I-IV, 12 prints per set for $14.95.
Scott, Randall W. *Comic Librarianship: A Handbook.* 1990. $32 50.
Smallwood, Carol. *Current Issues Resource Builder.* 1989. $19.95.
_____. *Free Resource Builder for Librarians and Teachers.* 1986. $19.95.
_____. *Health Resource Builder.* 1988. $15.95.
Smith, Adeline M. *Free Magazines for Libraries.* 3d ed. 1989. $19.95.

McKinley Memorial Library Niles, Ohio 44446.
Stout, Chester. *Measurement of Document Exposure Time Distributions at a Small Public Library*. No longer available.

Metro Graphic Arts, Incorporated P.O. Box 7035, Grand Rapids, Michigan 49510.
City maps in pocket or booklet format. $1.95 to $3.50 each.

Metropolitan Life and Affiliated Companies. One Madison Avenue, New York, New York 10010-3690.
Health & Safety Educational Materials Catalog 1987-88; 1990 update. Free.

Metropolitan Museum of Art 82nd Street and Fifth Avenue, New York, New York 10028.
Metropolitan Museum of Art Bulletin. Quarterly magazine. $22/year. Some back issues available $1 to $4.75 each.
Publications catalog. Includes teachers' packets for several topics with kits of booklets, slides, posters, activities, etc.
Videotapes, booklets, school picture sets.

Michelin Travel Publications P.O. Box 19001, Greenville, South Carolina 29602-9001.
Free catalog of maps and guides. Most under $10.

Modern Talking Pictures 5000 Park Street North, St. Petersburg, Florida 33709 (800-243-MTPS) FAX 813-546-0681.
Free-loan films and videos.

Money Management Institute, Household International 2700 Sanders Road, Prospect Heights, Illinois 60670.
Personal Money Management Materials Catalog.
MMI Memo. Newsletter. Semiannual.
Booklets at $1.25 each or $12 set of 12.

Moonbeam Publications 18530 Mack Avenue, Grosse Pointe, Michigan 48236 (313-884-5255).
Distributes the bound collection of more than 200 Cliffs Notes booklets. *See* **Cliffs Notes** for individual booklets.

Music Stand 1 Rockdale Plaza, Lebanon, New Hampshire 03766 (802-295-7044) FAX 802-295-5080.
Catalog of gift ideas from the performing arts including posters, audio- and videotapes.

Nancy Renfro Studios P.O. Box 164226, Austin, Texas 78716 (512-472-2140).
Hand puppets, finger puppets, puppet books, and other miscellaneous puppet things.

National Aeronautics and Space Administration Code XEP, Washington, D.C. 20546.
NASA Report to Educators. Quarterly. Free.
NASA Educational Publications. Catalog of available materials.
Discover Aeronautics and Space: A Coloring Book. 1990.

National AIDS Information Clearinghouse P.O. Box 6003, Rockville, Maryland 20850 (800-458-5231) FAX 301-738-6616.
America Responds to AIDS. Catalog of pamphlets, booklets, posters, displays.
Catalog of HIV/AIDS Materials for Professionals. Catalog of brochures, pamphlets, etc.

National Archives and Records Administration Washington, D.C. 20408.
Sets of photographs and pictures from the National Archives.
Cartographic and Architectural Branch lists finding aids relating to cartographic and architectural records.
Series of booklets on milestone documents in United States history including a number of famous speeches such as the Emancipation Proclamation. 25 pages each. $2.50 each.
See also **Social Issues Resources Series (SIRS)** (Document Series).

National Association of Trade and Technical Schools 2251 Wisconsin Avenue N.W., Washington, D.C. 20007 (202-333-1021).
Career booklets.

National Audubon Society 613 Riversville Road, Greenwich, Connecticut 06831 (203-869-5272).
Audubon Adventures. Bimonthly; single issues $2.
"Wild Habitat" posters.
Other educational materials available.

National Clearinghouse for Alcohol and Drug Information, Office for Substance Abuse Prevention P.O. Box 2345, Rockville, Maryland 20852 (800-729-6686).
NCADI Publications. Catalog of posters, flyers, stickers, books, capsules, research monographs, updates and fact sheets, magazines, guidelines, reprints, free-loan videos. $1 per item, first 10 items free.

National Committee for the Prevention of Child Abuse 332 South Michigan Avenue, Suite 1600, Chicago, Illinois 60604-4357 (312-663-3520).
Materials for parents, children, educators.
NCPCA Catalog.

National Concrete Masonry Association P.O. Box 781, Herndon, Virginia 22070 (703-435-4900).

National Cotton Council of America P.O. Box 12285, Memphis, Tennessee 38182-0285 (901-274-9030).
List of booklets and leaflets, posters and charts, teaching kits, audiovisual aids.

198 / Appendix—Vendors

National Council for the Social Studies 3501 Newark Street N.W., Washington, D.C. 10016 (202-966-7840).
Publications catalog.
How to Do It Series. Classroom methods and techniques. $1.75-$2 each.
Social Education. 7/year. Individual issues focus on a specific topic. $5 each.

National Dairy Council 6300 North River Road, Rosemont, Illinois 60018-4233 (708-696-1860 ext. 220).
Nutrition educational materials for children, young adults, and adults. Curriculum materials, posters, pamphlets, videotapes, slides, and food models. Free and inexpensive.

National Education Association (NEA) P.O. Box 509, West Haven, Connecticut 06516 (203-934-2669).
Catalog including booklets, leaflets, and audiocassettes.

National Endowment for the Arts Public Information Office Room 803, Washington, D.C. 20506 (202-682-5400).
Publications List.
Research Reports. Many are free.

National Exchange Club 3050 Central Avenue, Toledo, Ohio 43606-1700 (419-535-3232).
National Crime Prevention Kit.

National Gallery of Art Publications Service, Washington, D.C. 20565 (202-737-4215).
Color Reproductions Catalogue. Various sizes. $.35 to $1 each.
Extension Programs. Slides, videotapes, 16mm films for loan.
Slides available for purchase. $2.50 each.
Videos available for purchase.

National Gallery of Canada 380 Sussex Drive, P.O. Box 427, Station A, Ottawa, Ontario, Canada K1N 9N4.
The Bookstore: Retail List. Postcards, posters, reproductions & assorted sidelines.
Fine Art Publications. Lists catalog for special collections. Many under $5.
Slide Catalogue. $12.

National Genealogical Society Education Division, 4527 17th Street North, Arlington, Virginia 22207-2363 (703-525-0050).
Genealogical charts and forms; research aids. Order form and price list.
Suggestions for Beginners in Genealogy. Leaflet.

National Geographic Society Educational Services, Department 90, Washington, D.C. 20036 (800-368-2728) FAX 301-921-1380.
Educational Services Catalog. Lists maps and charts $6 and under.
National Geographic. Monthly. $21/year. Maps.
National Geographic World. Monthly. $10.95/year. Posters, charts.

National Home Study Council 1601 18th Street N.W., Washington, D.C. 20009.
Facts about the National Home Study Council. Flyer. Includes NHSC publications order form.
Directory of Accredited Home Study Schools. Free.

National Mental Health Association 1021 Prince Street, Alexandria, Virginia 22314-2971 (703-684-7722) FAX 703-684-5968.
Coping series. Pamphlet series of nine titles. $2.75 sample set.
Federal Program and Legislative Summaries. $2 each.
Feelings and Your Child series. Pamphlet series of 14 titles. $3 sample set.
NMHA Publications and Merchandise Catalog. Pamphlets, clip art, posters, etc.

National Research Bureau, Inc. 310 South Michigan Avenue, Chicago, Illinois 60604 (800-456-4555).
Internal Publications Directory. Vol. 5 of *Working Press of the Nation.* $140.

National Science Teachers Association 1742 Connecticut Avenue N.W., Washington, D.C. 20009-1171 (202-328-5800).
NSTA Publications. Catalog of inexpensive print materials, posters, etc.
NSTA Supplement of Science Education Suppliers. 100-page directory; $3.

National Wildlife Federation Department 308, 1400 Sixteenth Street N.W., Washington, D.C. 20036-2266 (800-432-6564) FAX 703-442-7332.
NatureScope series. $7 each.
Nature games, puzzles, posters, etc. for elementary-age children.

National Women's History Project 7738 Bell Road, Windsor, California 95492-8518 (707-838-6000) FAX 707-838-0478.
Posters on Women Series. Five sets of eight 11"x17" posters/set. $28/set.
Woman of the Month Display Kit. Two sets of twenty-four 8"x10" photos with short biography. $12 per set.
Women from History Postcard Sets. Four sets of 10 cards per set 5½"x7¼" for $5.95 each.
Women Writers and Their Visions. 20 postcards, 4"x6", for $11.95.
Women's History Resources. Catalog of posters, display kits, classroom materials, books, videos, teacher training materials, buttons, balloons, pins, etc.

Neal-Schuman Publishers, Inc. 23 Leonard Street, New York, New York 10013 (212-925-8650).
Information America. 3 issues each year for $80.
Information America: Sources of Print and Nonprint Materials Available from Organizations, Industry, Government Agencies and Specialized Publishers. 2d ed. 1990. $150.

New Readers Press Publishing Division of Laubach Literacy International, 1320 Jamesville Avenue, Box 131, Syracuse, New York 13210 (800-448-8878) FAX 315-422-6369.
Catalog of life skills booklets and workbooks for new adult readers.

NewsBank, Inc. 58 Pine Street, New Canaan, Connecticut 06840-5408 (800-243-7694).
NewsBank. Newspaper clippings from more than 450 U.S. cities on microfiche with indexing available in paper or CD-ROM. Additional support materials include "Notes for the Reference Librarian," orientation materials for transparencies, bulletin-board displays, handouts, pathfinders, and promotional ideas.

Newsweek Education Program P.O. Box 414, Livingston, New Jersey 07039 (800-526-2595).
Programs for social studies, economics, English, English as a second language. Maps, resource units, videocassettes, computer software, curriculum guides, handbooks, resource files, skills-builders units, quizzes, and interaction newsletters. Free with classroom subscription to *Newsweek*. Directed to secondary schools.

Nystrom Division Herff Jones, Inc. 3333 Elston Avenue, Chicago, Illinois 60618 (800-621-8086) FAX 312-463-0515.
Atlas Moderno Universal. Spanish text. $3.75.
Richard Scarry's *Our Busy World*. 12 thematic posters in 3 sets of 4 each $39/set.
World Atlas: A Resource for Students. $3.75.
Catalog of resources for social studies, science, health, early childhood. Charts, models, maps, form-a-globe, flash cards, copymasters, markable study prints.

Oblique Division National Service Industries, Inc., P.O. Box 5735, Columbia, South Carolina 29250 (800-845-7068).
Filing systems in a variety of sizes.

Oceana Publications 75 Main Street, Dobbs Ferry, New York 10522 (914-693-5956) FAX 914-693-0402.
Gould, Geraldine, and Ithmer C. Wolfe. *How to Organize and Maintain the Library Picture/Pamphlet File*. 1968. Out of print.

Oryx Press 2214 North Central Avenue, Phoenix, Arizona 85004-1483 (800-457-6799).
Thesaurus of ERIC Descriptors. 12th ed. 1990.

Oxford Furniture division of **Esselte Pendaflex Corporation** 10 Caesar Place, Moonachie, New Jersey 07074 (800-733-4537).
Filing systems available through most office furniture suppliers.

Panhandle Eastern Corporation P.O. Box 1642, Houston, Texas 77251-1642 (713-627-5400).
Panhandle Magazine. Ceased publication.

Pendulum Press, Inc. 237 Saw Mill Road, Box 509, West Haven, Connecticut 06516 (203-933-2551).
Illustrated Classics Series includes novels, Shakespeare, biography, American history, and Spanish-language materials illustrated in a style appealing to comic book readers.

Penguin Inc. 40 West 23rd Street, New York, New York 10010 (800-331-4624).
  Lesko, Matthew. Information U.S.A. 3d edition, 1991. $24.95.

Perfection Form Company 1000 North Second Avenue, Logan, Iowa 51546 (800-831-4190) FAX 712-644-2392.
  International Readers' Newsletter. 8-page quarterly newsletter $5.95.
  Mythology Pictures. Set of 30 10"x13" for $10.95.
  Newbery Posters. Set of 20 posters 17"x22" for $52.
  United States Authors. 43 pictures 8½"x11" for $35.95.
  World Authors. 24 pictures 8½"x11" for $18.95.
  Author bookmarks, French and Spanish posters and charts, many language arts poster sets, literature posters, American literature maps, author bookmarks, British and American literature period posters, Shakespeare posters and bulletin-board kit, Globe Theater model, mythology bookmarks, Shakespeare illustrated classics (comic-style illustrations), games, muralettes, student journals, blank books, cassette tapes, transparencies, and other audiovisual items.

Permaseal Corporation 2124 Jody Road, Florence, South Carolina 29501 (800-845-4369).
  Pouch laminators and supplies.

Phi Delta Kappa Eighth Street and Union Avenue, P.O. Box 789, Bloomington, Indiana 47402-0789 (812-339-1156).
  Publications Catalogue. Lists education materials including Fastbacks, instructional programs, books, monographs, periodicals, videotapes, reports and reprints.
  Fastback Series. 16 booklets each year $.90 each or $8/year; back issues are available; liberal discounts.
  Hot Topics Series. 8½"x11" reprints of articles/reports; $20 each; discounts.
  Profiles of Excellence Series. $3-$5 each.
  Research Bulletins. Single copies free.

Playful Puppets Inc. 9002 Stoneleigh Ct., Fairfax, Virginia 22031 (703-280-5070).
  Hand puppets.

Public Affairs Committee, Inc.
  Public Affairs Pamphlets. No longer available.

Public Affairs Information Service (PAIS) 512 W. 43rd St., New York, New York 10036-4396 (800-288-PAIS).
  PAIS International in Print. Print, CD-ROM, or online.
  PAIS Subject Headings. 2d ed. $65.

Putnam Publishing Group 200 Madison Avenue, New York, New York 10016 (212-951-8400) FAX 212-213-6706.
  Free Things for Gardners. Out of print.

Q-Data Corporation 3336 36th Avenue North, St. Petersburg, Florida 33713.
  Q File of annual reports for corporations.

Quill Corporation 100 Schelter Road, Lincolnshire, Illinois 60069-3621 (708-634-8000) FAX 708-634-5708.

General office supplies including file folders, envelopes, packets, vertical-file frames, and hanging folders.

Booklets 40-60 pages each; discounts for quantity orders.
How to Compile and Maintain a Mailing List. 1988. $3.95.
How to File and Find It.
How to Save Money on Office Supplies. 1986. $3.95.
How to Win through Great Customer Service.
How to Write Effective Business Reports. 1987. $3.95.

R. R. Bowker. *See* **Bowker, R. R.**

Rand McNally & Company Box 7600, Chicago, Illinois 60680-9915 (800-678-7263).

Educational Publishing Catalog. Outline maps, globes, teaching kits, city and state road maps, flash cards, activity cards, wall maps, floor maps, and others.
China in Maps. $2.50.
Classroom Atlas. $3.30.
Historical Atlas of the World. $5.21.
Quick Reference World Atlas. $3.25.
Soviet Union in Maps. $2.50.
These United States. $3.30.
"United States Factfinder. Wheel." $5.21.
World Facts & Maps. 1990. $7.46.

Reader's Digest Reprint Department-HB, Box 406, Pleasantville, New York 10570 (914-241-5374/5369).

Reprints, posters, booklets.

Readex 58 Pine Street, New Canaan, Connecticut 06840 (800-223-4739) FAX 203-966-6254.

Readex Publications. U.S., United Nations, and international documents on microfiche and CD-ROM; current and historical collections.

Replogle Globes, Inc. 2801 South 25th Avenue, Broadview, Illinois 60153-4589 (708-343-0900) FAX 708-343-0923.

Globes and sundials.
The "3 in 1" Sundial. Cardboard, folds flat. $2.95.

Resources for the Future 1616 P Street N.W., Washington, D.C. 20036 (202-328-5000).

Reprint Series. Articles from journals and books; free.

Right on Programs 755-A New York Avenue, Huntington, New York 11743 (516-424-7777) FAX 516-424-7207.

Computer programs.
Magazine Article Filer. IBM and compatibles. $99.
Vertical File Locator. For IBM and compatibles and Apple series. $89.

Rivershore Library Store P.O. Box 3916, 2005 32nd Street, Rock Island, Illinois 61201 (309-788-7717).
Animal hand mask assortment. 13 masks for $13.
Clip-art books. 4 for $20.
Dinosaur hand masks. 9 masks for $9.
Inflatable globe. 16" for $8.95.
Newspaper poster set. 32 posters 17"x22" for $49.
Promotional items including buttons, puzzles, puppets, stamps, postcards, stickers.

Robert Morris Associates One Liberty Place, 1650 Market Street, Suite 2300, Philadelphia, Pennsylvania 19103-7398 (215-851-9155).
Products and Programs. Catalog of books, pamphlets, folders, cards, and videos.
Reprints from *Journal of Commercial Bank Lending.* $6 each.

Roth Publishing, Inc. 185 Great Neck Road, Great Neck, New York 11021 (516-466-3676).
Core microfiche collections.

Royal Bank of Canada Monthly Letter Department, Box 6001, Montreal, Quebec, Canada H3C 3A9.
Royal Bank Letter. Available in French or English. Free.

Running Press Book Publishers 125 South Twenty-second Street, Philadelphia, Pennsylvania 19103 (800-345-5359) FAX 215-568-2919.
Postcard Book Series. More than 30 titles available with 30 cards per book. $6.95-$7.95 each. There are many different topics covered.
Miniature Books series.

Samuel French Inc. *See* **French, Samuel Inc.**

Scarecrow Press, Inc. 52 Liberty Street, P.O. Box 4167, Metuchen, New Jersey 08840 (800-537-7107).
Crothers, J. Frances. *The Puppeteer's Library Guide: The Bibliographic Index to the Literature of the World Puppet Theater.* 1983. 2 volumes; $47.50 set.
Index of American Periodical Verse.
Smallwood, Carol. *An Educational Guide to the National Park Systems.* 1989. $39.50.
VOYA Occasional Papers Series.

Scholastic, Inc. Box 7502, 2931 East McCarty Street, Jefferson City, Missouri 65102 (800-325-6149).
Art and Man.

Seal Products, Incorporated 550 Spring Street, Naugatuck, Connecticut 06770-9985 (203-729-5201) FAX 203-729-5639.
Dry-mounting, laminating presses, Chartex cloth backing, mounting tissue, laminating film, laminating pouches.
Mounting, Laminating and Texturing. $11.95.

Seymour, Dale Publications P.O. Box 10888, Palo Alto, California 94303 (800-USA-1100).
    Posters, portraits, art, math, science, social studies, health, fine arts.
    Artist's Color Wheel and *The Pocket Guide to Mixing Color.* $5.75.
    Portraits for Classroom Bulletin Boards. 9 sets of 15 portraits for $6.95 each set.

Shaffer, Dale E. 437 Jennings Avenue, Salem, Ohio 44460 (216-337-3348).
    Career Education Pamphlets. Out of print.
    Library Picture File: A Complete System of How to Process and Organize. Out of print.
    Pamphlet Library: Use of the Sha-Frame System. Out of print.
    Posters for Teachers and Librarians. Out of print.
    Sourcebook of Teaching Aids Mostly Free. 4th ed. 1984. Out of print.

Shoe String Press, Inc. 925 Sherman Avenue, P.O. Box 4327, Hamden, Connecticut 06514 (203-248-6307).
    Dane, William J. *The Picture Collection: Subject Headings.* Out of print.
    Hill, Donna. *Picture File: A Manual and a Curriculum-Related Subject Heading List.* Out of print.

Simon & Schuster Inc. 1230 Avenue of the Americas, New York, New York 10020 (800-223-2348) FAX 800-445-6991.
    Big Book of Animal Masks. 1990. 12 die-cut masks for $8.95.
    Big Book of Monster Masks. 1990. 12 die-cut masks for $8.95.
    Color Craft Book series. 1990. $4.95 each.
    Nash, Bruce. *Freebies for Sports Fans.* 1990. $4.95.
    NOVABOOK series. 1990. $5.95 each.
    Planet Earth: A Pop-up Guide. 1989. $13.95.
    Pop-up Atlas of the World: A Globe in a Book. 1988. $12.95.
    Weather Pop-up Book. 1987. $12.95.

Smithsonian Institution Washington, D.C. 20560
    _____. **Office of Elementary and Secondary Education** Arts and Industries Building, Room 1163, Smithsonian Institution, Washington, D.C. 20560 (202-357-3049).
    List of resources.
    Art to Zoo. 4 per school year. Free.
    Generations: The Study Guide. Example of a study guide based on an exhibit.
    _____. **Office of Telecommunications** Natural History Building, Room C222B, Smithsonian Institution, Washington, D.C. 20560.
    Tapes of "Radio Smithsonian" (weekly radio program), "Smithsonian Galaxy" (short radio spots), television public service announcements, and feature films in art, history, and science.

Smithsonian Institution Press Blue Ridge Summit, Pennsylvania 17294-0900 (717-794-2148).
    Smithsonian Coloring Books Series. 1990. 10 titles for $2.95 each.
    Smithsonian Postcard Books Series. $4.95 each.

Social Issues Resources Series, Inc. (SIRS) P.O. Box 2348, Boca Raton, Florida 33427-2348 (800-232-7477).
Reprints, documents.
SIRS Global Perspectives. History, government, economics, and world affairs. 4 vols. annual. Loose-leaf or CD-ROM. New in October 1991.
SIRS Social Issues Resources Series basic set. 34 subjects; reprints of periodical and newspaper articles, special reports, and other relevant materials. Available in print and microfiche, updated every March. CD-ROM format beginning with 1989 articles.
SIRS Digest Series. Several subjects based on basic set with summaries of articles. For younger reader or new readers.
Science series.
Critical Issues series.
Documents Series. American historical documents units prepared by the Education Branch staff of the National Archives, about 50 reproductions each. 10 units at $40 each.
Photo Essays. 16 units with photos, map, study guide. $28 each.

Social Studies School Service 10200 Jefferson Boulevard, Room P7, P.O. Box 802, Culver City, California 90232-0802 (800-421-4246) FAX 213-839-2249.
Charts, posters, models, puzzles, games, flash cards, factfinder wheels, maps, pictures, and other materials related to social studies.

Society for Visual Education (SVE) 1345 Diversey Parkway, Chicago, Illinois 60614-1299 (800-829-1900).
Instructional materials.
Study prints. More than 40 different 18"x13" sets of 6 for $19.95.

T. S. Denison & Company, Inc. See **Denison, T. S., & Company, Inc.**

3-M Audio-Visual Division (800-328-1371 or 800-792-1072).
How to Present More Effectively and Win More Favorable Responses from More People in Less Time. Free.

Toronto Public Library Community Information Coordinators, 281 Front Street East, Toronto, Ontario, Canada M5A 4L2 (416-393-7516) FAX 416-393-7782.
Subject Headings for Vertical Files. 2d ed. 1971. New edition expected in 1992.

U.S.A. Today/Classline P.O. Box 500-CL, Washington, D.C. 20077-1575 (800-USA-0001).
Educational materials.

U-File-M Binder Mfg. Co., Inc. P.O. Box 183, Lafayette, New York 13084 (315-677-3310) FAX 315-677-5308.
Variety of custom designed file folders with various pockets, fasteners, binder strips, adhesive clips, color-coding systems, and tabs.

United Nations 2 United Nations Plaza, Sales Section, Publishing Division Room DC2-853, Department 701, New York, New York 10017 (800-553-3210) FAX 212-963-4116.
Publications Catalogue.
UNESCO Publications Catalogue.
United Nations Family; A Selected Bibliography. Annotated bibliography. 1990.
United Nations Film, Video, Television Catalogue. 1990-91.
United Nations Member States. Press Release. 90-13215.
United Nations Headquarters. Press Feature No. 217. 86-21978.
United Nations Conferences and Special Observances. Press Release, Reference Paper No. 29. 90-04651.
Flags of member states. $1.50 each; $2.10 with stand; complete set $240, $340 with stands. Also flag chart for $4.95; UN flag postcards $.20 each; $19.95 per set. From United Nations Gift Centre (212-963-7702).

U.S. Agency for International Development, Bureau for External Affairs Washington, D.C. 20523 (202-647-4330).
Front Lines. Monthly except January.

U.S. Department of Agriculture Washington, D.C. 20250-1300.
List of Available Publications. 1987. Reports, handbooks, bulletins, bibliographies, leaflets, and audiovisual aids. Inexpensive.
_____. **Agricultural Stabilization and Conservation Service** Field Office, P.O. Box 30010, Salt Lake City, Utah 84130-0010.
Aerial maps.
_____. **Forest Service** P.O. Box 96090, Washington, D.C. 20090-6090.
Investigating Your Environment; teaching materials. 1980.
Posters, flyers, booklets.
_____. **Soil Conservation Service** P.O. Box 2890, Washington, D.C. 10013.
Directory of State Offices. 1990. Address and telephone number for each state.
List of Published Soil Surveys. 1989.

U.S. Department of Commerce
_____. **Bureau of the Census.** Washington, D.C. 20233-0001 (301-763-4100) FAX 301-763-4794.
Census Catalog and Guide. Annual.
Factfinder series CFF 1-22. $5 for 22 brochures each describing the range of materials available on a given subject.
Special Maps of the United States. GE-70 Series.
Statistical Maps of the United States. GE-50 Series.
(Series titles may change with 1990 census materials.)
_____. **National Oceanic & Atmospheric Administration** National Ocean Service (N/CG33), Riverdale, Maryland 20737 (301-436-6990) FAX 301-436-6829.
Aeronautical Charts and Related Products. Catalog. Includes a list of NOAA authorized aeronautical chart sales agents. Most charts $2.75 to $5.25 each.

Nautical Charts & Miscellaneous Maps. Quarterly list. Most charts $13.25 each.
World, United States, and Historical Maps. Bibliography.

U.S. Department of Education
_____. **Office of Educational Research and Improvement** Information Services, Washington, D.C. 20208-5641.
OERI Publications Catalog.
Selected Current Publications of the Department of Education.
Effective Schools, Practices and Programs. Series of 5 titles for $3-$9 each.
Helping Parents Help Their Kids. Series of 10 titles for $.50-$1.75 each.
_____.**Educational Resources Information Center (ERIC)** 1600 Research Boulevard, Rockville, Maryland 20850 (1-800-USE ERIC).
ACCESS ERIC.
Resources in Education. Document collection on microfiche including curriculum guides.

U.S. Department of Energy National Energy Information Center, EI-231, Energy Information Administration, Forrestal Building, Washington, D.C. 20585 (202-586-8800).
EIA Publications Directory 1977-1989. A 398-page directory of documents with abstracts, indexed by subject, report number, and title. Instructions for ordering from the Government Printing Office (GPO) or the National Technical Information Service (NTIS). 1990. Free.
Energy Information Sheets (from NEIC) on various aspects of coal, electricity, petroleum, or natural gas. 20 titles 1 to 1½ pages each. Free.
Selected Sources of Energy-Related Material for School Children and Educators (from NEIC). Lists sources of free or low-cost energy-related educational materials. Free.

U.S. Department of Health & Human Services
_____. **National Institute of Mental Health** Office of Scientific Information, Room 15C-05, 5600 Fishers Lane, Rockville, Maryland 20857.
Publications list. Information on specific disorders, research, disaster assistance.
Plain Talk Series. 2-4 page leaflets.
_____. **Public Health Services. National Library of Medicine** 8600 Rockville Pike, Bethesda, Maryland 20894.
Current Bibliographies in Medicine Series. $2.50 each; $47 for 20/year.
Medical Subject Headings—Annotated Alphabetic List, 1992. $40.
National Library of Medicine News. Monthly. Free.
National Library of Medicine Publications. Catalog.
Specialized Bibliography Series. Available on request.
Recurring bibliographies, brochures, reports, fact sheets, pocket cards, hotlines.

U.S. Department of Labor, Bureau of Labor Statistics Washington, D.C. 20212.
Dictionary of Occupational Titles.
Occupational Outlook Handbook Reprints. 20 reprints for $24.

208 / Appendix – Vendors

U.S. Department of the Interior
　　_____. **Geological Survey** Reston, Virginia 22092.
　　　Catalog of Published Maps. Most maps under $10.
　　　Index to Topographic and Other Map Coverage. Available for each state.
　　　New Publications of the U.S. Geological Survey.
　　　Topographic Map Symbols. (National Mapping Division) Flyer.
　　_____. **National Park Service** P.O. Box 37127, Washington, D.C. 20013-7127.
　　　Publications from the National Park Service. Lists handbooks, brochures, posters, charts. Most publications under $6.
　　　National Parks: Index. 1989. 112-page book on the National Park Service. $3.
　　_____. **U.S. Fish and Wildlife Service**
　　　Wetlands Coloring Book (available from the Superintendent of Documents)
　　　Good example of copyright-free line drawings easily used for transparencies.

U.S. Department of Transportation
　American Honda presents DC Comics' Supergirl in cooperation with the U.S. Department of Transportation's National Safety Belt Campaign. "Super" comic book style addressed to young people.

U.S. Department of the Treasury
　　_____. **Bureau of Engraving and Printing** 14th and C Streets S.W., Washington, D.C. 20228.
　　　Bibliography of Numismatic Books & Periodicals. Free.
　　　Gettysburg Address. 10"x13". $10.
　　　Government Seals. $1.50.
　　　Large Presidential Portraits. 9"x12" $4.50 for set of 20.
　　　Portraits of Chief Justices. 6"x8" $4 for set of 14.
　　　Small Presidential Portraits. 6"x8" $4 for set of 39.
　　　Vignettes of Buildings. 6"x8" $4 for set of 16.
　　　Uncut currency for sale.
　　　Miscellaneous information. Free.
　　_____. **Internal Revenue Service**.
　　　Reproducible Federal Tax Forms for Use in Libraries. Annual. $31.

U.S. Government Printing Office Superintendent of Documents, Washington, D.C. 20402-9325.
　　Subject Bibliographies Series.
　　Government Organization Manual.
　　Congressional Directory.
From the Public Documents Distribution Center, Pueblo, Colorado 81009.
　　Consumer Information Catalog. Quarterly. Free.
　　Consumer's Resource Handbook. 1990. Free.
　　List of Federal Consumer Publications in Spanish. 1989. Free.

U.S. National Archives Trust Fund NEPS Dept. 725, P.O. Box 100793, Atlanta, Georgia 30384.
Aids for Genealogical Research. Catalog.
Documents Series. American historical documents units prepared by the Education Branch staff of the National Archives, about 50 reproductions each. 10 units at $40. Available from Social Issues Resources Series, Inc.
Family Tree. Chart.
Milestone Document Series. Booklets on great documents that have shaped the course of U.S. history. 10 to 36 pages each $2.50.
Photograph series.
Posters, facsimiles, postcards, booklets. $.25-$5.
Using Records in the National Archives for Genealogical Research. 25 pages.

U.S. News and World Report 2400 N Street N.W., Washington, D.C. 20037-1196.
Reprints such as "Report on America's Best Colleges."

U.S. Postal Service 475 L'Enfant Plaza S.W., Washington, D.C. 20260-0010 (202-268-2000).
See your local post office.

United States Space Foundation P.O. Box 1838, Colorado Springs, Colorado 80901-1838 (719-550-1000) FAX 719-550-1011.
Many free materials including guides, information sheets, photographs, fact sheets, booklets, posters, lesson-plan books. Numerous videotape programs available for the price of a videotape.

University Microfilms International 300 North Zeeb Road, Ann Arbor, Michigan 48106.
PhoneFiche and other microfiche and microfilm collections.

University of Washington Press P.O. Box 50096, Seattle, Washington 98145-5096 (800-441-4115).
Art Books and Exhibition Catalogues. Most exhibit catalogs at least $10.

University Prints 21 East Street, P.O. Box 485, Winchester, Massachusetts 01890 (617-729-8006).
Art reproductions.
The University Prints Catalogue. 246-page catalog listing 7,500 basic art history subjects by period, school, and artist. Available 5½"x8" around $.06 each in black-and-white or $.12 each color. Can be ordered in loose-leaf sets or custom-bound for visual textbooks or special collections. 1989. $3.
History of Painting in Color. 300 prints $36.
Special topics include visits to the ancient world, various countries and cities; literature and the classics; history and social studies; religion; fine arts and architecture; theater and performing arts; costumes; masks; photography and film; dance; and general topics including animals, birds, flowers, Indians, sports, and games.

Upstart 32 East Avenue, Hagerstown, Maryland 21740 (800-448-4887) FAX 301-797-1615.
Promotional posters, picture sets, bookmarks, buttons, bulletin-board materials, games, idea books.
Dewey Brochures. 50 for $9.95.

Vance Bibliographies 112 North Charter St., P.O. Box 229, Monticello, Illinois 61856 (217-762-3831).
Bibliographies. Most $3-$12.

Vocational Biographies P.O. Box 31, Sauk Centre, Minnesota 56378-0031 (800-255-0752) FAX 612-352-6750.
Career Titles Catalog. 875 career biographies in 4-page briefs suitable for filing (can also be ordered spiral-wire bound or hardbound) 20 percent revised each year.

Washington National Insurance Company Evanston, Illinois 60201 (312-570-5506).
George Washington material.

WatchMe Blossom Theater Works 109 SE Adler, Portland, Oregon 97214.
Puppets, puppet theaters, teaching aids.

Weber Costello 200 Academic Way, Troy, Missouri 63379 (800-238-6009) FAX 800-242-5329.
Educational materials including posters, study prints, maps, charts.

Wilson, H. W. Company 950 University Avenue, Bronx, New York 10452 (800-367-6770) FAX 212-590-1617.
For subject headings: *Art Index, Biological & Agricultural Index, Business Periodicals Index, Education Index, General Science Index, Humanities Index, Index to Legal Periodicals, Library Literature, Readers' Guide to Periodical Literature, Religion Indexes,* and *Social Sciences Index* available in paper and other formats.
Ball, Miriam Ogden. *Subject Headings for the Information File.* Out of print.
Basic Map Library. 30 maps $59.95.
Biography Index.
Canadian Supplement. 12 maps $29.95.
City Map Library. 37 maps $69.95.
Current Biography. Subscription $54/year.
Flannel Board Storytelling Book. $37.
How to Use the Readers' Guide Abstracts. Booklet. Free.
How to Use the Readers' Guide to Periodical Literature. Booklet. Free.
Sears List of Subject Headings. 1991. $42. Also Canadian, Spanish.
Vertical File Index. Subscription $47/yr. print; online.
Wilson Library Bulletin. Includes *Booktalker* insert.

World Book, Inc. Educational Services, Station 8, Merchandise Mart Plaza, Chicago, Illinois 60654 (800-621-8202).
A Student Guide to Better Writing, Speaking, and Research Skills.
Teaching Materials Catalog. Lists reprints of selected articles from World Book, posters, additional teaching/learning aids. Free and inexpensive items.

World Newsmap of the Week. *See* **Curriculum Innovations.**

World Wide Directory Product Sales Inc. 44 Kimler, Suite 100, St. Louis, Missouri 63043 (800-792-2665) FAX 800-848-9012.
Telephone directories and specialty directories starting at $3.

Zoobooks Wildlife Education, Ltd. P.O. Box 85271, San Diego, California 92138 (800-334-8152).
Zoobooks. Subscription for 10 monthly issues each year is $15.95 per year. Back issues are available in soft or hard cover for $2.25 and $10.95 each. Also posters, time chart, masks, stickers.

Glossary

A glossary is provided because the author assumes that some readers will be unfamiliar with some of the library and educational terms used in the acquisition, processing, and management of vertical-file materials. The words and phrases included are those encountered during the preparation of this volume. Sources for definitions are listed at the end of the section. The definitions given are those related to vertical files, special collections, and supplementary materials and are not intended to include all meanings.

abstract — A summary, usually 50 to 150 words.

academic library — A library of a college, university, or other academic institution for postsecondary education.

accession number — The number assigned to provide a numerical count of the total collection. Accessioning books, recording in a ledger, and assigning a consecutive number to each new item was a common practice some years ago but has been eliminated by many libraries today.

acid-free paper — Permanent, durable paper made to resist the effects of aging.

aerial chart — A special map showing geographic features required for air navigation. Essentially the same as an aeronautical chart.

aerial view — The view from the air; usually taken from a helicopter or plane.

aeronautical chart. *See* **aerial chart.**

ALA — American Library Association.

almanac — A publication with factual and statistical data; usually published every year.

alphameric. *See* **alphanumeric.**

alphanumeric — A combination of letters and numbers; the same as alphameric.

alternative publications — Publications that express views or treat subjects not normally presented in the daily or establishment press. May be politically or culturally right or left of center, but the left is usually emphasized. Sometimes called underground publications. (ALA)

annotation, annotated—A descriptive or explanatory note; with an accompanying note.

annual—Once a year (see also biannual and semiannual).

annual report—A report of the preceding year's activities. Publicly owned companies send annual reports, including financial statements, to all shareholders, in accordance with requirements of the Securities and Exchange Commission; nonprofit organizations send them to members, contributors, and other entities. (*Webster's*)

archives—1. The organized body of noncurrent records made or received in connection with the transaction of its affairs by a government or a government agency, an institution, organization, or other corporate body, and the personal papers of a family or individual, which are preserved because of their continuing value. 2. The agency responsible for selecting, preserving, and making available such materials. 3. The repository itself. In American usage, the term "archives" is a collective noun, though the form "archive" is increasingly seen. (ALA)

art paper—A high-grade printing paper with a highly finished surface good for reproducing halftones.

art print—An engraving, etching, lithograph, woodcut, etc. printed from the plate prepared by the artist. Compare with art reproduction. (ALA)

art reproduction—A mechanically reproduced copy of a work of art, generally as one of a commercial edition. Compare with art print. (ALA)

authority file—A file showing the accepted form of heading used for author or subject headings.

back file—The file of back issues of a periodical. (ALA)

back issue—A copy of a periodical earlier than the current one.

back order—An order that is not completed but is expected to be filled when missing items are available.

bar-coded label—A label containing machine-readable data in the form of vertical bars of varying widths and distances apart representing binary digits. (ALA)

bar code—The vertical bars containing machine-readable code representing a number. Bar-code numbers can be attached to library records for patron and library items.

biannual—Twice a year. Compare with biennial.

bibliographic information — The bibliographic information includes information such as the author, title, place of publication, publisher, and date of publication for the item.

bibliography — A list of resources usually including the author, title, place of publication, publisher, and date of publication. An annotated bibliography includes notes about each resource.

biennial — Every two years. Compare with biannual.

bimonthly — Every two months.

bindery — A company that binds materials.

binding — 1. Various methods by which leaves, sheets, sections, signatures, etc. are held together or affixed so that they will be usable and resistant to wear for a prolonged period. Major subcategories of binding are machine binding, mechanical binding, and hand binding. Binding operations often are grouped into three large series of operations; sewing or leaf affixing, forwarding, and finishing. Synonymous with book-binding. 2. The cover of a volume. (ALA)

biography file — A file with information about individuals.

biweekly — Every two weeks. Compare with semimonthly.

blanket order — A plan by which a vendor or wholesaler agrees to supply to a library one copy of all publications as they are published.

blind reference — A reference in a catalog or index to a heading that does not appear in the catalog or index. (ALA)

blurb — A description and recommendation of a book prepared by the publisher and generally appearing on the book jacket.

book jacket — A detachable, protective paper jacket placed around a book by the publisher. The jacket fits flush with the head and tail of the cover and is attached to the book by flaps folded over the fore-edges of the cover. Commonly contains a blurb, a biographical sketch of the author, quotes from reviews, and a list of other books by the author or issued by the same publisher. Synonymous with dust cover, dust jacket, dust wrapper, jacket, jacket cover. (ALA)

book-talk — A talk about a book or books usually given in the library by school librarians and children's and young adult librarians but also done in the classroom.

broadside — Originally a sheet of paper printed only on one side to be read unfolded. Now also used for various folded sheets printed on one or both sides. Synonymous with broadsheet. (ALA)

brochure — A pamphlet or booklet usually stapled or stitched; from the French *brocher*, "to stitch."

bug — The process of placing a theft detection strip in or on an item. *Tattle-tape*, a 3-M security system detection device, is an example of a "bug."

bulletin — 1. A periodical issued by a government department, a society, or an institution. 2. In a special library, a selective dissemination of information service in fields of interest to the host organization, produced and issued by the library, usually weekly or monthly, and with some form of subject arrangement. (ALA)

calligraphy — The art of beautiful writing.

CD-ROM — Compact Disc-Read Only Memory.

chapbook — 1. A small, cheap paperback book, usually containing a tale, legend, poem, or ballad of a popular, sensational, juvenile, moral or educational character. Chapbooks were sold by hawkers or "chapmen" in the 16th-18th centuries. 2. A modern pamphlet suggestive of this type of publication. (ALA)

chart — 1. An opaque sheet that exhibits data in the form of graphs or tables, or by the use of contours, shapes, or figures. 2. A special-purpose map, generally designed for navigation or other particular purposes, in which essential map information is combined with various other data critical to the intended use, e.g. aeronautical chart, hydrographic chart. (ALA)

checklist — 1. A finding list. 2. A finding aid, usually for a particular accession, created by an archival agency and consisting of a preliminary listing of records with or without summary description of their informational content. With the development of the record group concept, this finding aid evolved into the inventory. (ALA)

chronological order — Arranged by date, usually beginning with the earliest date.

citation — 1. A note referring to a work from which a passage is quoted or to some source as authority for a statement or proposition. 2. Especially in law books, a quotation from, or a reference to, statutes, decided cases, or other authorities. (ALA)

classification — 1. A series or system of classes arranged in some order according to some principle or conception, purpose, or interest or some combination of such. The term is applied to the arrangement either of the class names, or of the things, real or conceptual, that are so classified and the use of the name for the classifying or arranging of classes, or things, as a process or method. (ALA)

clip art — Previously existing drawings or other art that is cut out and used as illustration in a publication as opposed to art especially commissioned for the purpose for which it is drawn.

clipping file—A file of clippings from current newspapers, periodicals, and other sources arranged in some definite order in a vertical file. Its scope is usually determined by anticipated needs of potential users. (ALA)

cloth-back—A woven backing that can be applied to the back of a map or poster using a dry-mount press to bond it to the item. The cloth-back makes the paper less likely to tear.

cold lamination—Applying a protective plastic film on material without using a heat process.

comic book—A magazine, often printed on newsprint, consisting of a series of cartoon strips in a narrative sequence.

contour map—A topographic map that uses contour lines to show relief.

copyright—The legal provision of exclusive rights to reproduce and distribute a work. Under U.S. Public Law 94-553 (Sec. 106) these rights are granted to the author, composer, artist, etc. and with certain limitations are those of (1) reproduction; (2) preparation of derivative works; (3) distribution to the public by sale, rental, lease or lending; (4) public performance; and (5) public display. These rights may be transferred to others. (ALA)

copyright date—The year as it appears in the copyright notice. The 1976 U.S. Copyright Act (Public Law 94-553, Sec. 401) specifies that this will be the year of first publication. (ALA)

copyright-free—Not protected from copying. Copyright-free materials may be copied and used without getting permission from the author or publisher.

corporation file—In a special library, a file of materials about the activities, securities, etc. of individual companies, such as annual reports and other publications issued by the corporations, stock exchange listings, prospectuses, and clippings. In a financial library the term "corporation file" is generally used; in other kinds of special libraries the term "company file" is sometimes used because it covers any type of business enterprise. (ALA)

CREW—Continuous Review, Evaluation, and Weeding

cross-reference—A direction to another heading; either *see* or *see also*.

cumulation, cumulated—Combined into one. A cumulated index is one in which several earlier indexes are combined into one list.

curiosa—Books containing curious or unusual subject matter; sometimes used euphemistically for erotica.

curriculum guide—A written plan including one or more aspects of curriculum and instruction such as goals and objectives, resources, a variety of learning activities, and evaluation techniques. This plan may cover a single unit of instruction or may be used to describe the entire curriculum of a school district or an entire state. (ALA)

cut-corner pamphlet file—A box file that has the upper-back corners of the sides cut away diagonally to half the height of the box and with the upper half of the back and the top unenclosed. The file is designed to hold pamphlets, unbound issues of periodicals, and other materials unbound or in paper covers. (ALA)

Cutter number—An alphanumeric code for a main entry heading, the first word other than an article of the bibliographic description, the name of a biographee, etc., taken from or based on a Cutter Table or the Cutter-Sanborn Table and forming part of the book number assigned to a bibliographic item. (ALA)

Cutter Table—Either one of two tables constructed by Charles A. Cutter to provide an alphanumeric code for author names which, when included in call numbers as author marks, provides under each class number an alphabetical subarrangement by author. One of the tables uses two numerals in the author mark, the other, three. (ALA)

Cutter-Sanborn Table—A modification of the two-figure Cutter Table by Kate E. Sanborn; uses single letters and three numbers to provide symbols to be used as author marks. (ALA)

Dewey Decimal Classification—A system of dividing books into ten main subject areas with further subdivisions in each group.

dictionary arrangement—An alphabetical arrangement using one alphabet; as used in a dictionary.

digest—A summary or condensation of a work.

document—In its broadest sense a document can be any work or part of a work. It is often used to refer to government publications.

DOT—*Dictionary of Occupational Titles.*

drawing—An original representation by lines. A sketch or design made by pencil, pen, ink, crayon, or typewriter drawn on transparent or translucent material. (ALA)

dry mounting—The process of bonding two paper surfaces with a paraffin-treated sheet between them and heat and pressure applied. The sheet—dry mount tissue—is commonly used to bond a photograph or other art to a surface using a dry-mount press.

dummy—A piece of wood or other material shelved in the regular place of an item to indicate an alternate location.

dust jacket—*See* **book jacket.**

encapsulation—The process whereby a flat item is held between two sheets of transparent plastic film and sealed around the edges, providing protection. The process is a quick, simple, and completely reversible process that has become popular and has found wide acceptance among paper and other conservators.

ephemera—Materials of transitory interest and value, consisting generally of pamphlets or clippings that are usually kept for a limited time in vertical files.

ERIC—Educational Resources Information Center, an education-based center sponsored by the U.S. government.

ESL—English as a second language.

festschrift—A complimentary or memorial publication in the form of a collection of essays, addresses, or biographical, bibliographical, scientific, or other contributions, often embodying the results of research, issued in honor of a person, an institution, or a society, usually on the occasion of an anniversary celebration. (ALA)

file—A collection of related materials treated as one item and organized or arranged in a specific sequence to facilitate their storage and retrieval. It might be a group of library materials kept together for certain reasons or purposes, e.g., a group of extra large books in a file called oversize.

financial report—A report of an organization, giving income received and expenditures made, with balances of budget accounts for the period covered, with explanatory remarks.

finding aid—A guide or index to locating information.

finding code—A set of letters, numbers, or symbols used to arrange materials. In this case it refers to a classification system such as Dewey Decimal or Library of Congress.

finding list—A list of items in a collection, often with a brief description. A finding list for vertical files might simply list subject headings.

flannel board—A display panel or board covered with cotton flannel or wool cloth, which is used to display messages or cut-out images to tell a story.

flash card—A small card containing an image (words, numbers, pictures, etc.) designed to be displayed briefly for drill, recognition training, or in a teaching presentation. (ALA)

flipchart — A set of illustrations, usually hinged at the top so they can be flipped over during a presentation.

flowchart — A diagram using standard symbols to indicate a step-by-step process.

fugitive literature — Material printed in limited quantities and usually of immediate interest at the time of, or in the place of, publication, such as pamphlets, programs, and processed publications. (ALA)

geographic filing method — Arrangement by place: continent, country, state, city, etc.

graphic — A two-dimensional representation that can be opaque (e.g., art originals and reproductions, flash cards, photographs, drawings) or projected without motion (e.g., filmstrips, slides, transparencies).

gray literature — Difficult-to-define publications that are not usually available from book vendors. Examples are reports, technical notes, proceedings, reprints, and translations.

guidebook — A handbook for travelers that gives information about a city, region, or country, or a similar handbook about a building, museum, etc. (ALA)

handbill — A small sheet containing an advertisement, to be distributed by hand. (ALA)

hard copy — Data printed in human-readable form on paper or card stock by a machine such as a computer. Also in reprography, the original paper document or an enlarged copy of a microimage, usually on paper. Compare with soft copy. (ALA)

hearings — United States government publications in which are printed transcripts of testimony given before the various committees of Congress. Many hearings are not published. (ALA)

hierarchical classification system — A classification system in which classes divide from the general to the specific by gradations of likeness and difference. It begins with the assembly of groups of the principal divisions of knowledge into main classes, which form the basis for the development of the classification system. A characteristic of classification is used to divide main classes into divisions, which form a second hierarchical level of classes. The process is continued to divide divisions into subdivisions, subdivisions into sections, and sections into subsections, until further subdivision is impossible or impractical. (ALA)

holdings card — The catalog card which lists the parts received of a serial or multipart item. (ALA)

house organ, house magazine — Free publications of groups (companies, associations, and other groups) that promote the interest of the group. They can be "internal" or "external." The internal publications are intended for employees only and the external ones are for customers, stockholders, "friends" or the general public. Sometimes the magazine is designed for both audiences. It has been estimated that there are about 50,000 house magazines in the United States and Canada.

housing — How or where things are stored such as a box or file cabinet.

iconography — The study of the pictorial representation of persons or objects in portraits, statues, coins, etc.

index — A way to find material; generally an alphabetical list of subjects, authors, or titles with a reference to locate them.

indexed periodicals — Magazines, journals, or periodicals that have been analyzed by subject resulting in some form of index.

index vocabulary — A list of terms used in indexing. Example: *The Thesaurus of ERIC Descriptors*.

integrated shelving — Shelving materials — such as books and audiovisual materials — together regardless of format.

interfiling — The practice of filing together.

inverted subject headings — A subject heading with the words transposed, such as POETRY, AMERICAN.

IRA — International Reading Association.

issue — A single part of a periodical or newspaper, individually numbered and dated.

jobber — A wholesaler.

journal — Interchangeable with *magazine*, though the more scholarly ones are usually called journals.

Kardex — A metal cabinet of shallow drawers that hold cards for checking in materials that are received in successive parts.

lamination — A process of adhering a special transparent protective film to the image surface of a piece of two-dimensional material. The process usually involves some type of acetate, vinyl, or mylar film that has a transparent adhesive coating on one side. The film, depending on the type being used, may be applied by either a cold process or heat process and by hand or by machine. (ALA) See also **cold lamination**.

LC — Library of Congress.

leaflet — In a limited sense, a publication of two to four pages printed on a small sheet folded once, but not stitched or bound, the pages following the same sequence as in a book. In a broader sense, a small thin pamphlet. (ALA)

letterhead — Stationery on which the library's name and address is printed.

Library of Congress Classification — A subject classification system using an alphanumeric (alphabet letters and numbers) notation system.

libretto — The text of a musical work such as an opera or musical comedy.

LINK — Library Information NetworK (Anchorage).

local history — History of the community or the area.

manual — A compact book or handbook that serves as a guide for doing something.

map — A representation, normally to scale and on a flat medium, of a section of material or abstract features on, or in relation to, the surface of the earth or of another celestial body. (ALA)

microfiche — A 4"x6" sheet of film that can hold many pages of text; sometimes called fiche.

microfilm — A microform roll of film usually 32mm wide.

microform — A general term applied to all forms of microreproduction on film or paper, e.g., microfilm or microfiche.

monograph — An item complete in one part such as a book.

mounting. *See* **dry mounting.**

NCR paper — No carbon required.

newsbook — 1. A pamphlet of the sixteenth through seventeenth centuries relating current events. 2. After 1640 in England, a serial, usually weekly, consisting of various kinds of news and called *Diurnall, Mercurius, Intelligence,* etc. (ALA)

newsletter — A serial consisting of one or a few printed sheets containing news or information of interest chiefly to a special group.

offprint — A separately issued article, chapter, or other portion of a larger work, printed from the type or plates of the original, usually at the same time as the original. Synonymous with separate. Compare with reprint. (ALA)

OP — Out of print.

opaque projectors — A projector that projects flat, opaque objects including pictures, maps, books.

open shelves — Shelves with unrestricted access.

oral history — An aural record, or the transcript of an aural record, originally recorded on a magnetic medium, and the result of a planned oral interview. (ALA)

OS — Out of stock. The publisher has run out but may have it later.

outdated — No longer current.

overhead projector — A piece of equipment used to project transparent materials, usually 8½"x11".

PAIS — Public Affairs Information Service.

pamphlet — 1. An independent publication consisting of a few leaves of printed matter fastened together but not bound; usually enclosed in paper covers. 2. As defined by Unesco, a complete, unbound nonperiodical publication of at least 5 but not more than 48 pages, exclusive of the cover. Also called a brochure. 3. A brief controversial treatise on a topic of current interest, usually religious or political, common in England from the 16th to the 18th century. (ALA)

pamphlet boxes — A box for holding pamphlets. Sometimes called pam box.

pathfinder — A guide arranged in search-strategy order indicating various types of library resources.

periodical — A regularly published work; one that is issued periodically at regular intervals. Periodical and magazine are often used interchangeably.

photocopy — A reproduction, usually on paper.

photograph — A picture produced by light on a photosensitive material.

picture — A representation of an object, person, or scene usually produced by painting, drawing, or photographing. Or a printed reproduction of a painting, drawing, or photograph.

picture file — A collection of pictures, photographs, illustrations, art prints, and/or clippings.

picture loan collection — A collection of art reproductions that are available to borrow.

policy — An administrative plan or series of guidelines, preferably written, which delineate acceptable practices and actions for a wide range of activities within an organization. A library might have policies covering specific areas of activity, including circulation, information service, gifts, collection development, and cataloging, as well as system-wide policies in such areas as personnel. (ALA)

preservation — The activities associated with maintaining library and archival materials for use, either in their original physical form or in some other usable way. Compare with conservation, frequently used as a synonym, though distinction between the two terms seems to be emerging — at least in North America in the library and archive world. (ALA)

Princeton file — A box with the back, top, and lower portion of the front unenclosed, used for holding pamphlets, unbound issues of periodicals, and other material unbound or in paper covers. (ALA)

procedure — An administrative plan, either written or formalized by practice, which establishes the acceptable sequence of steps, actions, and methods for accomplishing a narrowly defined task in an efficient and effective manner.

realia — Actual items such as specimens, models, and other real items.

relief map — A map showing land or submarine bottom relief in terms of height above or below, by any method, such as contours, shading, or tinting.

remainder — The unsold copies of a book which the publisher disposes of as a lot to a distributor who will offer them for sale at a reduced price. (ALA)

replica — A copy or reproduction of an object, especially of a work of art produced by the artist of the original or under the supervision of the artist. (ALA)

report — 1. An official or formal record, as of some special investigation, of the activities of a corporate body, or of the proceedings of a legislative assembly. 2. A separately issued record of research results, research in progress, or other technical studies. In addition to its unique, issuer-supplied report number, it may also bear a grant number and accession or acquisition number supplied by a central report agency. 3. In the plural, publications giving judicial opinions or decisions. (ALA)

reprint — For vertical files: A separately issued article, chapter, or other portion of a previously published larger work, usually a reproduction of the original but sometimes made from a new setting of type. Compare with offprint.

rotary card file — A card file attached to a revolving drum or wheel that is rotated to view individual cards.

scope note — A note that explains the use of the term. Scope notes are found in subject-headings lists and classification systems to explain how the term relates to related subjects.

score — Printed music with all instrumental and/or vocal parts displayed.

script — The text of a play or motion picture.

semiannual — Twice a year.

semimonthly — Twice a month.

semiweekly — Twice a week.

serial — A publication issued in successive parts with numbers or dates indicated and intended to be continued indefinitely. Examples: periodicals and newspapers.

serial shelving — Shelving in sequence or in order of publication.

series — A group of separate items related to one another by the fact that each, in addition to its own title, shares a collective title applying to the group as a whole.

shelf list — Records for materials in the library arranged in the order in which the materials sit on the shelf. Generally a card file with one card for each title.

SIC — Standard Industrial Code.

SIRS — Social Issues Resources Series.

sleeve — A protective envelope sometimes called a jacket.

small presses — Specialized, regional, or alternative publishers that do a limited number of publications.

soft copy — Something not in final or hard-copy form, such as a manuscript. In computers it represents the visual representation on the computer screen as opposed to the hard copy on paper.

software — 1. The computer programs, routines, procedures, and other documentation associated with operating a computer system. 2. Audiovisual materials, such as motion picture films, slides, and video recordings, that require the use of audiovisual equipment for projection or playback. (ALA)

spine — The backbone of a book; the part of the book that faces the reader as the book stands on the shelf.

standing order — An order to a vendor for all publications of a certain series or type of publication as they are published.

226 / Glossary

star map — A map representing the heavens; a celestial map.

subject heading — An access point to a bibliographic record, consisting of a word or phrase which designates the subject of the work(s) contained in the bibliographic item. (ALA)

subscription — The arrangement by which, in return for a sum paid in advance, a periodical, newspaper, or other serial is provided for a specific number of issues. (ALA)

SuDocs number — The **Su**perintendent of **Doc**uments number assigned by the Government Printing Office for each individual document. The number indicates the issuing agency, office, series, etc. Some libraries organize their documents by the SuDocs number.

tabs — The top section of the file folder that extends for the purpose of providing a place for the label. You may also have side tabs in a notebook.

Tattle tape — The detection strip to mark materials when using a 3-M security system.

TDD — Telecommunications devices for the deaf.

tickler file — A memorandum file of matters (inquiries, requests, forthcoming publications, etc.) which should be followed up at a definite date in the future. Synonymous with follow-up file. (ALA)

time lines — A chronological list of events.

topical guides — Bibliographic guides that arrange in search-strategy order the various types of library resources available for doing a literature search on particular topics. Synonymous with pathfinders. An example of such a guide is the Library of Congress-produced *Tracer Bullets*.

topographic map — A map that shows the features of the earth's surface.

trade catalog — A catalog distributed by a manufacturer or publisher.

transparency — A transparent sheet of acetate or other material with printed, pictorial, or other graphic matter which can be displayed by means of transmitted rather than reflected light. (ALA)

underground publications — 1. Printed publications issued secretly by a group or movement organized usually to overthrow or undermine a governing authority or, in time of war, the power in authority. Synonymous with clandestine publications. 2. Sometimes used synonymously with alternative publications. (ALA)

vendor — A company or its representative that sells products or services.

vertical file—1. A collection of materials such as pamphlets, clippings, and pictures, which because of their shape and often their ephemeral nature, are filed vertically in drawers for easy reference. 2. A case of drawers in which materials may be filed vertically. (ALA)

videodisc—A video recording on a disc, usually plastic. The videodisc can be played back to reproduce pictures and sound, using a television receiver or monitor and a playback device similar to an audiodisc player. Synonymous with optical disc. (ALA)

visible index—1. A filing unit containing a series of metal frames, panels, or flat trays fitted with pockets for holding card records. The pockets are so arranged that approximately one-fourth inch of each card, which contains the index entry, is exposed. The units come in a variety of designs and configurations. Synonymous with visible file. 2. The collective records kept in such a file, mostly serial records and holdings information. (ALA) See also **Kardex**.

vocal score—In music, a score showing all vocal parts, with accompaniment, if any, arranged for keyboard instrument. (ALA)

weeding—The removal of unwanted items; items are usually weeded because they are old, worn, unused, out-of-date, or unsuitable. Weeding is based on content, age, need, use, and condition.

workbook—A learning guide, which may contain exercises, problems, practice materials, space for recording answers, and, frequently, means of evaluating work done. (ALA)

ALA—*The ALA Glossary of Library and Information Science*. Chicago: American Library Association, 1983. Material reprinted with permission.

ALAT—Soper, Mary Ellen. *The Librarian's Thesaurus*. Chicago: American Library Association, 1990.

Webster's—Weiner, Richard. *Webster's New World Dictionary of Media and Communications*. New York: Webster's New World, 1990.

Bibliography

The bibliography contains references to some of the literature about vertical files and free materials that the author encountered in this study. It is selective and does not contain everything found on vertical files. Some of the references in Shirley Miller's *The Vertical File and Its Satellites* are included, but most entries are new references from periodicals. Most sources of free and inexpensive materials are included in the list of vendors under the name of the company.

"ED" numbers indicate publications available on microfiche from the ERIC Document Reproduction Service (1-800-443-ERIC).

Abbott, Randy L., and Jonette Aarstad. "Vertical Files Still Standing Tall." *Unabashed Librarian* 72 (1989): 25-27.

Anthony, Susan C. *Facts Plus: An Almanac of Essential Information*. Anchorage, Alaska: Instructional Resources, 1991. An example of a compilation of the kinds of information that might be found in a vertical file in an elementary school.

Applegate, Rachel. "WordStar and the Vertical File." *Small Computers in Libraries* 7 (July 1987): 41-42.

Aubrey, Ruth H. *Selected Free Materials for Classroom Teachers*. 6th ed. Belmont, California: Fearon-Pitman Publishers, 1978. Out of print.

Automating the Newspaper Clipping Files: A Practical Guide. Washington, D.C.: Special Libraries Association, 1987.

Ball, Miriam Ogden. *Subject Headings for the Information File*. 8th ed. New York: H. W. Wilson, 1956. Out of print.

Bator, Eileen F. "Automating the Vertical File Index." *Special Libraries* 71 (November 1980): 485-91.

Bloomberg, Marty. "Reference Services: Special Materials and Services," in *Introduction to Public Services for Library Technicians*. 3d ed. Littleton, Colorado: Libraries Unlimited, 1981, 281-83.

Bolt, Nancy M. "The Vertical File Collection," in *The How-To-Do-It Manual for Small Libraries*. New York: Neal-Schuman Publishers, 1988, 185-89.

Book Preservation and Repair Guide. Madison, Wisconsin: Demco, 1989.

Buckingham, Betty Jo. "The Vertical File." Library Media Centers Mini-Bibs. Mini-Bib #13. Des Moines: Iowa State Department of Public Instruction, 1984. ED 247 955. A brief bibliography.

Carleton, Maureen O., and Catherine G. Cheves. "The Vertical File Enters the Electronic Age." *Medical References Services Quarterly* 8 (Winter 1989): 1-10. Report of integrating the vertical-file headings in the library's on-line catalog.

Cataloging Special Materials: Critiques and Innovations. Edited by Sanford Berman. Phoenix, Arizona: Oryx Press, 1986. Discusses special materials including comics and government documents.

Cernahan, Luella. *Subject Guide for the Vertical File of the Church Library.* Milwaukee, Wisconsin: Our Savior's Lutheran Church, 1961. Out of print.

Chang, Catherine S. "The Vertical File: Versatile Library Tools, So Why Aren't You Using Them?" *The Reference Librarian* 7-8 (Spring-Summer 1983): 201-4.

Classification System of the Public Affairs Reference Service. Rev. ed. Bloomington: Indiana University Bureau of Public Discussion, 1971. Out of print.

Collins, Barbara, and Ann Rogers. "Have You Tried the Vertical File?" *Tennessee Librarian* 33 (Fall 1981): 20-24.

Czopek, Vanessa. *The Vertical File.* Staff Report. Mesa, Arizona: Mesa Public Library, 1986. ED 275 344. Includes vertical-file guidelines.

Dane, William J. *The Picture Collection: Subject Headings.* 6th ed. Hamden, Connecticut: Shoe String Press, 1968. Out of print. First edition was in 1910 by John Cotton Dana.

Data Informer (Information U.S.A., P.O. Box 15700, Chevy Chase, MD 20815; 301-657-1200, $128 per year). Monthly newsletter from Matthew Lesko on sources of federal and state information sources.

"Dating Maps." *Unabashed Librarian* 74 (1990): 13-14. Suggestions to help understand the codes used by map publishers to date maps.

Davis, Nancy Harvey, and Pam Fitzgerald. "Literacy Clearinghouse." *Library Journal* 115 (9) (May 15, 1990): 25. Suggestions for collections of vertical file materials for new readers.

DeCandido, Keith R. A. "Get the Picture? A Serious Look at Comics in Libraries." *Library Journal* 116 (8) (May 1, 1991): 46-49.

Dennie, Donald D. "Pamphlets," in *Simplifying Work in Small Public Libraries.* Philadelphia, Penn.: Drexel Institute of Technology, 1965, 59-60.

"Developing a Curriculum-Based Vertical File." *School Librarians' Workshop* 12 (September 1991): 7-8.

Dixon, Rebecca, and Edmund D. Meyers, Jr. "Initial Experiences with an Online Catalog at the Boys Town Center Library." *Cataloging and Classification Quarterly* 2 (1982): 59-76.

Ehrenberg, Ralph E. *Archives and Manuscripts: Maps and Architectural Drawings*. Chicago: Society of American Archivists, 1982. Contains a good discussion of organization options and conservation techniques.

Ferguson, Elizabeth. "Pamphlets Are Worth the Trouble." *Wilson Library Bulletin* 33 (September 1958): 35-47.

Free Materials for Schools and Libraries (Department 284, Box C34069, Seattle, Washington 98124-1069; 604-734-0255). Five issues each year for $20. A selected number of materials have been reviewed by professionals and are recommended.

Freebies Magazine (P.O. Box 20283, Santa Barbara, California 93120. Bimonthly, $10.95/year). Includes many free samples as well as some items for library collections; of interest to the general public.

Freedman, Barbara. "Solving the Vertical File Buildup." *School Library Journal* 31 (January 1985): 41.

Garoogain, Andrew. "Freebie Cards Get Free Documents." *Unabashed Librarian* 11 (Spring 1974): 29.

_____. "Pamphlet Power." *LACUNY Journal* 3 (Spring 1974): 11-13.

George Peabody College for Teachers, Office of Educational Services. *Free and Inexpensive Learning Materials*. Nashville, Tennessee: Incentive Publications. Out of print.

Giganti, Carl J. "Pictures in a Small Library." *Wilson Library Bulletin* (November 1940): 225-29.

Goldsmith, S. "Defense Rests: Don't Sell Pamphlet Collections Short." *School Libraries* 18 (Summer 1969): 17-19.

Gould, Geraldine N. *How to Organize and Maintain the Library Picture/ Pamphlet File*. Dobbs Ferry, New York: Oceana Publications, 1968. Out of print.

Greenfield, Jane. "Pamphlet Binding," in *Books: Their Care and Repair*. New York: H. W. Wilson, 1983, 108-28. Detailed instructions for binding pamphlets.

Hahn, Doyne M. *Vertical File Selection Policy and Procedure Policy Manual*. Muncie, Indiana: Bracken Library, Ball State University, 1986. ED 285 583.

Haring, Jacqueline. "The College Arrangement" *Illinois Libraries*. 57 (March 1975): 226-30.

Haycock, Ken. *Free Magazines for Teachers and Librarians.* 2d ed. Toronto, Canada: Ontario Library Association, 1977. Out of print.

Hennepin County Library. *HCL Authority File.* Minnetonka, Minnesota: Hennepin County Library, quarterly microfiche. $7.50/year.

_____. *HCL Cataloging Bulletin.* Minnetonka, Minnesota: Hennepin County Library, bimonthly. $12/year.

Hill, Donna. *Picture File: A Manual and a Curriculum-Related Subject Heading List.* 2d rev. ed. Syracuse, New York: Gaylord Professional Publications, 1978. Out of print.

Hodgson, Tom, and Andrew Garoogain. "Special Collections in College Libraries: The Vertical File." *RSR* 9 (July/September 1981): 77-84. Includes good discussions of sources and use of vertical-file materials.

_____. *The Vertical File in the Libraries of the City University of New York: A Survey.* New York: City University of New York, 1981. ED 221 216. Report of 1974/75 survey.

Hughston, Milan. "Preserving the Ephemeral: New Access to Artists' Files, Vertical Files and Scrapbooks." *Art Documentation* 9, no. 4 (Winter 1990): 179-81.

"Index to Free & Inexpensive Materials," in *Information America.* New York: Neal-Schuman Publishers, 3/year.

Information America: Sources of Print and Nonprint Available from Organizations, Industry, Government Agencies and Specialized Publishers. Neal-Schuman Publishers. 3 issues/year for $80. Includes "Index to Free and Inexpensive Materials."

Information for Everyday Survival: What You Need and Where to Get It. Chicago: American Library Association, 1977. Out of print.

Intner, Sheila S., editor. *Policy and Practice in Bibliographic Control of Nonbook Media.* Chicago: American Library Association, 1987.

Ireland, Norma Olin. *The Pamphlet File in School, College, and Public Libraries.* Rev. enl. ed. Boston: F. W. Faxon, 1954. Still in print.

_____. *The Picture File in School, College and Public Libraries.* Rev. enl. ed. Boston: F. W. Faxon, 1952. Still in print.

Knowles, Em Claire, and others. "Vertical File Subject Headings KWIK List." Davis: University of California, Davis, 1984. ED 244 627.

Kouns, Betty. "Clipping and 'Sweet Talk' for Free Information." *Library Journal* 104 (April 15, 1979): 897.

Lane, D. "Your Pamphlet File Supports Apartheid; To Avoid Misinformation about South Africa, Use Alternative Sources." *Library Journal* 115 (September 1, 1990): 174-77.

Lee, Frank. "Dead End for Documents—Alternatives to the Vertical File." *Public Library Quarterly* 6 (Fall 1985): 51-55. Practical suggestions for processing, publicizing, and using government documents.

Lesko, Matthew. *Information U.S.A.* Rev. ed. New York: Viking, 1986. The third edition was due in 1991.

Library of Congress. *Free and Inexpensive Materials: A Selected List of Guides to Sources.* GR & B Series, no. 3. Rev. ed. 1980.

Lovenburg, Susan L., and Frederick W. Stoss. "The Fugitive Literature of Acid Rain: Making Use of Nonconventional Information Sources in a Vertical File." *RSR* 16 (1988): 95-104.

Makepeace, Chris E. *Ephemera: A Book on Its Collection, Conservation, and Use.* Brookfield, Vermont: Gower, 1985.

Malyshev, Nina Alexis. "Concept and Reality: Managing Pikes Peak Library District's Community Resource and Information System." *RSR* 16 (1988): 7-12. Library information databases for agencies, calendars, clubs, courses, daycare, local documents, local authors, senior housing options, and socioeconomic indicators. An alternative to vertical files for certain types of community information.

Mason, Robert S. *Free and Cheap Resources for Schools.* London: The Library Association, 1984. British focus.

McVety, Margaret A. *The Vertical File.* Woodstock, Vermont: Elm Tree Press, 1915. Out of print.

Miller, Bruce. *Sources of Free and Inexpensive Teaching Aids.* Riverside, California: Bruce Miller, 1959. Out of print.

Miller, Shirley. "From Abacus to Zoos, or the Care and Feeding of the Vertical File." *Library Journal* 92 (December 15, 1967): 447-79.

_____. *The Vertical File and Its Satellites: A Handbook of Acquisition, Processing, and Organization.* 2d ed. Littleton, Colorado: Libraries Unlimited, 1979. Out of print.

_____. *The Vertical File and Its Satellites: A Handbook of Acquisition, Processing, and Organization.* Littleton, Colorado: Libraries Unlimited, 1971. Out of print.

Myers, Mildred, and Jean S. Adelman. "Pamphlets," in *Encyclopedia of Library and Information Science.* Vol. 21. New York: Marcel Dekker, 299-309.

Nonbook Media: Collection Management and User Services. Chicago: American Library Association, 1987. An excellent resource.

Noordhof, Margaret. "Indexing with AUTHEX." *Computers in Libraries* 11, no. 1 (January 1991): 25-26.

Pearson, Otillia M. "Planning for Preserving the Schomburg Center Vertical File via Microfiche." *Microform Review* 5 (January 1976): 25-33.

Pepe, Thomas J. *Free and Inexpensive Teaching Aids*. 4th rev. ed. New York: Dover, 1970. Out of print.

Phalen, Heather. "Supplementary Resources for Enhancing Reference Service." *Ohio Library Association Bulletin* 55 (July 1985): 17-19.

Schmidt, Jean M., and John S. Wilson. "Out of the Shoebox: Publishing a Regional Periodical Index Using a Microcomputer." *RSR* 16 (1988): 13-20. An alternative to the vertical file.

Shaffer, Dale Eugene. *Library Picture File: A Complete System of How to Process and Organize*. Salem, Ohio: D. E. Shaffer, 1970. Out of print.

_____. *The Pamphlet Library (Use of the SHA-FRAME System)*. [Salem, Ohio]: D. E. Shaffer, 1972. Out of print.

_____. *Posters for Teachers and Librarians: A SourceBook of Free and Inexpensive Items*. Salem, Ohio: D. E. Shaffer, 1978. Out of print.

Slote, Stanley J. *Weeding Library Collections*. 3d edition. Englewood, Colorado: Libraries Unlimited, 1989.

Smallwood, Carol. "Physical Management Tips," in *Free Resource Builder for Librarians and Teachers*. Jefferson, North Carolina: McFarland, 1986, 250-53.

_____. "School Library Vertical File." *School Library Media Activities Monthly* 6 (7): 34-35. Carol Smallwood's books are listed in the vendor section, under Libraries Unlimited, McFarland, and Scarecrow Press.

Snyder, Doris. "A Supplementary Pamphlet File in an Academic Library." *Oklahoma Librarian* 24 (October 1974): 8-17ff.

Stavis, Ruth. "Creating a Publisher's Catalog Database in a Curriculum Materials Center." *Education Libraries* 14 (Spring 1989): 68-70.

Still, Julie. "The Vertical File in Academic Libraries." *Show-Me Libraries* 39 (Spring 1988): 36-38.

Strauss, Diane Wheeler. "Free Vertical File Materials for Business Collections," in *Handbook of Business Information: A Guide for Librarians, Students, and Researchers*. Englewood, Colorado: Libraries Unlimited, 1988, 480-99.

_____. "Vertical File Collections," in *Handbook of Business Information: A Guide for Librarians, Students, and Researchers*. Englewood, Colorado: Libraries Unlimited, 1988, 143-54.

Subject Bibliographies of Government Publications: A Compilation of Books, Reports, and Pamphlets Available from the U.S. Government Printing Office at the Time of Their Publication. Detroit, Michigan: Omnigraphics, 1989.

Subject Headings for Vertical Files. 2d ed. Toronto, Canada: Toronto Public Libraries, 1971.

Thomas, Joy. "Rejuvenating the Pamphlet File in an Academic Library." *Library Journal* 110 (October 15, 1985): 43-45.

Thompson, Enid T. *Local History Collections: A Manual for Librarians.* Nashville, Tennessee: American Association for State and Local History, 1978. Still in print.

Vertical File (Videotape). Denver, Colorado: University of Denver Center for Communications and Information Research, 1976.

Vertical File Index. See the vendors section.

Weihs, Jean Riddle. *Nonbook Materials: The Organization of Integrated Collections.* 3d ed. Ottawa, Canada: Canadian Library Association, 1989.

Weisinger, Thelma. *1001 Valuable Things You Can Get Free.* 12th ed. New York: Bantam Books, 1982. Out of print.

Wells, Dorothy. "Vertical File Sources." *RQ* 10 (Winter 1970): 150-55.

_____. "Vertical File Usage: A Comparative Study." *Focus on Indiana Libraries* 29 (Spring 1975): 26-27.

Woodbury, Marda. "Free Materials and Their Costs," in *Selecting Materials for Instruction.* Littleton, Colorado: Libraries Unlimited, 1980, 13-30.

Worden, Diane D. "A Cooperative Conversion Project from Vertical File Hardcopy to Jacketed Microfiche." *Special Libraries* 73 (July 1981): 270-76.

Index

ABC School Supply, Inc., 144
Abstract, defined, 213
Academic library, defined, 213
Accents Publications Service, Inc., 31, 181
Access, 62
Accession number, 34, 39, 67
   defined, 213
Acid-free paper, 115
   defined, 213
Acquisition order, 40
Adhesive, 51
Advertising, 62
Aerial chart
   defined, 213
   sources, 188, 206
Aeronautical chart, 213
Aeronautical Charts and Publications, 188
Aeronautical Charts and Related Products, 206
Age of materials, 69. See also Weeding
Agency for International Development, 206
Agricultural Stabilization and Conservation Service, 206
AIDS
   education, 195
   sources of material, 17, 136, 195, 197
AIDS Information Clearinghouse, 197
Airlines, 132
ALA. See American Library Association
ALA bibliographies, 79
ALA Glossary of Library and Information Science, 227
ALA Graphics, 154
ALA Graphics Catalog, 183
Alcohol and Alcoholism, 181, 195, 197
Alcoholics Anonymous World Services, 181. See also National Clearinghouse for Alcohol and Drug Information
Almanac
   association information, 77
   defined, 213
   embassy information, 141

Alphabet styles, 166
Alphabetical arrangement, 37
Alphameric. See Alphanumeric
Alphanumeric, 37, 222
   defined, 213
Alternative publications, 1, 226
   defined, 213
Aluminum Recycling: Your Next Assignment, 181
Amazing Spider-Man, 89
America Responds to AIDS, 197
American Association for State and Local History, 23, 182, 235
American Association for the Advancement of Sciences, 122, 182
American Association of Petroleum Geologists, 23, 169, 182
American Automobile Association, 169
American Bar Association, 23, 182
American Classical League, 20, 182
American Fiber Manufacturers Association, 20, 182
American Historical Image on File series, 134, 136, 189
American history, 90, 184
American Hospital Association Library, 22, 182
American Hospital Association Resource Center, 22
American Humane Association, 21, 182
American Library Association (ALA), 1, 55, 71, 79, 134, 150, 151, 157, 183 213, 227, 232
American Psychological Association, 43, 183
American Quarter Horse, 183
American Trade Schools Directory, 187
Annotated, defined, 214
Annual reports, 6, 74-75, 217
   circulation, 65, 75
   defined, 214
   housing, 56, 75
   orders, 30

Annual reports—*Continued*
  orders, 30
  sources, 134, 185, 188, 201
  special collections, 167-68
    career collections, 173
    local history, 175, 176, 177
Annual weeding, 70. *See also* Weeding
Annual, defined, 214
Appeal, 62
Architecture, 184
Archives, defined, 214
Archives & Manuscripts: Maps and Architectural Drawings, 54
Argus Communications, 117, 118, 119, 184
Argus Posters, 117
Aristoplay, 144, 184
Arizona Educational Information System, 31, 184
Arizona State University, 31, 184
Art, 43, 61, 117, 143-44
Art & Man, 76, 203
Art Books and Exhibition Catalogues, 209
Art Extension Press, 184
Art Index, 43, 210
Art paper, defined, 214
Art print, 184, 195, 223. *See also* Art reproductions
  defined, 214
Art reproductions, 6, 7, 75-76, 134. *See also* Art print
  defined, 214
  picture loan collections, 223
  pictures, 225
  postcards, 117, 118
  slides, 148
  sources, 183, 184, 193, 195, 209
Art teachers, 77
Art to Zoo, 104, 204
Artext. *See* Art Extention Press
Articles of Confederation, 93
Artists, 144
Artist's Color Wheel and The Pocket Guide to Mixing Color, 204
Artists Files, 186
Artists Scrapbooks, 61
Asian Agenda Reports, 184
Asian Updates, 184
Association for Supervision and Curriculum Development, 135, 193
Association information, 77
Association publications, 181
Atlas Moderno Universal, 200
Audiotapes, 103, 110, 126, 138, 155. *See also* Cassette tapes
Audubon Adventures, 197

Austrom, Liz, 158
Authority file, defined, 214
Authors, 154
Automated circulation, 36, 66
Avery, 110, 184
Avery Easy-Reference System, 110

Back file, defined, 214
Back issue, defined, 214
Back order, defined, 214
Background Notes, 97
Backup copies, 101
Badge-a-Minit, 166, 184
Bailey, William G., 193
Ball, Miriam Ogden, 40, 210
Ballet, 183
Bar code, 34, 36, 40, 66
  defined, 214
  label, 214
  numbers, 67
Basic Map Library, 210
Bauer, Caroline Feller, 155
Beattie, Kathleen, 136
Best Books for Young Adults Series, 79, 183
Biannual, defined, 214
Bibliographic information, defined, 215
Bibliographies, 6-7, 20, 78-80, 91
  as sources of information, 10, 14, 20-21
  career collections, 171
  computer programs, 140-41
  government documents, 97
  microforms, 145
  bookmarks, 153
  defined, 215
  handbooks, 160
  sources, 166, 183, 192, 206, 207, 208, 210, 235
Biennial, defined, 215
Big Book of Graphic Designs and Devices, 158
Bill of Rights, 92, 93
  sources of information, 182
Bill of Rights Bicentennial Resource Book, 182
Bimonthly, defined, 215
Bindery, defined, 215
Biographical sketches, 80-81, 116
Biographies, 6-7, 80-81
  bibliographies, 79
  book jackets, 215
  buttons, 157
  clippings, 85-86
  comic books, 90

Biographies—*Continued*
　festschrift, 219
　guides, 98
　interviews, 101
　pamphlets, 112
　photographs, 114
　portraits, 116
　sources, 120, 134, 183, 190, 195, 199, 200, 210
Biography file, defined, 15
Biography Index, 81, 210
Biological & Agricultural Index, 210
Biweekly, defined, 215
Blanket order, 30
　defined, 215
Blind reference, defined, 215
Blueprint, 84
Blurb, defined, 215
Bodart, Joni, 155
Book covers. *See* Book jacket
Book jacket, 152-53
　biographical sketches, 80
　blurb, 215
　defined, 215
Book of Business Forms, 135
Book of Personal Forms, 135
Book of Time Lines, 137
Book Preservation and Repair, 49
Bookcraft: Protection, Maintenance and Repair of Library Materials, 49, 191
Bookmarks, 153-54
　clip art, 158
　sources, 20, 21, 182, 188, 201, 210
　speeches, 126
Books for Children, 194
Books in Print, 81, 163
Booktalker, 155, 210
Book-talks, 7, 155
　bibliographies, 80
　bookmarks, 154
　sources, 210
Border Clip Art for Libraries, 193
Bowker, R. R., 79, 81, 104, 105, 134, 136, 163, 185
Bowker Annual, 81, 163
Bradbury, Phil, 193
Broadside, 1
　defined, 215
Brochures, 111
　defined, 216
Bryan, Carol. *See* Carol Bryan Imagines
Budgets, 96
Bug, defined, 216
Building Bridges, 185
Bulk mailing, 30, 74, 132

Bulletin, defined, 216
Bulletin boards, 156-57
　association information, 78
　book jackets, 152-53
　buttons, 157
　calendars, 81
　career collections, 174
　cartoons, 83
　charts, 84
　ideas, 151, 166
　maps, 169
　materials, 7, 156-57
　portraits, 116-17
　postcards, 118
　protection, 55
　sources, 81, 136, 188, 190, 200, 201, 204, 210
Bulletin of Bibliography, 79
Bumper stickers, 152, 157-58
Bureau for External Affairs, 206
Bureau of Engraving and Printing, 116, 208
Bureau of Labor Statistics, 207
Bureau of the Census, 206
Business in Brief, 186
Business Periodicals Index, 210
Business study, 234
Button Art: Reading and Libraries, 193
Buttons, 7, 157-58, 193
　sources, 23, 152, 166, 183, 187, 188, 189, 199, 203, 210

Caldecott Medal Books, 79, 183
Calendars, 6, 7, 82-83, 190, 194
　biographical information, 80
　pictures, 115
California Medical Association, 185
Calligraphy, 161, 188
　defined, 216
Camera-ready sheets, 79, 183
Canada Today/Canada d'Aujourd'hui, 185
Canada Travel Information, 186
Canadian Library Association, 186, 235
Caplan, Frank, 185
Captain Atlas and the Globe Riders Series, 191
Car rental companies, 132
Card file, 100
　rotary, 224
Card games, 144, 184
Card index, 45
Cards, 107
Care & Repair: Book-Saving Techniques, 49, 192
Career Briefs, 172, 186

Career collections, 7, 171-74
　biographical sketches, 80
　college catalogs, 88
　government documents, 97
　interviews, 101
　magazines, 104
　ordering, 29
　sources, 17, 134, 135, 186, 188, 191, 197, 204, 210
　special collections, 166-69
Career Education Pamphlets, 204
Career Guidance Foundation, 135, 186
Career Guidance Index, 186
Career Job Guides, 186
Career Reprints, 186
Career Summaries, 186
Career World, 188
Careers, Inc., 172, 186
Careers in the Paper Industry, 183
Carleton, Maureen O., 134
Carol Bryan Imagines, 154, 158, 186
Carrier envelopes, 67
Cartographic and Architectural Branch Lists, 197
Cartoons, 6, 7, 83-84, 115, 117, 135, 193. *See also* Slides; Transparencies
　pictures, 115
　postcards, 117
Cartoons by Kids, 193
Cassette tapes, 138-39. *See also* Audiotapes
　oral history, 110
　sources, 201
Catalogs, 111
CD-ROM, 60, 61, 134, 151
　defined, 216
Census Catalog and Guide, 206
Center for Applied Research in Education, 135
Center for Research and Development in Law Related Education, 186, 187
Center for the Book, 194
Chadwyek-Healey, 60, 186
Chambers of commerce, 21, 132, 169
Chapbook, 1
　defined, 216
Chartex cloth backing, 119, 203
Charts, 6, 7, 84, 112. *See also* Drawings
　aeronautical, 206
　defined, 216
　mileage, 169, 170, 179
　nautical, 207
　organizational, 176
　protection for charts, 50, 52, 84

　sources, 10, 13, 17, 20, 134, 135, 182, 187, 188, 189, 190, 192, 193, 197, 198, 200, 201, 205, 208, 210
　study guides, 127
Charts on File, 190
Chase's Annual Events: Special Days, Weeks, and Months, 193
Check-in card, 30, 87
Checklist, defined, 216
Check-out card circulation system, 65
Cheves, Catherine G., 134
Chief justices, 116
Child abuse, 44, 89, 197
Children's Choices, 192
Children's Literature Center of the Library of Congress, 194
China in Maps, 202
Chronicle Guidance Publications, Inc., 172, 187
Chronicle Occupational Briefs, 172
Chronicle Occupational Reprints, 172
Chronological order, 37, 50
　defined, 216
Church, Frank P., 99
CINAHL. *See* Cumulative Index to Nursing and Allied Health Literature
Circulation, 34, 36, 66
Citation, defined, 216
Citizenship manuals, 107
City Map Library, 210
City maps, 196
Clandestine publications, defined, 226
Class schedules, 87, 123
Classification
　defined, 216
　job families, 173
　pamphlet material, 38
Classroom Atlas, 202
Cliffs Notes, 127, 128, 137, 187, 196
Clip art, 7, 158-59
　bibliographies, 80
　bookmarks, 154
　coloring books, 88
　defined, 216
　pictures, 115
　sources, 21, 183, 186, 187, 188, 193, 194, 199, 203
ClipArt & Dynamic Designs for Libraries & Media Centers: Vol. 1 & Vol. 2, 194
Clipping, 115, 120
Clippings, 6, 7, 49, 85-86
　biographical information, 80-81
　cartoons, 83

Clippings—*Continued*
  CD-ROM, 60, 186, 200
  corporation file, 217
  court cases, 90
  file, defined, 217
  instructions, 100
  labels for, 34
  obituaries, 80
  preservation, 48-51
  reference materials, 120-21
  special collections, 167
Cloth-backed, 84
Coins
  iconography, 221
  sources, 20, 182, 183
Cold lamination, 52, 221
  defined, 217
College Blue Book, 87
College catalogs, 6, 7, 87-88
  circulation, 64, 88
  housing, 57
  microfiche, 151
  ordering, 27, 30, 87
  processing, 33, 87
  sources, 186
  special collections, 167-68, 173
  weeding, 69, 88
Color, 57, 62
Color Reproductions Catalogue, 198
Color wheels, 133
Color-coding, 34, 164
  book cards, 66
  dots, 107
Colored folders, 58
Coloring books, 88
  flannel boards, 159
  sources, 188, 204
Comic books, 89-90, 135, 230
  cataloging, 230
  clippings, 83
  defined, 217
  sources, 200, 208
Comics Librarianship: A Handbook, 135, 195
Community calendar, 134
Community file, 77, 134
Complete Book of Forms for Managing the School Library, 135
Composers, 144, 184
Compton's Encyclopedia, 122
Computer
  index, 45, 47
  programs, 7, 130, 140-41, 150, 158, 182, 189, 202
  record keeping, 31

Concerts, 123, 183
Congressional Directory, 208
Congressional Quarterly, Inc., 112, 187
Constitutions, 177. *See also* U.S. Constitution
Consumer Information Catalog, 12, 208
Consumer Information Center, 12
Consumer's Resource Handbook, 208
Contour map, defined, 217
Coping Series pamphlets, 199
Copyright
  clearance, 60, 64
  date, 217
  defined, 217
  guides, 107
  Office, 194
Copyright-free
  defined, 217
  illustrations, 189
Core microfiche collections, 203
CoreFiche, 137, 203
Corporation file, defined, 217
Correspondence, 178
Coty, Patricia Ann, 151
Counselor's Information Service, 171
Court cases, 6, 7, 90-91
Creative Media Services, 166, 187
Creative Publications, 157, 187
CREW, 71, 217
Critical Issues Series, 205
Cross-references, 44, 45
  defined, 217
Crothers, J. Frances, 203
Culturgram Series, 185
Cumulation, defined, 217
Cumulative Index to Nursing and Allied Health Literature, 185
Cunningham, Willis F., 135
Curiosa, 1
  defined, 217
Currency (uncut), 208
Current Bibliographies in Medicine Series, 207
Current Biography, 81, 120, 210
Current Consumer & Lifestudies, 188
Current Health I, 149, 188
Current Health II Sexuality Supplement, 188
Current Issues Resource Builder: Free and Inexpensive Materials for Librarians & Teachers, 17, 18, 195
Curriculum
  guides, 102, 135, 176
  defined, 218
  materials, 127

Curriculum Innovations Group, 169, 188
Cut It Out, 189
Cut-corner pamphlet file, defined, 218
Cut-outs, 159
Cutter, Charles A., 218
Cutter code, 60
Cutter Table, 193
  defined, 218

Dale Seymour Publications. *See* Seymour, Dale, Publications
Dale E. Shaffer. *See* Shaffer, Dale E.
Dane, William J., 204, 230
Data-Guide, 110, 188
Date stamps, 33
"Day of Infamy" address, 93, 126
DeCandido, Keith, 135
Declaration of Independence, 93
Dedications, 120, 178
Dell, 185
Demco, 49, 57, 154, 157, 162, 165, 188, 229
Deposit account, 30, 97
Design on File, 190
Dewey brochures, 210
Dewey Decimal Classification, 37, 174
  defined, 218
Diagrams, 84, 109
Diaries, 178
Dictionary arrangement, 38
  defined, 218
Dictionary of Occupational Titles, 39, 167, 173, 207, 218
DiFelice, Clara L., 136
Digest, defined, 218
Dinosaurs, 117, 144, 162, 184
Directions, 100
Directories, 91-92
  as sources of information, 9, 21-22
  association information, 77
  guide to organization, 37
  sources, 151, 211
  special collections, 168, 179
    local history, 176
Directory of Accredited Home Study Schools, 199
Discarded reference books, 84-85
Disclosure, Inc., 134, 188
Discover Aeronautics and Space, 88, 197
Display boards, 156
Document
  defined, 218
  facsimile, 92-93
Donations, 87

DOT. *See Dictionary of Occupational Titles*; U.S. Department of Transportation
Doubleday, 185
Double-sided tape, 51
Dover Publications, 88, 100, 103, 113, 114, 117, 158, 161, 162, 163, 188, 234
Dow Jones & Company, 20, 188
Drama, 119
Dramatists Play Service, 124, 189
Drawings, 84, 115
  defined, 218
Drill and practice, 143
Drivers' manuals, 108
Dry mounting, 52
  defined, 218
  press, 52
Dummy, 153
  defined, 219
Dummy books, 153, 219
Dust cover (dust jacket or dust wrapper). *See* Book jacket

Easy Cover, 193
Easy Hold, 53, 193
Easy Lam, 193
Editorial Research Reports, 112, 120, 187
Education curriculum. *See* Curriculum
Education Index, 43, 210
Educational Guide to the National Park System, 17, 19, 203
Educational Press Association of America, 106
Educational Resources Information Center, 207. *See also* ERIC
Educational Services Catalog, 198
Educators Grade Guide to Free Teaching Aids, 13, 189
Educators Guide to Free Audio and Video Materials, 16, 189
Educators Guide to Free Films, 16, 189
Educators Guide to Free Filmstrips and Slides, 16, 189
Educators Guide to Free Guidance Materials, 17, 171, 189
Educators Guide to Free Health, PE and Recreational Materials, 17, 189
Educators Guide to Free Home Economics and Consumer Education Materials, 16, 189
Educators Guide to Free Science Materials, 17, 189
Educators Guide to Free Social Studies Materials, 17, 189

Index / 243

Educators Index of Free Materials, 13, 189
Educators Progress Service, 12-13, 16-17, 88, 102, 140, 141, 189
Ehrenberg, Ralph E., 54
EIA Publications Directory 1977-1989, 207
Ekhaml, Leticia T., 97, 193
Election issues, 94
  games, 144, 184
  sources of information, 21, 193
Elementary Teachers Guide to Free Curriculum Materials, 13, 102, 189
Ellison Lettering Machine, 154, 156, 166, 189
"Emancipation Proclamation," 93, 126
Embassies, 21, 30, 132, 185
  films, 141
  flags, 142
  map collections, 169
Emergency Librarian, 158
Encapsulation, 52
  defined, 219
Encyclopedias, 120, 122
Encyclopedia of Associations, 21, 77, 134, 172, 191
Encyclopedia of Associations; Regional, State & Local..., 191
Encyclopedia of Careers and Vocational Guidance, 172
Encyclopedia of Library and Information Science, 233
Energy Information Sheets, 207
English (vocabulary), 143
Engravings, 116
Envelopes, 50
Ephemera, 1
  defined, 219
ERIC, 102, 219. *See also* Educational Resources Information Center
ERIC Document Reproduction Service, 145
ESL (English as a second language), 90, 219
Esselte Pendaflex Corporation, 200
Ethnigram Series, 185
Evaluating and Weeding Collections ... The CREW Method, 71, 183
Exceptional Free Library Resource Materials, 13, 194
Exhibition catalogs, 95
  local history, 177
  sources, 209
Extension Programs, 198

Face masks. *See* Masks
Faces of America, 134, 136, 189

Facsimiles
  children's books, 163
  documents, 126
Factfinder, 206
Facts on File, 134, 135, 136, 137, 150, 151, 189-90
Fairy tales, 184
Family tree (chart), 209
Fastback Series, 112, 201
Faxon, F. W., Company, 40, 190, 232
Federal Consumer Publications in Spanish, 208
Federal Program and Legislative Summaries, 199
Feelings and Your Child Series, 199
Felt boards and figures, 159
Festschrift, 1
  defined, 219
Fieldstaff Reports Series, 183
File
  cabinets, 56
  defined, 219
  guides, 58
  systems, 200
Filing, 34
Films, 141-42, 150, 220. *See also* Filmstrips; Microfiche; Microfilm; Slides; Videos
  preservation, 54
  sources, 13, 16-17, 76, 150, 183, 189, 196, 198, 204, 206
Filmstrips, 54, 141-42, 150
Financial reports, defined, 219
Finding aid, defined, 219
Finding code, defined, 219
Finding list, defined, 219
Finger puppets. *See* Puppets
Finishing Prints on Kodak Water-Resistant Papers, 189
Flags, 7, 142-43
  sources, 183, 190, 206
  state, 117
Flags Unlimited, 142, 190
Flannel-board
  defined, 219
  materials, 159-60
Flash cards, 6, 7, 143-44
  art reproductions, 75
  defined, 219
  games, 144
  sources, 181, 183, 200, 202, 205
Flipcharts, defined, 220
Flowcharts, 113
  defined, 220
Flyers, 111

Focus on Asian Studies, 184
Folders, 50
For You, an American Quarter Horse, 183
Foreign language study, 142, 143, 164, 183
Forest Service, 206
Form letters and postcards, 27-28
Forms, 96
　circulation, 64
　sources, 135, 190, 194, 208
　tax, 96, 135, 208
Forms on File, 190
Formulas, 71, 109
Foundation for Traffic Safety, 181
Framed art, 77
Framed reproductions, 134
Frames, 57-58
Free and Inexpensive Learning Materials, 192
Free Audio and Video Materials, 16, 189
Free Films, 16, 189
Free Filmstrips and Slides, 16, 189
Free Guidance Materials, 17, 189
Free Health, P.E. & Recreational Materials, 17, 189
Free Home Economics and Consumer Education Materials, 16, 189
Free literature rack, 160
Free Magazines for Libraries, 79, 104, 195
Free Magazines for Teachers and Librarians, 232
Free Materials for Schools and Libraries, 231
Free Publications for U.S. Government Agencies: A Guide, 194
Free Publications from U.S. Government Agencies, 97
Free Resource Builder for Librarians and Teachers, 13, 14, 195
Free Science Materials, 17, 189
Free Social Studies Materials, 17, 189
Free Stock Photography Directory, 136
Free Things for Gardners, 201
Freebies for Sports Fans, 23, 204
Freebies Magazine, 237
Freeman, W. H., 122, 190
French, Samuel, Inc., 124, 190
Front Lines, 206
Fugitive
　literature, defined, 220
　materials, 1
Full cataloging, 48
Funding for vertical-file collections, 6
Futas, Elizabeth, 135

Gale Research Inc., 21, 77, 108, 171, 191
Galleries (art)
　art reproductions, 76
　exhibition catalogs, 95
　postcards, 117
　slides, 148
　sources, 198
Games, 6, 7, 144-45, 166
　art reproductions, 75
　calendars, 82
　flags, 142
　flash cards, 144
　holiday items, 99
　puzzles, 147
　sources, 20, 182, 183, 184, 186, 188, 190, 199, 201, 205, 209
Gaylord Bros., 22, 49, 191, 232
Genealogical charts and forms, 198
Genealogical Research, 209
Genealogy, 96
General merchandise catalogs, 107
General Science Index, 210
Generations: The Study Guide, 95, 203
Genovese, Sandi, 189
Geographic filing method, defined, 220
Geography and Map Division, 194
Geography on File, 190
Geography study, 184
Geological Survey, 208
George Peabody College for Teachers, 192
Gettysburg Address, 153, 208
Giant Photos, 116, 118, 119, 133, 161, 191
Gifts, 175
Gilbert, K., 195
Global Perspectives, 205
Glossary of Library and Information Science, 1
Glove puppets. *See* Puppets
Glow in the dark, 186
Gold Files, 31, 184
Goldsmith's Music Shop, 183
Gotsick, Priscilla, 183
Gould, Geraldine H., 31, 200
Government Books for You, 12, 97
Government documents, 96-98
Government Organization Manual, 208
Government Printing Office, 208
Graphic, defined, 220
Gray literature, 1, 121
　defined, 220
Great Performances on Video, 183
Greek
　alphabet, 166
　culture, 182
　myths, 144, 184

Index / 245

Greenfield, Stanley, 185
Greenhaven Press, 136, 191
Groundbreakings, 120, 178
Guide to Federal Career Literature, 171
Guide to Free Computer Materials, 16, 140, 189
Guide to Popular U.S. Government Publications, 193
Guide to Selected Federal Agency Programs, 14, 15, 97, 194
Guidebook, defined, 220
Guides as vertical-file material, 6, 7, 98-99
   career, 186
   curriculum, 102, 176, 193, 200, 207
   films, filmstrips & videotape, 141
   instructional, 100
   lettering, 161
   manuals, 207
   notebook inserts, 109
   stencil, 159
   study, 110, 127-28, 187
   teacher, 149
   test preparation, 187
   topical, 226
   travel, 196
Guides to library materials, 98-99

Haddad's Fine Arts, Inc., 76, 191
Haddad's Reproductions Catalog, 191
Hand printing headings, 34, 35
Handbill, 1
   defined, 220
Handouts, 6, 7, 98, 160-61
   bibliographies, 62
   charts, 79
   coloring books, 89
   guides, 98
   microform information, 146
   promotion of vertical files, 62
   schedules, 123
   sources, 185, 200
   speeches, 126
   test information, 130
   transparency masters, 150
Hanging folders, 57-58
Hard copy, defined, 220
Haycock, Ken, 158
HCL Authority File, 48, 192
HCL Cataloging Bulletin, 48, 192
Headings. *See* Subject headings
Headline Focus Wall Maps, 169, 188
Health & Safety Educational Materials Catalog, 196
Health Resource Builder, 20, 195

Health study, 43, 96, 164
Health Tips, 185
Hearings, defined, 220
Hennepin County Library system, 48, 192, 232
Herring, Billie Grace, 134
Hierarchical classification system, defined, 220
Highsmith Book Repairs, 192
Highsmith Co., Inc., 49, 57, 192
Highway map series, 182
Hill, Donna, 204
Historical Atlas of the World, 202
Historical Maps on File, 151, 190
History of Measurement, 190
History of Painting in Color, 209
History of your institution, 114. *See also* Local history
   study, 110, 143
   teachers, 111
HIV/AIDS Materials for Professionals, 197
Hobbies, 105
Hobbyist Sourcebook, 191
Holdings card, defined, 220
Holiday and Seasonal Border Clip Art, 193
Holiday collections, 99
   bulletin-board materials, 155
   calendars, 82
   scripts, 124-25
   sheet music & song sheets, 126
Home Study Council, 199
Home study schools, 199
Hook & loop, 156
Hospital Literature Index, 22, 182
Hot Topics Series, 201
House organ (house magazine), 104, 177
   defined, 221
House planning, 113
Housing, defined, 221
How Paper Came to America, 183
How to Compile and Maintain a Mailing List, 202
How to Do It Series, 198
How to File and Find It, 58, 59, 202
How to Organize and Maintain the Library Picture/Pamphlet File, 31, 200
How to Present More Effectively..., 205
How to Save Money on Office Supplies, 202
How to Use the Readers' Guide, 210
How to Win through Great Customer Service, 202
How to Write Effective Business Reports, 202

How to's, 100, 138
How You Can Make Paper, 183
Human anatomy, 184
Human Body on File, 151, 190
Humanities Index, 210
Humidity, 54, 139, 142

"I Have a Dream" speech, 126
Iconography, defined, 221
Illustrated Classics Series, 90, 200
Images of Excellence, 80, 192
In the Field, 190
Inaugural addresses, 93, 126
Index, 10-12, 44
  computer, 45, 46
  defined, 221
  vocabulary, defined, 221
Index Medicus, 43
Index of American Periodical Verse, 203
Index to Free Periodicals, 105
Index to Legal Periodicals, 210
Index to Nursing & Allied Health Literature, 43
Indexed periodicals, defined, 221
Inexpensive materials, defined, 3
  or free, 12-13, 16-17, 23
Infogram Series, 185
Information America, 10, 22, 199, 232
Information for Everyday Survival, 183
Information U.S.A., 22, 201, 233
Instructional Aids Series, 192
Instructions as vertical-file materials, 6, 100
Integrated shelving, defined, 221. *See also* Shelving
Interesting People (Black history), 195
Interfiling, defined, 221
Internal filing devices, 57
Internal Revenue Service (IRS), 96, 135, 208
International documents, 202
International Portrait Gallery, 191
International Readers' Newsletter, 201
International Reading Association (IRA), 106, 192
Inverted subject headings, defined, 221. *See also* Subject headings
Interviews, 101, 111
IRA. *See* International Reading Association
Ireland, Norma Olin, 40, 190
IRS. *See* Internal Revenue Service
Issue, defined, 221

Jacket. *See* Book jackets
Jenkins, Lee, 189
Jobber, defined, 221
Jones, Diane Rovena, 104
Journal Graphics, 131, 193
Journal of Commercial Bank Lending (reprints), 203
Journalism study, 92
Journals, defined, 221

Kapco Library Products, 53, 193
Kardex, 87, 227
  defined, 221
Katz, Bill, 104, 105
Katz, Linda Sternberg, 104, 105
Kennedy, John F. (inaugural address), 93, 126
King, Martin Luther, 126
Kodak Index to Photographic Information, 189
Kraus International Publications, 95, 135, 193

Labels for files, 34
Lambert, Shirley, 194
Lamination, 52
  defined, 221
Lamp, 189
Landmark cases, 91. *See also* Court cases
Language teachers, 132
Larsgaard, Mary Lynette, 179, 193
Late or lost materials, 67
Lateral cabinets, 56
Latin, 182
Laubach Literacy International, 199
Laughlin, Mildred Knight, 151
LC. *See* Library of Congress
LC Science Tracer Bullets, 194
Leaflets, 111
  defined, 222
League of Women Voters, 21, 94, 193
Learning, 149
Ledger book circulation system, 64
LEI, Inc., 158, 193
Lesko, Matthew, 22, 201
Lesson plans, 102, 127
Letterhead, 29, 98
  defined, 222
Lettering. *See also* Patterns; Stencils; Templets
  guides, 6, 161
  machine, 154, 156, 166, 189
  transparencies, 149

Librarian's Thesaurus, 227
Libraries Unlimited, 13, 14, 60, 71, 97, 158, 166, 176, 179, 193-94, 233, 234, 235
Library Forms Illustrated Handbook, 135
Library Imagination Paper, 154, 158, 186
Library Information NetworK (LINK), 98, 222
Library Learning Resources, Inc., 166, 194
Library Literature, 210
Library of Congress, 219, 222
  catalog, 21
  classification
    career materials, 174
    defined, 222
    organization, 37-38
    Preservation Leaflet No. 5, 51, 178
  publications, 79, 163, 194, 226, 233
  subject headings, 41-42, 45, 194
Library Picture File: A Complete System of How to Process and Organize, 204
Library PR News, 158, 193
Library Reference Service, 31, 195
Library supplies, 57
Librettos, 103
  defined, 222
Life cycle materials, 68
Lincoln, Abraham, 126
LINK. *See* Library Information NetworK
Literacy programs or projects, 108, 160
Literary works, 127
Literature rack, 98
Literature section, 124
Loan period, 67
Local history, 175-78
  annual reports, 75
  association information, 78
  biographical sketches, 80
  checklist of ingredients, 176
  clippings, 86
  collections, 175-78
  defined, 222
  directories, 92
  election issues, 94
  oral history, 110
  ordering, 30
  preservation, 48
  programs, playbills and reviews, 119-20
  sources of information, 23, 182, 195, 235
  special collections, 167-69
  weeding, 69
Louisiana Purchase, 93
LRS Vertical File Update, 195

Magazine Article Filer, 202
Magazines. *See also* Journals; Periodicals
  clipping, 85, 101
  free, 104-5
  home and craft, 113
  pictures, 115
  reprints, 122
  sample, 105-6
Magazines for Children, 106, 192
Magazines for Libraries, 79, 104, 105, 185
Magazines for Young People, 105, 185
Magic Plus tape, 51
Magna Carta, 93
Mail-order catalogs, 6, 56, 106-7
Making the Grade, 127
Malin, Fran, 22
Malyshev, Nina Alexis, 134, 233
Mancarella, Michael, 194
Manipulatives, 133, 189
Man-Made Fiber Producers Association, 20
Man-Made Fibers Guide, 20, 182
Manuals, 107-8
  computer, 139-40
  defined, 222
  study guides, 127
Map Librarianship: An Introduction, 179, 193
Maps, 6, 167-71
  aerial, 206, 213
  cases, 84, 116, 119
  census, 206
  collections, 169-71, 179
  contour, defined, 217
  defined, 222
  drawings, 117
  floor, 202
  historical, 20, 151, 190, 207
  literature, 201
  local history, 175
  microforms, 146
  nautical, 207
  news, 169, 179, 188, 200
  outline, 191, 202
  protection, 50, 54
  relief, defined, 224
  sources, 13, 17, 151, 169, 182, 183, 190
  special collections, 169-71
  star, defined, 226
  state, 189, 202
  street, 184, 196, 210
  symbols, 208
  topographic, 188
    defined, 226
  travel files, 132
  vendors list, 181-211
  wall, 184, 191, 202

248 / Index

Maps on File, 151, 190
Marketing Information Guide, 195
Marking Paper Manuscripts, 194
Masks, 7, 152, 162-63
  sources, 188, 203, 204, 209
Master-card circulation system, 65
Matthews, Judy Gay, 194
McCaughe, Lori, 189
McFarland, 13, 17-18, 20, 79, 104, 135, 195, 234
McKinley Memorial Library (Niles, Ohio), 60, 196
Measurement of Document Exposure Time Distributions at a Small Public Library, 196
Media Briefing Series, 184
Medical Subject Headings—Annotated Alphabetic List, 43, 207
MEDLINE (SilverPlatter), 134
Metropolitan Life and Affiliated Companies, 20, 196
Metropolitan Museum of Art, 76, 196
Metropolitan Museum of Art Bulletin, 76, 196
Microfiche, 60, 134, 135, 145, 151
  defined, 222
  sets, 87
Microfilm, 60, 151
  defined, 222
Microforms, 54, 145. *See also* Microfiche; Microfilm
  defined, 222
Miller, Shirley, 60, 176, 181, 229, 233
Miller, Suzanne M., 194
Miniature books, 152, 162-63
  sources, 203
Miniexhibit, 82
Miniposters, 153
MMI Memo, 196
Modern Talking Pictures, 141, 196
Monograph, defined, 222
Monroe Doctrine, 93
Monthly Catalog of U.S. Government Publications, 10, 97, 98
Moonbeam Publications, Inc., 137, 187, 196. *See also* Cliffs Notes
More Science Experiments on File, 190
Motion pictures, 54
Mounting, 50, 222. *See also* Dry mounting
Mounting, Laminating and Texturing, 203
Museum of Modern Art Artists Scrapbooks, 186
Museum of Modern Art in New York, 61
Museum publications, 105
Museums, 117, 148

Music Stand, 118, 196
Music, 125-26, 164
Musical instruments, 184
Musicians, 126
MUSTY, 71
Mythology Pictures, 201

Nancy Renfro Studios, 165, 196
NASA. *See* National Aeronautics and Space Administration
NASA Educational Publications, 197
NASA Report to Educators, 197
Nash, Bruce, 23, 204
National Aeronautics and Space Administration (NASA), 88, 197
National Archives, 93, 116, 126, 135, 197, 205, 209
National Archives and Records Administration, 197. *See also* National Archives
National Clearinghouse for Alcohol and Drug Information (NCADI), 197. *See also* Alcoholics Anonymous World Services
National Committee for Prevention of Child Abuse (NCPCA), 89, 197
National Crime Prevention Kit, 198
National Directory of Addresses and Telephone Numbers, 185
National Education Association (NEA), 198
National Energy Information Center, 207
National Gallery of Art, 76, 198
National Gallery of Canada, 76, 95, 198
National Geographic, 85, 169, 198
National Geographic Society, 169, 198
National Geographic World, 198
National Institute of Mental Health, 207
National Library of Medicine, 207
National Library of Medicine News, 207
National Library of Medicine Publications, 207
National Oceanic & Atmospheric Administration (NOAA), 206
National Park Service, 208
National Park System, 17
National Parks Index, 208
National Science Teachers Association (NSTA), 199
National Women's History Project, 116, 199
Nature games, puzzles, posters, etc., 199
NatureScope series, 199
Nautical Charts & Miscellaneous Maps, 207

Index / 249

NCADI. *See* National Clearinghouse of Alcohol and Drug Information
NCADI Publications, 197
NCPCA. *See* National Committee for the Prevention of Child Abuse
NCPCA Catalog, 197
NCR paper (no carbon required), 64
NEA. *See* National Education Association
Neal-Schuman Publishers, Inc., 22, 135, 199, 229
New adult readers, 108, 199
New Book, 12, 97
New topics in subject headings list, 44
New York Gallery of Art, 95
New York Public Library Artists File, 60, 186
New York Public Library Print File, 61, 186
New York Sun, 99
New York Times Index, 175
New Yorker, 83
Newbery Medal Books, 79, 183
Newbery Posters, 201
NewsBank, 60, 200
Newsbooks, 1
  defined, 222
Newsletters, 77, 108-9, 111
  defined, 222
Newsletters in Print, 108, 191
Newspaper Indexing for Historical Societies, Colleges and High Schools, 195
Newspapers, 21, 85, 101, 114
  poster set, 203
Newsprint and Its Preservation, 51, 194
Newsweek, 200
NMHA Publications and Merchandise Catalog, 199
NOAA. *See* National Oceanic & Atmospheric Administration
Nonbook materials, 150
Nonbook Materials: The Organization of Integrated Collections, 196
Nonbook Media Collection Management & User Services, 49, 55, 134, 136, 150, 151, 183
Notable Books, 79, 183
Notebook inserts, 109-10
  sources, 188
  study guides, 127
Notes to files, 36
NSTA. *See* National Science Teachers Association
NSTA Publications, 199

NSTA Supplement of Science Education Suppliers, 199
Numerical arrangement, 37
Numismatic Books & Periodicals, 208
Nystrom Division Herff Jones, Inc., 169, 200

Obituaries, 80-81, 175
Occupational Briefs, 187
Occupational Outlook Handbook, 97, 172, 207
Occupational Outlook Quarterly, 171
Occupational Reprints, 187
Office of Educational Research and Improvement, 207
Office of Elementary and Secondary Education, 204
Office of Scientific Information, 207
Offprints, 122
  defined, 222
OP (out of print), defined, 223
Opaque projectors, 117
  defined, 223
Open shelves, defined, 223
Opera
  librettos, 103
  videos, 183
Opposing Juniors Viewpoints Series, 191
Opposing Viewpoints: Sources, 136, 191
Opposing Viewpoints Pamphlet Series, 112, 191
Oral history, 110-11
  cassette tapes, 138-39
  defined, 223
  interviews, 101
  transcripts, 131
Oryx Press, 43, 200, 230
OS (out of stock), defined, 223
Our Busy World, 200
Outdated, defined, 223
Outline maps, 202
Outlines for white- and blackboards, 114
Outstanding Theater for the College Bound, 124
Overhead projectors, 149
  defined, 223
Overheads. *See* Transparencies
Ownership stamp, 50

PAIS. *See* Public Affairs Information Service
PAIS International in Print, 12, 22, 79
PAIS Subject Headings, 43

250 / Index

Pam box. *See* Pamphlets: boxes
Pamphlet File in School, College, and Public Libraries, 40, 190
Pamphlet Library: Use of the Sha-Frame System, 204
Pamphlets
  binders, 54
  boxes, 57, 223
  defined, 223
  jobbers, 31
  reinforcements, 53
  series, 111-13
Paper and Paper Manufacture, 183
Parents' Yellow Pages, 185
Passport to Legal Understanding, 182
Pastes and glues, 51
Patents, 177
Pathfinders, 98
  defined, 223
Patterns, 113-14
  sources, 190
Pendaflex Corporation, 200
Pendulum Press, Inc., 90, 200
Perfection Form Company, 127, 154, 201
Perica, E., 195
Periodicals. *See also* Magazines
  defined, 223
  free materials listed, 21
  indexed, 221
Personal files, 102
Personal information files for librarians and teachers, 40, 102-3, 152-66
Personal Money Management Materials Catalog, 196
Personalities in History Series, 116, 191
Personalized individual letters, 29
Phi Delta Kappa, 112, 201
PhoneFiche, 135, 209
Photo Essays, 205
Photocopy, defined, 223
Photographs, 6, 7, 114-18, 220, 223
  defined, 223
  local history, 178
  sources, 135, 136, 189, 197, 209
Picture Collection: Subject Headings, 204
Picture File: A Manual and a Curriculum-Related Subject Heading List, 204
Picture Indexing for Local History Materials, 195
Picture loan collection, defined, 223
Pictures, 1-4, 6-7, 31, 33, 115-16
  aids, 31, 200, 203, 204, 230, 231, 232, 234
  bulletin boards, 156
  calendars, 82-83
  career collections, 174

  defined, 223
  flannel boards, 159
  flash cards, 144, 219
  games, 144
  housing, 56
  indexing, 195
  local history, 175
  organization, 39
  photographs, 114, 223
  portraits, 80
  postcards, 117-18
  posters, 119
  preservation, 50, 52
  slides, 148
  sources, 12, 13, 81, 85, 196, 197, 200, 205
  videodisc, 227
Pikes Peak Library District (Colorado Springs), 134
Plain Talk Series, 207
Planet Earth: A Pop-up Guide, 204
Plastic sleeves, 50
Playbills, 119-20, 186. *See also* Programs
Playful Puppets, 165, 201. *See also* Puppets
Plays, 99, 124, 139, 189, 190
  scripts, 124
Poetry, 99, 175
Pokorny, Elizabeth J., 194
Policy, defined, 224
Pollution, 184
Popular culture, 83, 135
Pop-up Atlas of the World: A Globe in a Book, 204
Portraits, 6, 7, 81, 115, 116-17, 118
  iconography, 221
  posters, 118, 208
  preservation, 50
  sources, 80, 134, 136, 189, 191, 204, 208
Portraits for Classroom Bulletin Boards, 81, 204
Postal Service, 209
Postcard books, 117
Postcards, 27, 29, 117-18, 136, 184, 188
  pictures, 115
  portraits, 116
Posters, 6, 7, 118-19
  art reproductions, 75-76
  book jackets, 153
  charts, 84
  clip art, 158
  documents (facsimile), 93, 135
  flags, 142
  government documents, 96
  lettering guides, 161
  local history, 177
  patterns, 113

Index / 251

pictures, 115
postcards, 117
preservation, 50
sources, 10, 13, 17, 20
special collections, 167
time lines, 130
travel information, 132
Posters for Teachers and Librarians, 204
Preservation, 49-50
  defined, 224
Preservation Office, 194
Presidential Portraits, 208
Presidents of the United States, 116, 144, 208
  sources of information, 181
Prime Time, 183
Princeton file, defined, 224
Print Shop Graphics for Libraries, 194
Prints, 118
Procedure, defined, 224
Professional Articles, 187
Professional Careers Sourcebook, 171, 191
Profiles of Excellence Series, 201
Programs, 7, 119-20. *See also* Career collections; Computer programs
  association information, 77
  holiday information, 99
  local history, 176-77
  television programs, 131
Prospectuses, 217
Psychology, 43, 110
Public Affairs Information Service (PAIS), 22, 43, 121, 201
Public Affairs Pamphlets, 201
Public Documents Distribution Center (Pueblo, Colorado), 208
Public Domain Software on File, 150, 190
Public Health Services, 207
Public relations, 157
Public television, 127
Publishers' catalogs, 163-64
Punch and bind systems, 54
Punctuation, 109, 110
Puppeteer's Library Guide: The Bibliographic Index to Literature, 203
Puppeteers of America, 166
Puppets, 164-65
  sources, 186, 187, 188, 190, 196, 201, 203, 210
Puzzles, 6, 7, 147-48
  sources, 190, 199, 203, 205

Q-Data Corporation, 134, 201
Quatrefoil, 184

Quick Chart series, 110, 188
Quick Clips, 183
Quick Reference World Atlas, 202
Quick Speller's Guide, 110, 184
Quill Corporation, 58-59, 202

Radio spots sources, 181, 204
Rand McNally, 169, 202
Reader's Digest, 122, 147, 202
Readers' Guide to Periodical Literature, 42, 210
Readers' service postcards, 29
Ready-to-Use Humorous Illustrations of Children, 158
Ready-to-Use Humorous Sports Illustrations, 158
Ready-to-Use School and Education Illustrations, 158
Ready-to-Use Whimsical Illustrations of Animals, 158
Realia, 4
  defined, 224
Reference books, discarded, 120-21
Reinforcements, 53
Relief map, defined, 224
Religion Indexes, 210
Remainder, 139
  defined, 224
Replica, defined, 224
Report covers, 54
Reports, 121-22. *See also* Annual reports; Pamphlets; Reprints
  association information, 77
  circulation, 64
  defined, 224
  interviews, 101
  local history, 176
  microforms, 145
  ordering, 31
  series, 112, 181, 183, 184
  sources, 22, 136, 198, 201
  special collections, 167
Reprints, 6, 7, 111, 122-23, 220, 222. *See also* Offprints; Pamphlets
  bibliographies, 79
  defined, 224
  election materials, 94
  government documents, 97
  sources, 136, 182, 183, 187, 190, 195, 197, 201, 202, 203, 205, 207, 209, 211
  speeches, 126
  study guides, 127
Reproducible Federal Tax Forms, 208

252 / Index

Reproducible tax forms, 135, 208
Research Reports, 181
Resources in Education, 102, 145, 207
Return mailing labels (peelable), 29, 30
Reviews, 3, 119-20
　of books, 155
Rivershore Library Store, 162, 203
Roosevelt, F. D., 93, 126
Rose Bowl Parade, 132
Rotary card file, 45
　defined, 224
Rough sort materials, 33
Royal Bank Letter, 203
Rubber cement, 51
Rubber stamp, 33
Running Press, 1 7, 163, 203

Safety Belt Campaign, 208
Sample questions for tests, 128
Samuel French. *See* French, Samuel, Inc.
Sanborn, Kate E., 218
SASE (self-addressed, stamped envelope), 30, 225
Scarecrow Press, Inc., 17, 19, 234
Scarry, Richard, 200
Schedules, 6, 123-24
　college catalogs, 87
　handouts, 160
　tests, 128
Scholastic, Inc., 76, 203
School Librarian's Workshop, 147, 151, 156, 166, 194
School Library Media Folders of Ideas for Library Excellence, 166, 194
Science, reprints, 182
Science, study, 122, 182
Science and Technology Division (Library of Congress), 194
Science Experiments on File, 190
Science series, 205
Scientific American, 122, 190
Scope notes, defined, 225
Scores (music), 188
　defined, 225
Scotch Brand Magic Transparent Tape, 51
Scott, Randall W., 135, 195
Scripts, 6, 120, 124-25
　circulation, 65
　defined, 225
　sources, 161, 189, 190
　special collections, 167
Seal Products, Inc., 52, 203
Sears List of Subject Headings, 40, 41, 45, 210

Segal, Joseph P., 71, 183
Selected Sources of Energy-Related Material for School Children and Educators, 207
Self-indexing, 45, 58
Semiannual, defined, 225
Semimonthly, defined, 225
Semiweekly, defined, 225
Sequence, 67
Sequence (accession), 36
Sequential system, 39-40
Serial
　arrangement, 40
　defined, 225
　shelving, 225
Series, defined, 225
Sermons, 178
Seymour, Dale, Publications, 81, 116, 133, 204
Shaffer, Dale E., 40, 204, 234
Sha-Frame system, 40
Shakespeare, William, 90
Shape-books, 163
Shareware, 140
Sharing Lessons in Citizenship Education (SLICE), 186
Sheet music, 5, 7, 125-26, 167, 195. *See also* Songs and song sheets
Shelf life, 2, 3, 103
Shelf list, 45
　defined, 225
Shelving, integrated, 221
Shoe String Press, Inc., 204, 230
Short Report, 127
SIC (Standard Industrial Code) number, 168
Sign language alphabet, 153, 161
Signage, 36, 62
Sign-out sheet circulation system, 64
SilverPlatter MEDLINE, 134
Simon & Schuster Inc., 23, 162, 204
SIRS. *See* Social Issues Resources Series
SIRS Critical Issues Series, 136, 205
SIRS Digest Series, 136, 205
SIRS Documents Series, 197, 205
SIRS Global Perspectives, 205
SIRS Photo Essay, 136, 205
SIRS Science Series, 136, 205
Sleeves, defined, 225
SLICE. *See* Sharing Lessons in Citizenship Education
Slide Buyers' Guide: An International Directory..., 194

Slides, 6, 7, 54, 148-49, 220. *See also* Cartoons; Transparencies
  art reproductions, 75-76
  postcards, 117-18
  preservation, 54
  sources, 13, 16, 17, 20, 181, 182, 189, 196, 198
Slip law, 35
Slote, Stanley J., 71, 194, 234
Small Business Reporter Series, 185
Small press publications, 1
Small presses, defined, 225
Smallwood, Carol, 16, 88, 97, 194, 195, 203, 234
Smart Chart Series, 191
Smith, Adeline Mercer, 79, 104, 195
Smithsonian Coloring Books Series, 204
Smithsonian Institution, 95, 204. *See also* Smithsonian Institution Press
Smithsonian Institution Press, 204. *See also* Smithsonian Institution
Smithsonian Postcard Books Series, 204
Social Education, 198
Social Issues Resources Series (SIRS), 31, 114, 123, 135, 136, 197, 205, 209, 225
Social Sciences Index, 210
Social studies, 92
Social Studies School Service, 114, 130, 144, 205
Soft copy, defined, 225
Software, 150
  defined, 225
Soil Conservation Service, 206
Soil Surveys, 206
Songs and song sheets, 125-26, 175, 188. *See also* Sheet music
Soper, Mary Ellen, 227
Source file, 30
Sourcebook of Teaching Aids Mostly Free, 204
Sources: A Guide to Print and Nonprint Materials Available from Organizations..., 22
Soviet Union in Maps, 202
Space Foundation, 209
Spanish language, 90
Special classification schemes, 38
Special collections, 37
Special events, 132
Special students, 164
Speeches, 6, 92, 126-27. *See also* Inaugural addresses
  bookmarks, 154
  cassette tapes, 138-39

local history, 177
  sources, 197
Spencer, Michael, 97, 194
Spencer S. Eccles Health Sciences Library, 134
Spine (book), defined, 225
Sports, 23
Sports schedules, 123
Spot weeding, 70
Stamps,
  daters, 34
  rubber, 33
Standard Subject Headings for the Book Collection, 41
Standing orders, 173
  defined, 225
Stanzi, Richard, 22
Star maps, defined, 226
State Administrative Officials Classified by Function, 187
States, 144
  documents, 97
  flags, 117
  sources of information, 182
  visitor centers, 117
Stencils, 113-14, 188
  flannel boards, 159
  lettering, 161
  sources, 188
Stickers, 119
Storytelling, 159, 162, 163, 164, 165
  aprons, 165, 188
Stout, Chester B., 60, 196
Strategies for Study, 127
Street maps, 184
Student Guide to Better Writing, Speaking, and Research Skills, 127, 211
Student Quick Reference for Social Studies, 187
Study aids. *See* Study guides
Study guides, 6, 7, 110, 127-28. *See also* Flash cards; Manuals: study guides; Notebook inserts; Tests: sources
Study photos. *See* Study prints
Study prints, 114
Subdivisions, 43
Subject Bibliographies, 79, 97, 208
Subject Bibliography Index, 20, 79
Subject classification, 37
Subject headings, 34, 43
  defined, 226
  inverted, 43, 221
Subject Headings for the Information File, 40, 210
Subject Headings for Vertical Files, 40, 205

254 / Index

Subscription, defined, 226
SuDocs (Superintendent of Documents) number, 35, 39, 97
  defined, 226
Suggestions for Beginners in Genealogy, 198
Sundial, 202
Super Bowl, 132
Supergirl, 208
Superintendent of Documents, 208
Superintendent of Documents number. *See* SuDocs
Supplies for libraries, 57
Supreme Court decisions, 91
Supreme Court Reporter, 90, 91
Surgery on File Series, 190

Tabs and file cuts, 58-59
  defined, 226
Tape, 51
Tattle Tape, defined, 226
Tax forms, 96, 135, 208
TDD. *See* Telecommunications devices for the deaf
Teacher Aids, 190
Teachers' Choices, 192
Teaching Materials Catalog, 211
Technical drawings, 84
Telecommunications devices for the deaf (TDD), 20, 226
Telephone books, 92
Telephone orders, 29
Television programs, 131
Temperature, 54, 142
Templets, 113-14
Test preparation guides, 187
Tests, 6, 7, 128-29
  career collections, 172
  puzzles, 147
  sources, 186, 187
  study guides and worksheets, 127
Theater. *See also* Plays
  bibliography, 183
  performances, 123
  programs, playbills, reviews, 119
  showcard posters, 118
Thermal-adhesive binding system, 54
Thesaurus of ERIC Descriptors, 43, 200
Thesaurus of Psychological Index Terms, 43, 183
These United States, 202
Three-ring notebooks, 54
Tickler file, 30, 74, 78, 92, 108, 123
  defined, 226

Time lines, 6, 7, 130-31
  defined, 226
  sources, 137, 189, 190
Time Lines on File, 190
Timeliner, 189
Toor, Ruth, 135
Topical guides, defined, 226. *See also* Guides
Topographic map, defined, 226
Topographic Map Symbols, 208
Topographic Maps and Publications, 188
Toronto Public Libraries, 40, 205
Tourist information bureaus (foreign), 21
Trade catalogs, defined, 226
Traffic signs and symbols, 144, 181
Transaction form circulation system, 64, 65
Transcripts, 111, 131, 220
  interviews, 101
  oral history, 111, 223
  sources, 93, 182, 192
Transparencies, 7, 149-50, 151. *See also* Cartoons; Slides
  coloring books, 88-89
  defined, 226
  preservation, 54
  sources, 16-17, 200, 201, 208
Transportation, 144
  schedules, 123
Travel, 117, 148, 220. *See also* Maps; Posters; Schedules; Transportation
  agencies, 8, 118, 132
  brochures, 6, 132-33
  flags, 143
  postcards, 117
  slides, 148
  sources, 13, 186, 196
  special collections, 168, 169
  stamps, 34
Tubes, 50, 84
Typed list (index), 45

U.S. Agency for International Development, 206
U.S. Constitution, 92, 93, 187
U.S. Department of the Interior, 17, 208
U.S. Government Documents: A Practical Guide for Non-Professionals..., 194
U.S. Government Printing Office, 96, 126, 169, 208. *See also* SuDocs; U.S. Government publications; *specific agencies and bureaus*

U.S. Government publications, 10, 12, 21, 31, 79, 97, 98, 104, 118, 121, 171, 181, 193, 194, 235. *See also* U.S. Government Printing Office; *specific agencies and bureaus*
U.S. Government Publications for the School Library Media Center, 97, 193
U.S. National Archives Trust Fund, 209. *See also* National Archives; National Archives and Records Administration
U.S. News and World Report, 122, 209
U.S. Superintendent of Documents, 30. *See also* SuDocs
Uncut currency, 208
Underground publications, 1, 213
  defined, 226
Understanding and Creating Editorial Cartoons: A Resource Handbook, 193
UNESCO Publications, 206
United Nations, 96, 97, 135, 142, 202, 206
United Nations Family, 206
United Nations Film, Video, Television Catalogue, 206
United States Authors, 201
United States Government Manual, 21
University Microfilms International, 135
University of Utah, 134
University of Washington Press, 95, 209
University Prints, 76, 209
University Prints Catalogue, 209
Update on Law-Related Education, 182
Upstart, 154, 157, 210
Using Records in the National Archives for Genealogical Research, 209

Vance Bibliographies, 79, 210
Vendor, defined, 226
Vertical file, defined, 227
Vertical File (Videotape), 235
Vertical File and Its Satellites, 60, 176, 181
Vertical File Index, 10-11, 42, 112, 121, 122, 171, 210, 235
Vertical File Locator, 202
Vertical File on Microfilm (VFOM), 60
Vertical files
  defined, 227
  on microfilm, 186
Vertical-file treatment, 1, 3, 102

Video recording (videocassettes, videos, videotape), 101, 103, 110, 126, 141-42, 155
  sources, 181
Videodisc, defined, 227
Visible index, defined, 227
Vital Speeches, 126
Vocabularies, 109, 110, 143
Vocal score, defined, 227
Vocational Biographies, 134, 210
Vocational collections. *See* Career collections
Vocational Guidance Quarterly, 171
Vocations. *See* Career collections
Volunteers, 8, 110
Voting information, 94. *See also* Election issues
VOYA Occasional Papers Series, 203

W. H. Freeman. *See* Freeman, W. H.
Wall maps, 184
Wall Street Journal, 122, 188
Washington, George, 210
  Inaugural Address, 93, 126
WatchMe Blossom Theater Works, 165, 210
Weather Pop-up Book, 204
Webster's New World Dictionary of Media and Communications, 227
Weeding, 38, 68-71
  annual, 70
  continuous, 70
  defined, 227
  formula, 71
  spot weeding, 70
Weeding Library Collections, 71, 194
Weiner, Richard, 227
Weisburg, Hilda K., 135
Weisinger, Mort, 185
Wheels (manipulatives), 7, 133-34
  sources, 191, 202, 204, 205
Wide Directory Product Sellers Inc., 92
Wilson, H. W., Company, 10-11, 21, 40, 41, 81, 155, 210, 229, 231, 234, 235
Wilson Library Bulletin, 155, 210
Wittig, Alice J., 97, 193
Wolfe, Ithmer C., 31, 200
Woman of the Month Display Kit, 199
Women from History, 199
Women Writers and Their Visions, 199
Women's History Resources, 199
Workbooks and worksheets, 127-28
  defined, 227
Working Press of the Nation, 199

World Atlas, 200
World Authors, 201
World Book Encyclopedia, 122, 127, 211
World Chamber of Commerce Directory, 21, 132
World Facts & Maps, 202
World History Program, 112, 191
World Newsmap of the Week, 169, 179, 188
World Photography Sources, 136
World, United States, and Historical Maps, 207
Write in Style, 127
Writing, 188

Yearbooks, 114
Young Adult's Choices, 192

Zoobooks, 211
Zullo, Allan, 3